IN THE
HOT ZONE

IN THE HOT ZONE

ONE MAN, ONE YEAR, TWENTY WARS

KEVIN SITES

HARPER ● PERENNIAL

NEW YORK ● LONDON ● TORONTO ● SYDNEY

HARPER PERENNIAL

HarperCollins books may be purchased for educational, business, or sales promotional use. For information please write: Special Markets Department, HarperCollins Publishers, 10 East 53rd Street, New York, NY 10022.

FIRST EDITION

Designed by Jaime Putorti

Library of Congress Cataloging-in-Publication Data is available upon request.

ISBN: 978-0-06-122875-9
ISBN-10: 0-06-122875-3

07 08 09 10 11 DIX/RRD 10 9 8 7 6 5 4 3 2 1

This book is dedicated to the innocent victims of conflict worldwide.
You are not forgotten.

CONTENTS

Prologue: Blacksburg and Baghdad   1

PART I

THE REVELATION WILL NOT BE TELEVISED

1. Burdens of War: The Mosque Shooting   5
2. Holiday Hell: Reporting the Tsunami   28
    Intermission: Fathers and Sons   37
3. TV News or the Internet: Do I Yahoo!?   38

PART II

INTO THE ARMS OF MAMA *AFRICA:* REBELS, RAPE VICTIMS AND THE CHILDREN OF WAR

4. Somalia: Chew on This!   57
    Intermission: Khat Tales   70
5. Democratic Republic of the Congo: Worse Than the Guns   72
    Intermission: Hammering Rocks   82
6. Uganda: An Army of Children   84
7. Sudan: The Longest War   91
    Intermission: Young Woman and a Log   99

PART III

PHANTOMS OF FALLUJA, BROWN SUGAR JUNKIES, MARTYRS' MOMS AND OTHER *MIDDLE EAST* NIGHTMARES

8.	Iraq: What Cannot Be Left Behind	103
9.	Lebanon: Hanging with Hezbollah	115
	Intermission: Defendant "198964"	121
10.	Iran: Under the Hijab	128
	Intermission: Persians Can Jump	140
11.	Syria: Without Mouths	141
12.	Israel and Gaza: Burned, Blind and Reborn	147
	Intermission: Sami	153

PART IV

THE CHILD BRIDE, ENDLESS GRIEF AND MUSIC TO DISARM TO: LIVES AND LESSONS FROM *EUROPE, CENTRAL ASIA* AND THE *AMERICAS*

13.	Chechnya: Art Amid the Ruins	157
	Intermission: Bomb U	163
14.	Afghanistan: Smiling Through the Pain	165
15.	Colombia: The Right to Bear Arms	181
	Intermission: Email	189
16.	Haiti: Life Without a Net	192
	Intermission: The Art of Survival	196

PART V

MY *ASIAN* ODYSSEY: TAMIL TIGERS, NEPAL MAOISTS, KAREN REBELS AND A MISSED MOMENT WITH THE DALAI LAMA

17. Nepal: Where to Mao?   199

18. Kashmir: Trouble in Paradise   208
     Intermission: Learning to See   214

19. Sri Lanka: Tiger Don't Surf   216

20. Myanmar: Oldest Rebels Battle Ugliest Regime   225
     Intermission: Missing Chance: Oh, Hello Dalai   232

21. Cambodia: Does Justice Lie Among Those Bones?   235

22. Vietnam: Clockwork Orange   245

PART VI

THE THIRTY-FOUR-DAY WAR: PUTTING THE HOLE IN THE HOLY LAND

23. Lebanon: Dodging Drones and Dead Men's Pockets   253
24. Israel: The Equality of Fear   266

PART VII

MY THIRD-WORLD AMERICA: A WEALTH OF INFORMATION, A POVERTY OF KNOWLEDGE

25. Coming Home: Dreams, Death and the Hardest Truth   283

     Epilogue: What Did I Learn?   293
     Acknowledgments   295
     Appendix A: Open Letter to the Devil Dogs of the 3.1   299
     Appendix B: Email to Yahoo! About the China Situation   311
     Appendix C: Statistics   313
     Sources for Appendix C   351

IN THE
HOT ZONE

BLACKSBURG AND BAGHDAD

While I was writing this book, a Korean-American student named Seung-Hui Cho used two handguns to kill thirty-two people and then shot himself on the campus of Virginia Tech University in Blacksburg, Virginia, on April 16, 2007. Federal officials called it the deadliest shooting rampage in American history.

The American public seemed riveted to the story. The shared sense of tragedy, though on a smaller scale, seized their attention in the same way the events of 9/11 had; this, we believed, was about us.

In the days that followed, details about the victims began to emerge, the narrative of their lives took shape, they became people rather than the body count of a massacre. The story of their lives allowed us to make connections to them, to feel empathy for their families—choosing, if we wanted, to send messages of support, moving beyond the role of witnesses to participants in the healing process.

Meanwhile, in Iraq that very same week, 700 civilians were killed in shootings, bombings, executions and other war-related violence. Nearly half of those happened on one day, April 18, including a string of suicide bombings in Baghdad, which took the lives of nearly 200.

And while I watched media coverage of the memorial services for the students and teachers who were killed at Virginia Tech, I was troubled by a feeling that while we were rightfully absorbed by our own national tragedy, we had long been inured to the daily civilian death toll in Iraq and elsewhere in the world.

A violent death and the sorrow it provokes among those left behind is not something to try to equivocate—whether it occurs in Baghdad or Blacksburg. Each victim, regardless of place, leaves a ripple of pain that penetrates families, communities, even whole societies—traumatized by the loss.

But as I watched the images of grief televised from Virginia, I hoped that when our national mourning was over, we, as American citizens, might feel a renewed sense of empathy because of this incident—one robust enough to transcend our national boundaries and inspire us to see the rest of the world.

Kevin Sites

PART I

THE REVELATION

WILL NOT BE TELEVISED

CHAPTER 1

BURDENS OF WAR
The Mosque Shooting

FALLUJA, IRAQ | NOVEMBER 13, 2004

SUNBEAMS

The carpet of the mosque is stained with blood and covered with fragments of concrete. Tank shells and machine-gun rounds have pitted the inside walls. The rotting, sweet smell of death hangs in the morning air. Gunsmoke-laced sunbeams illuminate the bodies of four Iraqi insurgents. A fifth lies next to a column, his entire body covered by a blanket.

I shudder. Something very wrong has happened here.

Yesterday I had seen these same five men being treated by American medics for superficial wounds received during an afternoon firefight. Ten other insurgents had been killed, their bodies still scattered around the main hall in the black bags into which the Marines had placed them.

I was told by the commander of the 3.1 Marines, Lieutenant Colonel Willy Buhl, that these five wounded, captured enemy combatants would be transported to the rear. But now I can see that one of them appears dead and the three others are slowly bleeding to death from gunshots fired by one lance corporal, I will learn later, who used both his M-16 and his 9 mm pistol on them, just minutes before I arrived.

With my camera rolling, I walk toward the old man in the red kaffiyeh and kneel beside him. Because he was so old, maybe in his early sixties, and wearing the red headgear, he had stood out the most to me when I was vid-eotaping the day before, after the battle.

Now the old man is struggling to breathe. Oxygenated blood bubbles from his nose. Another man, stocky and dressed in a long gray shirt called a dishdasha, is slumped in the old man's lap. While I'm taping, the old man is bleeding to death in front of my camera. I look up to see the lance corporal who had just shot all of them moments before, now walking up to the other two insurgents against the wall, twenty feet away. One is facedown, appar-ently already dead. The other, dressed in an Iraqi Police uniform, is faceup but motionless, aside from his breathing.

The lance corporal says, "Hey, this one's still breathing." Another agrees, "Yeah, he's breathing." There is tension in the room, but I continue to roll on the man in the red kaffiyeh.

"He's fucking faking he's dead," the lance corporal says, now standing right in front of the man.

THE EMBED

As a freelance correspondent for NBC News, I embedded with the Third Battalion, First Marine (Regiment) for three weeks prior to the Battle of Falluja, or what the Americans code-named Operation Phantom Fury and what the Iraqi interim government called Operation Al Fajr, or "The Dawn."

The mission has a clear but complicated objective; take back the restive city of Falluja from the insurgents who had been running the place for the last eight months.

In the time leading up to the battle, I have developed a good relationship with my unit. The Marines see that I'm a television reporter working solo—shooting, writing and transmitting my reports without a crew—and they tell me they like my self-reliance. I tell them it's a necessity, because no one wants to work with me anymore. Television news is the ultimate collabora-tive medium, but by being recklessly aggressive, low on the network food chain (a producer turned reporter) and eager to go it alone to uncomfortable locations, it has not been difficult to convince news managers to let me do just that.

The Marines also like the fact that I write an independent war blog, which NBC allowed me to keep as a freelancer, where I post longer, more detailed and personal stories about my experiences.

Inspired by Tim O'Brien's book *The Things They Carried*, in which he describes the items, both literal and figurative, that each man in a U.S. Army platoon carried on a jungle march through Vietnam, I ask the Marines to show me the same. They pull out rosaries, Saint Christopher medals, photographs of their wives and children taped inside their Kevlar helmets.

I snap their pictures and post them on the site. Their families, eager for information about their loved ones, come to my blog in droves. They post responses, thanking me for allowing them to see the faces of their sons, husbands, brothers. Soon, however, those messages of gratitude will be replaced with hate mail and death threats.

CAMP ABU GHRAIB

We are on a small, dusty satellite base near Camp Falluja, the First Marine Expeditionary Force headquarters. Like the infamous, scandal-ridden prison, the base is named Camp Abu Ghraib. It is a sprawling compound ringed by dirt walls, large concrete slabs, concertina wire and gravel-filled wire baskets called HESCO barriers.

In this time of waiting, when I've finished filing my reports for the day, I sometimes jog around the base on a makeshift track just inside the walls. It's an incongruous but now-common experience to run in the golden light of dusk, passing the guard towers with their .50-caliber machine guns and the brig at a far end of the base quadrant where Iraqi prisoners are temporarily held before being transferred to the real Abu Ghraib prison.

Inside, I see Marines tossing a football, walking to the chow hall, cleaning their weapons. I hear the clank of weights being dropped and a boombox blasting from the tent that houses their surprisingly well-equipped gym. On the outside I see red skies over Falluja as the sun drops to the horizon.

FOUR HORSEMEN

I made friends with three country Marines and a navy medic who provide security for the base—and who, in the course of their duties, confiscated four horses from Iraqi men who came too close to the base with carts, supposedly to collect scrap metal.

Corporal David Harris, Lance Corporal Kenny Craig, Corporal Lloyd Williams and Corpsman Michael Driver use their own money to pay for hay brought in from Baghdad to feed those malnourished horses. In an effort to re-create a little piece of home, they're trying to train the cart-hauling horses to be ridden.

It's a risky undertaking. When Craig mounts a horse named Bandit, it quickly turns its head and bites down hard on Craig's leg. I ask him if the injuries are worthy of a Purple Heart.

But Craig is undeterred. He kicks his heels into Bandit's ribs and pushes him into an enthusiastic stroll around the base.

"When we ride them around camp, everybody wants to pet them," says Craig. "Everybody wants to see them. It brightens their day, even if they choose to deny that."

That same night, the four men build a roaring fire in a fifty-gallon metal drum and feed their horses granola bars from MRE (Meal, Ready-to-Eat) packets. I watch as they line-dance to Lynyrd Skynyrd's "Sweet Home Alabama" in their fatigues and combat boots, bathed in the orange firelight that warms the chilly Iraqi night.

THE FEINTS

Everyone knows the battle is coming, they just don't know when. In the meantime the Marines conduct operations known as feints, bluffing maneuvers in which they charge up to the city's edge with armor and infantry, both to fool the insurgents into thinking the real battle has begun and to draw them out of their urban hiding spots to kill them.

I am assigned to the CAAT (Combined Anti-Armor Team) Platoon, commanded by Lieutenant Ryan Sparks, a former enlisted man and member of the Marines' elite Recon Unit, similar to Army Special Forces and Navy SEALs.

The CAAT team consists of Humvees mounted with heavy, squad-operated weapons such as TOW antitank missiles and Mark 19 grenade launchers that can fire belted 40 mm grenades at a rate of sixty rounds per minute.

A week before Phantom Fury begins, Sparks's team is assigned to an operational feint on the south end of the city, where commanders believe foreign fighters, possibly from Al Qaeda, are concentrated.

The units rehearse the operation in a "rock drill" in which rocks and, strangely, large children's Lego blocks are arranged on the ground to approximate Falluja's buildings. Water bottles stand in as minarets for the mosques. Each unit commander involved in the operation, from captains to squad leaders, explains, in chronological order of the event, their mission objective, entry into the operation and exit.

On the evening of the feint, I ride in Sparks's Humvee. As we race across the desert, I shoot video out the front windshield, where my last name, along with those of the three crew members, is written in black marker along with our blood types.

There is a loud explosion as an insurgent mortar round lands a hundred yards behind us. Sparks orders his teams to find cover somewhere on the flat desert plains.

"There it is—right there, Johnson, eleven-thirty." Sparks directs his Mark 19 gunner to a flash point in the city where he believes the mortar came from.

The radio crackles as Sparks listens to the field artillery unit triangulating the mortar's firing grid more precisely. When another mortar lands nearby, Sparks no longer waits. He orders his squad and those in the other Humvees to return fire.

It is, on a small scale, what the Marines had hoped would happen—drawing insurgents out and then springing the trap. Though the insurgent response has been tepid so far—a couple of mortars and small-arms fire—the Marines ramp up the firepower.

Abrams M1A1 tanks fire their 120 mm main guns; Marine artillery units drop their own mortars; while the CAAT team shoots shoulder-launched Javelin and Humvee-mounted TOW missiles at the outlying houses.

TOW BACKBLAST

I leave Sparks and run seventy-five yards across the open field to where another CAAT Humvee is shooting TOWs. After several firings, Lance Corporal Joe Runion loads another missile into the launcher; the gunner yells "Fire in the hole" and pulls the trigger. But there is no launch—only a clicking sound.

It's a hang-fire. Runion waits for a full minute, Marine protocol in this situation, before climbing onto the Humvee to unload the faulty weapon. Just as he is about to reach for the tube, the missile fires, roaring to life at its target. The backblast concussion from the rear of the tube knocks Runion unconscious and he falls off the Humvee to the ground.

Others in his unit run to his aid, but, remarkably, he shakes it off, climbs back on the Humvee and reloads the weapon. I've recorded the entire sequence on my video camera.

"I'm glad you're safe, dog," says one of the Marines to Runion, whose head is still ringing from the explosion.

The moment is soon lost. Darkness falls and the fight continues. In my story I report the TOW malfunction and Runion's stubborn perseverance after being knocked out. I also say that while no American lives were lost in the operation, it did cost hundreds of thousands of dollars in manpower and munitions.

The next day, after my piece has aired on NBC *Nightly News,* a few of the Marines from the CAAT team tell me they're happy that I didn't use the TOW backblast incident to make them look stupid.

I feel that I have gained a little trust—but also begin to see the deep-rooted *mis*trust they have for my profession.

Some of that perception, they tell me, started with their fathers, who served in Vietnam and told them when they were growing up that the media helped lose that war by reporting only the "bad stuff."

I think about telling them that the United States dropped more bombs in Vietnam than in both World Wars I and II combined and that it had a determined foe, one willing to live in underground tunnels and endure the death of millions. It was the enemy who won that conflict, and not news reporting that lost it. I decide it is probably better left unsaid.

SLIPPING THE BIG FOOT

I am on a satellite phone call with an NBC desk assistant who says the foreign news manager, Danny Noa, needs to speak with me. She transfers me to his line and he's hesitant, then apologetic, telling me that they want to pull me out of Falluja and replace me with their Baghdad-based staff reporter, Richard Engle.

"That's bullshit, Danny," I say, getting angrier with every second. "I've been here for weeks, I've established a working relationship with the unit. You can't just yank me out days before the biggest battle of the war."

He listens but is firm—the network wants Engle, NBC's rising star and future Middle East Bureau chief, in the driver's seat when Falluja goes down.

"Danny," I press my case, "I know Engle is a good reporter and speaks Arabic, but he doesn't necessarily speak Marine. I've been embedded longer and with more units than anyone at the network. This is what I do best."

"The Pentagon says we can only have one embedded reporter for the operation," he says. "You can have Ramadi."

"Ramadi? This is where it's happening right now," I say. Silence on the other end. It's no use. I kill the call and think about my options. There do not seem to be many, but I am not ready to just step aside for something that I had worked so long and hard for.

The next day I go to Camp Falluja, First Marine Expeditionary Force headquarters, to talk to one of the public affairs officers with whom I had become friendly.

"Your network called me yesterday," he tells me. "They said they wanted to pull you out and replace you with Engle." I nodded.

"I told them they could yank you if they wanted, but no one would be allowed to take your place. NBC's embed slot would stay empty." I smile broadly, realizing the gift I've been given. "Guess you're the guy now," he says, without expression.

When it becomes clear that the Marines are serious about not letting Engle come in to take my place, NBC gets behind me as if I were their first choice all along. I get a bump in pay and—now that I'm going to be a real correspondent, not some one-man-band mutt—they're going to assign me a cameraman.

At first I'm not eager to work with someone else, but when I learn it's Boston native Kevin Burke, a talented shooter and freelance workhorse who has spent as much time in Iraq as me, I warm to the idea.

I also realize that I can continue to shoot. Kevin and I can attach to different squads and cover twice as much ground, then meet up at the end of the day.

While I am writing the story script, he can log and rough-edit our video from the day. Later, I will transmit the piece from my laptop using a phone-book-sized satellite modem called an RBGAN (Regional Broadband Global Area Network) to a computer server in Secaucus, New Jersey.

Other networks, like CNN, which I had worked for earlier in the war, have been sending video by FTP (File Transfer Protocol) like this since the invasion of Iraq. But at the time the Battle of Falluja is about to begin, I am the only correspondent at NBC who knows how to do it and has used it in the past.

There weren't going to be any convenient satellite dish feed points on the front lines when Operation Phantom Fury began, so anyone who didn't know how to send by satellite modem would be sitting on piles of videotape—unable to file their daily reports. Technology had shrunk the world to a much more manageable size just in time for this battle.

THE MOSQUE SHOOTING

After hearing the lance corporal say, "He's fucking faking he's dead," I raise my camera up from the bleeding old man to the Marine.

I see him in my viewfinder; he is raising his M-16 rifle and pointing it directly at the wounded insurgent's head. He peers down at him through his laser scope.

I don't know what he's going to do, but I hope he's just going to cover him while other Marines search him for weapons. But in this place, already filled with so much death, somehow, in this moment, I sense there will be more. The lance corporal squeezes the trigger, firing a 5.62 round into the man's head, which I watch explode on my screen.

His skull and brains splatter against the dirty white wall he was lying against. After firing the shot, the Marine (whom I have chosen not to name) turns on his heels and walks away.

The name of the man he shot was revealed later in an identification card recovered from his body by the Naval Criminal Investigative Service. The card, ironically, had been issued to the man under the authority of the First Marine Expeditionary Force in Falluja. His name was Officer Farhan Abd Mekelf, a member of the Iraqi Police.

I have seen people killed and wounded in combat, but never like this. Never at point-blank range. It stuns me to the point that instead of jumping up, I continue to videotape from my kneeling position. Maybe it was shock, but to this day, I still can't understand why I completed the shot sequence, panning back to the old man with the red kaffiyeh after the lance corporal killed Mekelf.

After the shooting, the fifth insurgent, who had been completely covered by the blanket, slowly pulls it down, raising his bandaged hands as he does. Two other Marines in the mosque immediately point their weapons at him.

This snaps me out of my trance. Thinking they might shoot him, too, I get up and confront the Marine who had pulled the trigger.

"Why did you do that?" I asked him. "What's going on? These were the same guys that were here yesterday. They were wounded."

"I didn't know, sir," he said. "I didn't know." The voice that had seemed so confident just a few moments ago is now filled with unsettling realizations. And then he walks out of the mosque followed by the other Marines.

The insurgent under the blanket begins speaking to me in Arabic. He's the only one of the five wounded who had not been shot a second time by the lance corporal, somehow escaping that fate by hiding under the blanket. Because of the wounds on his legs from the Friday afternoon firefight, he's wearing only a blue-striped shirt and white underpants; his trousers are in a heap next to the mosque pillar.

He tries to talk to me, gesturing with his hands, but I can't understand what he's saying. He falls back on his upper arms, frustrated and scared.

It's only later, after my video is translated, that I will find out what he was trying to tell me. But it will be more than two years later before I learn the fate of this man, Taleb Salem Nidal, and my complicity in it.

As I walk away from the mosque, I'm not thinking of Nidal, but only of the shooting I just witnessed. There is a vehicle going back to the battalion field headquarters. I jump in and ride back to the 3.1 Battalion's field headquarters. I need to see Lieutenant Colonel Willy Buhl, tell him what has happened and show him the video.

When I first met Buhl at the beginning of my embed, I liked him right away. He seemed like an easygoing, no-bullshit kind of guy. Small and stocky, he was a former wrestler and, like Lieutenant Ryan Sparks, had been an enlisted man who became an officer. Guys like that, who have been there and know the business from the ground up, generally command a lot of respect. Buhl was no exception. I had interviewed him prior to Phantom Fury and he had said something to me that now, in retrospect, seems both sadly ironic on one level and prophetically true on another.

"We're the good guys. We are Americans. We are fighting a gentleman's war here—because we don't behead people, we don't come down to the same level of the people we're combating," he says during our interview at Camp Abu Ghraib. "And that's a very difficult thing for a young eighteen-year-old Marine that's been trained to locate, close with and destroy the enemy with fire and close combat, and that's a very difficult thing for a forty-two-year-old lieutenant colonel with twenty-three years' experience in the service who's trained to do the same thing once upon a time and now has a thousand-plus men to lead, guide, coach, mentor and to ensure we are the good guys and keep the moral high ground."

When I show Buhl the tape, he is not shocked so much as he is deflated. His comments are along the lines of "Ah, this is so bad." I think he felt that all he had accomplished up to that moment could be taken away by a single image.

THE REPORT

After I shoot the video, one of the first things I do is call the NBC News desk in New York and have them wake up the vice president of NBC News at the time, Bill Wheatley; the VP of foreign news, David Verdi; and the foreign news manager, Danny Noa.

Partly, this is a safety net for myself. If no one at NBC knows that I have the tape, I might be tempted to destroy it. It is the most soul-wrenching moral dilemma I have ever faced in my life. My professional code of ethics commands me to "seek and report the truth," but it also, as few outside the profession know, instructs us to "minimize harm." The Society of Professional Journalists' code requires that the "ethical journalist treat sources, subject and colleagues as human beings deserving of respect."

How, in this circumstance, can I possibly do both? I know that the videotape probably shows a violation of the Geneva Convention and Uniform Code of Military Justice regarding humane treatment of wounded enemy combatants.

And while that is the likely truth, I fear that releasing the video could have unintended consequences. The most obvious, it seems, is that once word of the video reaches insurgents, they might not be willing to surrender if they believe their fate is going to be similar to Farhan Abd Mekelf's.

A further inflamed insurgency might also take retribution through more suicide bombings on civilian and military targets. In addition, there are already slim hopes for merciful and humane treatment of American, Iraqi government and coalition forces prisoners by insurgent fighters, and now there will almost certainly be summary executions.

Reporting the truth is my professional responsibility, but so is consideration of its potential harm. If my employers know about the video, I will not be alone in my decision making.

Kevin Burke, who was videotaping with another unit while I was in the mosque, meets up with me at battalion headquarters. I ask him to start making duplicates of the shooting video, just in case someone tries to take it from us.

No one ever does.

TICKING CLOCK

My belief is that we should hold the tape for seventy-two hours to give the Marines a chance to investigate.

To their credit, they move quickly, pulling the lance corporal from the field and assigning Lieutenant Colonel Bob Miller from the judge advocate general's office to begin questioning witnesses in the case.

But there are other complications. Even though I am working for NBC News, the network has made a video-sharing agreement called a "pool" with a consortium of other television media, including the other four American networks, three British networks (including the BBC), as well as Reuters TV and Associated Press Television News. This pretty much guarantees that whatever footage comes out of the Battle of Falluja will be seen around the world, including the Middle East through Al Jazeera.

Part of the pool agreement requires me to turn over my footage as soon as possible. But I know that if I do that before allowing the Marine Corps to respond, the story could spin out of control without proper context.

As the seriousness of the incident begins to reverberate, I begin meetings with Marine Corps brass that swiftly take me from the front lines to the desk of the commanding general of the entire First Marine Division and first Marine Expeditionary Force, Major General Richard Natonski.

At the same time, NBC News VP Bill Wheatley is pressuring me to release the tape to the pool in forty-eight hours—otherwise, he tells me, "we'll look like we're holding out on them."

At Camp Falluja, the Marines billet Kevin Burke and me away from the other media so we can do our work quickly and quietly without stirring up questions about what I videotaped in the mosque.

Sunday, the day after the shooting, I'm sitting outside our quarters on a satellite phone with Danny Noa. I'm tired, frustrated and conflicted—and the pressure from Wheatley has pissed me off. I tell Danny that I've come to a decision.

"I'm not going to feed the tape, Danny."

"What do you mean, you're not going to feed the tape?"

"I didn't make this pool agreement and I have no idea how the other networks are going to use it and we don't have any control over it. I'll messenger it to our bureau in Baghdad but I'm not going to feed this tape to the pool."

Noa is understandably shocked and puzzled to the point that he hardly knows what to say. He and I had come up through the ranks as producers at NBC. *No* is not a word producers use or accept if they are going to have any kind of career. He pushes, pleads and finally lets me know just what kind of grave territory I have entered. When I still refuse to budge, he says he needs to get David Verdi on the phone when he's done with a meeting. He asks me to call back in a half hour.

When Verdi gets on the phone, he is calm and deliberate.

"I can understand how hard this is, Kevin," he tells me, "but we've already told the pool what we have and if you don't feed the tape it's going to look like we're trying to hide the truth or something—like we're collaborating with the government to bury this thing."

He pauses, then pushes a button that he knows will affect me. "It could become an even bigger incident. There will be a buildup and the demand for the video will turn into an outcry. When it's finally released, it could create an even more volatile situation than if we give it to them now and provide the context of what happened through your report."

It's exactly what I don't want to happen, for everything to spin out of control. I didn't want to be responsible for a massive wave of violence and bloodshed. By the end of the phone call, I relent. We decide the video will be released in two versions: the entire tape, then a second feed where I pause the video after the Marine raises his M-16 at the insurgent's head. The gunshot will be heard, but the image of the actual shooting won't be seen. The other networks can use their own discretion on which version they want to air.

Simultaneously, I will complete my packaged story for NBC *Nightly News* with a video interview of the JAG investigator, Bob Miller, responding to the facts of the case.

The process of putting together the script is painstaking, requiring multiple levels of oversight from news management, NBC lawyers, executive and senior producers.

By the time we're finished, the script is a Frankenstein's monster of caution and qualifications that violates the most basic rule of journalistic writing—tell the most important thing that happened first; do not bury your lede.

Also, we choose to censor ourselves and show the version with the paused image in the report. We justify it by saying it's too graphic for our viewers.

This is a decision that I not only support but push for. In hindsight, I know it was the wrong decision. We didn't trust the American public enough to let them see the video in its entire context. Instead we added to their confusion about the incident by toploading the story with all the mitigating factors such as insurgents using mosques to fight from and booby-trapping dead bodies—while not honestly evaluating the visual evidence that this shooting was both cavalier and without provocation.

Because they didn't get the whole story, viewers filled their lack of understanding with their own conclusions, based on personal perceptions, political beliefs and emotional reactions—almost anything but factual detail. The very thing we held back on.

On this basis, many viewers decided the Marine was justified. When the hate mail and the death threats started pouring into my email accounts, many people accused me of omitting the mitigating factors with which we actually began our report.

THE AFTERMATH

Since I haven't seen the actual broadcast, I don't learn until the next day what has happened. NBC anchor Brian Williams, in an incredibly generous gesture to me and the burgeoning blog movement, mentioned, at the end of my mosque shooting report, that I also keep an independent blog. He then read the Internet address on air to his ten million viewers, inadvertently sending thousands of rabid right-wingers to my electronic front door. I'm certain they could have found it anyway, but this kept them from having to search (his on-air promotion will actually help me reach millions a week later, when I write my Open Letter and post it on the site).

But the morning after the broadcast, when I wake up at Camp Falluja and connect my satellite modem to check my email, I have more than six hundred waiting for me. In a prolonged and ill-advised display of masochism, I sit on a concrete barrier smoking cigarettes and reading at least the first couple of lines of every one of them. While there are a lot of messages of support, the negative, more inherently dramatic responses tend to monopolize my attention.

After a while, they run together in a tone of hateful—even threatening—rhetoric:

> *You better sleep with one eye open, you anti-war asshole! You fuck with one Marine, you fuck with all of us Marines, douchebag! Semper Fi and sleep tight, you piece of shit!*
> *Mark*

> *We know where you live. We know what you drive. We know who your friends are. And we'll be waiting for you when you get back home. You made a big mistake.*
> *SMS*

May your entire family contract AIDS or die a painful death from cancer.
Anonymous

I imagine you didn't give a thought to the danger you put your family in, did you? Well, some whacko is probably fashioning a six pack of Molitov [sic] cocktails to deliver to them, but hey, lookit the money and fame you got at someone else's expense. You're dirt schmuck and I don't think there is anything too horrible that could happen to you.
Jim

We would love to be able to give thanks this Thanksgiving that you were killed by one of your Arab friends. When you get killed every American will dance in the streets. YOU ARE THE ENEMY! WE HATE YOU!!!
Annie

Hey Kev,
Waiting for the picture with your head laying on your back. So when do you suppose we will see that?
Bill

Sigh . . .
I wonder why the units who have imbedded [sic] journalists who rat them out do not frag them. There is absolutely no place for f*cking reporters in a combat zone. Plain and simple.
A Grandmother in Houston

If you were shadowing my unit in the field, I would personally put a round in the back of your head myself. . . . I am praying that some good Americans find out where you live and teach you a lesson or two about betraying your country.
Anonymous

O'REILLY AND NORTH

The emails will continue at the rate of about three hundred per day for the next year. The numbers will rise or fall depending on who has decided to fan the flames: right-wing bloggers or conservative Fox News Channel talk-show hosts such as Bill O'Reilly and ex-Marine and '80s Iran-Contra scandal figure Oliver North.

Fox was a part of the pool, so both men have had a chance to watch the entire video. They either misinterpreted the events or decided the facts were too inconvenient.

In either case, instead of reminding viewers that as citizens of a democracy, we are all responsible for what our military does in our name in a time of war, both bad and good, O'Reilly and North attack as unpatriotic anyone who believes we should live up to our national ideals of seeing truth revealed and justice served.

In his own blog post on November 28, 2004, O'Reilly makes several errors that create misconceptions that ripple through cyberspace and mobilize an army of chronically misinformed ideologues to come out swinging with erroneous emails and half-baked accusations.

O'Reilly writes (identifying the Marine as a soldier), *"On the tape you can see the insurgent move before the soldier pulls the trigger."*

I was closer to the insurgent than Bill O'Reilly ever could be—the insurgent never even twitched. His mistake, as one Marine said on tape: "Yeah, he's breathing."

O'Reilly continues, *"If that young Marine had homicide on his mind, he would have entered the Mosque shooting. But he did not."*

The truth is, regardless of his intentions, the Marine did enter the mosque and begin shooting. According to the Naval Criminal Investigative Service investigation, the same lance corporal admitted to shooting three of the wounded Iraqis when he entered the compound before me. He used his 9 mm pistol after first firing with his M-16, which jammed. I recorded on video the sound of the distinctive small-arm reports while waiting to go inside the mosque.

The shots were fired in a slow and methodical manner, not the frantic pattern of combat when the enemy is shooting back. A Marine Corps statement issued on May 4, 2005, five months after the incident, states: "During the assault, the corporal entered the building and shot 3 AIF [U.S. military parlance for anti-Iraqi forces or insurgents], one of whom was recorded on videotape by reporter Kevin Sites. The Marine admits in his sworn statements that he shot the 3 AIF in self-defense believing they posed a threat to him and his fellow Marines."

The report continues, "The ballistic reports indicate the projectiles removed from the bodies of three AIF were attributable to the corporal's weapon (M-16)."

O'Reilly concludes, *"The Pentagon is not releasing the name of the Marine, and is investigating. Both of these things are fair. But this case is not complicated, and anyone condemning that soldier should himself be condemned."*

The truth is that out of fairness to the Marine during the investigation I didn't release his name—nor have I now, after its conclusion. More importantly, the case *is* complicated, both in the small facts and intentions relating to the individual Marine and the larger facts and intentions relating to our military and nation as a whole.

OUR FAILING

For me, the problems following the incident are predictable. In the United States there is a loud outcry against me and against NBC and, to a lesser degree, the media overall for the perception of having betrayed the troops in a time of war.

All the other American networks follow NBC's lead in not showing the actual shooting on the mosque video, while in Europe at least one network in each country does. However, in the Middle East, nearly everyone is seeing the entire segment—over and over again. During the week following the release of the video, Al Jazeera airs it nearly once every hour.

Later, I would consider how sadly we failed the public in our responsibility to them, that it was not our government or military that censored us in this story; we, the American media, did it ourselves.

Everyone in the world had the potential to see one of the most important and controversial stories to come out of the war—except the citizens of the nation whose own military was directly involved.

NBC

As any corporate behemoth might, NBC responds to the outcry by slowly backing away from me. I had been a Murrow Award–winning staff producer for them in the past and a go-to freelance war reporter for them since Afghanistan in 2001. But now I begin to see Associated Press reports that have NBC referring to me as a freelance cameraman—or not even bothering to defend me at all. The silence became deafening.

I had reported the biggest and most controversial story in the world that week, but during this incredibly challenging moment, I never even merit a call of support from the NBC News president at the time, Neal Shapiro, until I complain to Verdi that I feel NBC has left me hanging in the wind.

Other reporters hound me around Camp Falluja as they try to get comments on the story for their own networks or publications. I refuse, feeling the story is still in play and that I don't want to be the central focus. I also feel that none of them, my own network included, will give me the time and space to tell the more complete and nuanced version of events.

NBC offers to let me do a *Nightly News* segment titled "Own Words," in which a subject tells his or her own story without a reporter interjecting other information, but the maximum amount of time the network is willing to give is less than two minutes. I know that the time will end before I can provide any significant detail. Then MSNBC.com, the network's news Web site, offers me the opportunity to post a story.

KEVINSITES.NET

But that is when I realize that I don't have to be beholden to anyone to get my unedited version of this story on record. I still have my own independent war blog.

I first launched the blog at the urging and with the support of southern California tech gurus Xeni Jardin and John Parres while still working for CNN covering the invasion of Iraq. At the time, I had only heard about blogs and had no idea how to start one. Jardin and Parres told me that if I sent them photographs and text that got behind the scenes of the war, they would create and maintain a site where they could be posted.

My blogging was completely counterintuitive. Instead of pithy diary entries, I began sending them long-form, highly detailed first-person accounts of what it was really like to be in northern Iraq covering the Kurdish territories both in the buildup to and during the invasion. People responded—in one very active point of the war, the site got a million hits and drew a loyal base of readers who created an ongoing dialogue.

Since I was a staff correspondent and had not cleared the idea with my bosses before I left for Iraq, they made me shut the blog down just a few weeks after we started. But the large response by people hungry for fresh, raw and personal reporting on the war made me realize its potential.

When I left CNN a year later in the fall of 2003 and went back to work for NBC as a freelancer in Iraq, part of our agreement required that they let me keep posting independently to kevinsites.net. Perhaps because of the MSNBC association with Microsoft, NBC had at the time a more sophisticated view of blogging's potential as an amplifier for both its coverage and its correspondents.

In hindsight, it was perhaps the most serendipitous deal I could have made to save my reputation and my career.

From my cot in Camp Falluja I stop looking at the hundreds of hate emails and hunker down to write what I title "Open Letter to the Devil Dogs of the 3.1." It is to be a full account of events leading up to, during and after the mosque shooting. In it I will explain not only what I witnessed but what I felt, as well as what my responsibilities were as a journalist and why it was not just the right choice but the *only* moral and ethical choice.

I have addressed it to the Marines, but it's also meant for the world. In an email, I ask my sister Shawn if she knows a lawyer who could look at the letter. With so much heated debate around the incident, I want to protect myself. In some ways, I look at the article as a kind of self-deposition.

Shawn contacts her former boss at Dick Clark Productions, Trudi Behr, who is married to the prominent Los Angeles attorney Joel Behr. According to my sister, Joel and Trudi are fans of my blog, and I had met them for dinner at their house once, prior to this trip to Iraq.

Both of them take me on as a kind of crisis communication project, helping me to think out what the article needs to accomplish—telling what I saw, what it meant and why as a journalist I had to tell the story.

In the meantime, a right-wing Web site called WorldNetDaily.com is claiming I am an antiwar activist. Citing this one "shred of evidence," an antiwar German Web site had, without my permission, taken photographs from my blog and posted them.

Shawn and Xeni Jardin contact the site and threaten legal action if the photos aren't removed.

OPEN LETTER TO THE DEVIL DOGS OF THE 3.1

On Sunday, November 21, 2004, I post the open letter on my blog. It is eight days after the actual incident. As a courtesy, I send a copy to NBC and MSNBC. (Neal Shapiro has advised me earlier not to write a response—or, if I am determined, to let them make suggestions. I decide it is best for me to do this on my own—with a little help from my friends.)

The original article is 2,600 words long with several photographs—but since we don't have a way to post the video, only the text is posted.

I conclude it with the following paragraph, which I believed sums up our differing roles:

> *So here, ultimately, is how it plays out: When the Iraqi man in the mosque posed a threat, he was your enemy; when he was subdued, he*

was your responsibility; when he was killed in front of my eyes and my
camera, the story of his death became my responsibility.

The burdens of war, as you so well know, are unforgiving for all
*of us.**

The response to the article is overwhelming. Media outlets from around
the world publish excerpts, or in some cases, such as Britain's *Guardian*
newspaper and *Marine Corps Times,* carry nearly the entire piece.

According to user statistics on kevinsites.net, readership skyrockets
from just 37,600 hits early in the month to more than two million the day
after the letter is posted.

Anecdotally, at least, the impact it has on the perceptions of the American public about the story seems even more remarkable. While the hate mail
and the death threats do not disappear, I am able to see the trend of hate
shift either to begrudging understanding of my actions or outright support
now that more information is available.

With a few exceptions,† even my own industry, which had been mostly
ambivalent in its support and defense of my journalistic integrity, now
seems to enthusiastically welcome me back into the fold. *Wired* magazine
will give me its first-ever Rave Award for blogging, specifically concerning
the mosque shooting, and the University of Oregon will honor me with its
Payne Award for Ethics for both my television and blog coverage of the
incident.

---

* Entire unabbreviated text of the open letter can be found in Appendix A.

† Shortly after the mosque-shooting video aired on NBC and the fallout began, reporter Darrin
Mortenson wrote an article titled *Blame the Messenger* in which he vigorously defended my actions
in Falluja, my reputation as a fair-minded reporter and the crucial role reporters play in a democracy during wartime. It also highlighted Mortenson's own courage, considering he was working for
California's *North County Times,* considered the hometown newspaper for the Marine Corps base
at Camp Pendleton and home of the 3.1 Marines. Story link found here: *http://www.nctimes.com/*
articles/2004/11/21/opinion/commentary/14_23_1711_20_04.txt

EDDIE ADAMS

At Camp Falluja, I'm too exhausted to feel vindicated and my difficulties are not over yet. When I leave and get back to NBC's Baghdad Bureau, I learn that the famous Vietnam photojournalist Eddie Adams has died. He was the one who snapped the incredible Pulitzer Prize–winning photograph of a Viet Cong fighter being summarily executed by a South Vietnamese general. Adams captured it just as the trigger was pulled and the man was beginning to grimace.

It was a poignant moment for Adams, who would later write, regretful of the photo, "the General killed the Viet Cong; I killed the General with my camera."

It seems relevant that Adams would die some thirty years after Vietnam and during a time when the challenges of telling the truth in war were revealing themselves again.

CHAPTER 2

HOLIDAY HELL
Reporting the Tsunami

BANDA ACEH, INDONESIA | JANUARY 4, 2004

ARMY OF CORPSES

For the moment it feels much better to be on a motorbike, hauling through the debris-strewn streets of Banda Aceh, than standing still, surrounded by the humid embrace of the ghosts of thousands who died here only a week ago.

Aceh province is the northern spear tip of Sumatra, which is part of the Indonesian island chain—and the province is ground zero for the tsunami triggered by an undersea earthquake just off its coast one day after Christmas.

Mohammed and I are headed to a small village southwest of Banda Aceh. The path is so muddy and rutted that it's sometimes impossible for us to get any traction with our motorbikes. We are looking for one of the mass graves being used to bury the victims here.

I am apprehensive for seventeen-year-old Mohammed, whom I have hired as an English translator after finding him standing in a water line a few days earlier.

Even though he has not had much opportunity to talk with native speakers, Mohammed's English is excellent. Remarkably, however, since his family's home is near the hills and was spared by the tsunami, he had not yet seen a dead body, despite the fact that they seem to be literally everywhere. I have seen them hanging from trees, protruding from the open doors of cars, buried facedown in ditches, arms and legs poking up through fields like withered crops. Yesterday, I made him come with me to Banda Aceh's devastated marina area, where the inescapable images burned themselves into his young mind. He covered his face with a piece of cloth and tried to avoid the smell as we interviewed families who were looking for the bodies of loved ones.

We see a fire a little way ahead and stop at a swampy opening of palm trees. Two brothers in their early twenties are sifting through the remains of a house about twenty yards across the water from us.

"We're looking for our parents," one says—before slipping off a downed tree trunk into the muck up to his waist. The others laugh. It seems a welcome sound, even if out of place in this ghoulish setting.

Seeing a flat, smoky fire nearby, I ask what it is that's burning.

"A body, but not someone they recognize," Mohammed translates.

The flesh burns, appropriately enough, like the tallow of a candle and melts slowly into a maze of branches below.

We ride farther down the trail, seemingly deeper into the heart of darkness. A brownish yellow foot sticks out of one of the many black body bags that line both sides of our path. Mohammed reacts with a groan and veers the bike to avoid running over it.

OUT OF IRAQ

Amid the remnants of tsunami-thrashed Banda Aceh, I consider how, only a month ago, this trip had started so differently.

Desperately needing a vacation, I left Iraq a few weeks after the mosque shooting and caught a plane out of Baghdad to Amman, Jordan, and then from Jordan to Bangkok, Thailand.

It had been an incredibly tense time for me, as well as my family and friends. Because of the constant death threats I was receiving, NBC News hired security guards to keep an eye on my last known address in the United States—a house in California that I owned with an ex-girlfriend.

Though I no longer lived there (we had broken up a few weeks before my latest deployment to Iraq), the threats were specific enough to warrant a few precautions despite the current awkward nature of our relationship.

My plan was to decompress in Asia for as long as I could afford. I didn't want to think, speak or write about war, Iraq or anything associated with news. I was so determined to make a clean break for a while that I shipped all my camera gear back to the United States.

CHINESE JUNK

My first stop was a week scuba diving off Thailand in the Andaman Sea while sailing on a traditional Chinese junk that had been converted from an old coal-running ship to a diving live-aboard. I had stored my scuba gear at a hotel in Jordan while I was in Iraq and picked it up after my flight out of Baghdad.

Since the invasion of Iraq in spring 2003, I had rotated into and out of the country for two or three months at a time, coming out for a month and then redeploying for another round.

It is an uncomfortable and isolating life—as anyone who has done this kind of rotation can tell you. But as a freelancer, the money is too good to pass up, and the opportunity to endear yourself to a network shorthanded on staffers who want to be there for any length of time makes saying no a very difficult thing indeed.

For me, scuba diving was the best way to forget temporarily the perpetual violence of Iraq. Underwater there are no explosions, no shouting, no guns, bombs, tanks or choppers. There are no MREs, IEDs, AIFs or any of the other relentless acronyms that invade your senses when you cover war and the American military for a living.

I spent a week on the junk, diving four times a day, eating amazing Thai food and, once, even climbing the rigging to stand on top of the mainsail. Thoughts of Falluja and the mosque began to fall away, at least during my waking hours.

After leaving the junk, I met up with some friends to explore more of Thailand, as well as Laos and Cambodia. In Siem Riep, Cambodia, we visited the twelfth-century Khmer temple ruins of Angkor Wat, with its marvels of engineering and design artistry that blend elements of Hinduism and Buddhism.

But in Phnom Penh, it is not the ancient but rather the modern history that envelops me sadly. On the day after Christmas, I visit both the Tuol Sleng Museum and the killing fields of Choeung Ek—heartbreaking memorials to the Cambodian genocide, in which an estimated two million people died at the hands of the Khmer Rouge communists and their leader, Pol Pot, during their four years in power from 1975 to 1979. In their efforts to transform Cambodia into a "utopian agricultural paradise," they left a wake of death and destruction from which the nation has not yet completely recovered.

On this day at Choeung Ek, I consider the magnitude of this crime by peering at the skulls and bones of eight thousand of their victims piled in a glass-walled pagoda—ten stories high.

When I return to the hotel, my friend Corey tells me that something huge has happened. He's watching CNN but has the remote in his hand. On the screen I see an image of Phuket, Thailand, the port of call for the Chinese junk and my recent scuba trip. I'm watching a group of people, bruised and bleeding, including one that I recognize as a man named Jim, a Brit who had dived with me. Another image pops up showing the island covered in a blanket of water. The crawl under the video reads, "Tsunami strikes Asia, 20 thousand dead."

RESCUING THE DEAD

While Mohammed and I are searching for the mass grave, we find an even more compelling story in a group of young professionals from Jakarta who call themselves the Islamic Community for Social Help.

They are doctors, lawyers, teachers, all volunteers, clad in rubber boots and surgical masks, focused on doing what few others will—wrestling away from the vultures, worms and soggy earth the remains of the tsunami dead.

We follow them as they move deeper into the jungle and into the more remote parts of the village. They have been busy. There are black bags everywhere. We pad through a small clearing where two more bodies are found; one, a man floating facedown in a large, fetid pool of water created by the tsunami; the second, a woman trapped in a cake of debris made of palm fronds, wood and mud.

The men split into teams and slowly, reverently work at freeing the two from nature's reckless grip—the bodies now remind me of baby sparrows, crushed by a clumsy, eager child.

The man's body is naked and floating near a patch of reeds. Five volunteers wade in to get him. One pulls a large plank from the water and uses it like a lever to loosen the suction of mud attached to the body. He slips it under the chest and poles it carefully, feet first into the end of a large black plastic bag that the others hold open.

Meanwhile, another group is uncovering the debris pile from around the woman. Only her arm is visible at the moment, but more is revealed with each piece they remove. Twenty minutes later, the body is fully exposed.

They slide a rectangle of plywood under the corpse. As they drag it out on the homemade stretcher, I can finally see her face. I want to look away but feel I owe her the courtesy of witnessing the pain of her experience. The face is already beginning to decompose in the tropical heat and her top and bottom lips are pulled back in a frozen grimace. It's clear to me that her death was neither quick nor painless.

Now the man's body is being carried from the water to firm ground. His feet are exposed and the white flesh is beginning to fall away after so many days of being immersed.

Once on shore, the men begin trussing the body up in more black plastic. I watch their uncalloused hands, hands not accustomed to such tasks, skillfully wrapping the bags with twine, transforming what had been a violent and chaotic death into something more orderly, more peaceful; something that the living could make sense of and that the dead may have ultimately wished for.

THANKS, BUT NO THANKS

When I call the NBC News desk in New York to tell them I'm still in Asia and in position to help them report on the tsunami, the producer working overnight seems relieved to have a reporter so close.

But when I speak to the desk producer again, a little later, she tells me she has spoken with Danny Noa, the foreign news manager. He said not to worry about it, that they already have a team heading to the region from Hong Kong.

"But this thing is huge," I tell the producer. "There's already twenty thousand dead and the numbers are going up every hour. You're going to need more than one team."

I don't wait to be told no again. I pack my clothes, head to the airport and buy a ticket back to Bangkok. Things are chaotic when I arrive, but there are still a few flights scheduled to Phuket. I buy another ticket and head south. In the meantime, I learn just how deadly the tsunami has been. According to news reports, it was unleashed by a massive 9.0-magnitude undersea earthquake whose epicenter was just off the west coast of Banda Aceh, Indonesia. While nations including Thailand, Sri Lanka and India suffered from the tsunami, Banda Aceh bore the greatest brunt, with a death toll already rising to about fifty thousand.

When I reach Phuket and call NBC again, things have changed, as I expected. Now they seem very happy to have me in place and ready to report, but there is one critical problem; I had sent my video camera and all my transmission gear back to the States. All I have left to report with is a pocket-sized Canon PowerShot digital still camera.

They tell me that the NBC News magazine *Dateline* has a crew en route to Phuket with extra cameras. Until then, I will do "live" reports from locations already set up by news agencies such as Associated Press Television and Reuters.

On my first night in Phuket, I walk down the devastated beachfront that I would later describe in my blog under the title "Paradise Tossed":

Patong Beach's usually bustling oceanfront Thuweewong Road— now looks like the apocalypse. A bright yellow speedboat sits in the middle of the street cracked in two like an eggshell, the sidewalk has disintegrated under the sledgehammer force of the water, cars defy gravity posed in every position imaginable with the exception of sitting on their four wheels, and the beach, littered with chunks of concrete has become the road, while the road covered in sand has seemingly turned into the beach. The ocean worm has burrowed through the island and in doing so, turned everything inside out.

As night falls—several immigrant men, tailors who specialize in turning out handcrafted suits for western tourists at lightning speed, sit around a makeshift table in front of what's left of their shop. They have only a couple of small lights, powered by a car battery—but it's still very easy to see—they have lost everything.

The owner, Gillan Rai, a Nepalese man married to a Thai woman says he's worried about how he'll support his wife and three children.

He says he's worked his entire life to build his business and in an instant, it's gone.

"The wave was like a cobra," he says, demonstrating with his hand, "it fanned out before crashing down on us."

One of Rai's employees—says he just arrived in Thailand a few weeks ago, happy about the prospect of a new job and a new life.

"I don't know what I'll do now," he says, "but I have to work."

Rai holds up a bottle of vodka that the men had been mixing with their colas as they talk. The bottle is scratched and the label half torn off.

"We found it," he says, "washed up on our doorstep the day after."

He smiles knowingly, the irony not lost. While the ocean has taken away all he's ever had—it has left him a way to toast his own misfortune.

After five days of my reporting in Phuket, NBC decides to send me to the tsunami's ground zero, Banda Aceh. Two days later, I arrive at the Banda Aceh airport, already busy as large transport aircraft arrive every hour with hastily arranged relief supplies from around the world.

NBC's new *Nightly News* anchorman, Brian Williams, has also arrived with a crew, dozens of boxes of television and transmission gear, as well as food, sleeping bags and toiletries to keep us fed, warm and clean while we work on this island-turned-graveyard.

NATURE'S DESTRUCTION VERSUS MAN'S

Everywhere I point my camera in Banda Aceh, there is death.

It is a tragedy multiplied out in figures beyond my imagination but, in some ways, still easier to take than the killing I had seen in war. This was nature at work. There is no recourse, no negotiation with nature. And nature's destruction, unlike war's, tends to unite people rather than divide them. Here people are coming together to help those victimized by the tsunami.

The United States has even sent an aircraft carrier to Indonesia, the USS *Abraham Lincoln,* which is now fully engaged, not in bombing sorties but in humanitarian relief.

Its shipboard desalinization plant is turning seawater into critical supplies of drinking water at the rate of ninety thousand gallons a day; the water is ferried to remote locations on the island by the ship's Seahawk helicopters.

THE GRAVE

After searching throughout the morning, Mohammed and I find one of the dozens of mass graves in Aceh province. In the hour that we stand over a pit the size of a swimming pool, we see Indonesian army trucks pull up nine times and unload body bags. There is no dignity here, but also no alternative. The gate is dropped and the bags heaved over the ledge into the hole like garbage.

They land with a solid, dull thud. On one occasion a dump truck simply backs up to the pit, raises its bed and the bodies slide in. A soldier lowers only one bag gently, a small one containing the remains of a child.

When the job is done, a backhoe scoops great heaps of red earth and drops it on top of the bodies, many of which will never be identified, leaving their family members wondering for the rest of their lives which hole in the ground holds the bodies of their loved ones.

When we leave the grave site, we throttle our motorbikes all the way back—twenty-five, thirty, forty miles an hour. We ride as fast as we can, trying to outrun the smell of death, but it stubbornly travels with us, gripping the fabric of our clothes. It will not let go—until we free it by fire.

INTERMISSION

Fathers and Sons

INDONESIA

I'm working with an NBC crew at an overcrowded hospital in Banda Aceh that has been turned into an extension of the children's wing to accommodate young tsunami victims.

I'm ready to do a stand-up, the portion of the television story where the reporter appears on camera saying something impressively intelligent, remarkably weighty—in other words, irrelevant, as a way to prove to viewers we were there.

But here's the problem: my cameraman, Duane, can't keep his rig steady on his shoulder because, at the moment, he's bawling his eyes out. There's good reason. Duane is a new dad and he's just been shooting video of a father singing to his sick son, who may be near death. The singing is the only thing that eases the boy's pain.

Duane is a veteran shooter, someone who has seen plenty of the world's ugly things in places like Haiti and Afghanistan. I've watched him trudge through a day of misery without flinching, then put his camera down and tell a joke to move past it. But this moment has forced his emotions to the surface from what I imagine is that indelible connection between parent and child.

It repeats itself in another room where another father named Saiful lies on a foam pad on the concrete floor next to his seven year-old son. Saiful lost his wife and and other two children and this boy is all he has left. Duane focuses his lens on the father's hand as he gently strokes the boy's hair. Duane is steady now, trying to honor the man's commitment—as well as his own. I can do nothing else but respect this moment and back away.

CHAPTER 3

TV NEWS OR THE INTERNET

Do I Yahoo!?

LOS ANGELES | FEBRUARY 2005

BOXES

As I roll up the corrugated metal door and peer inside, I am both comforted and unsettled by this moment. All my belongings, the material history of my life, are here. They are clean and protected and all nicely arranged in this one place—an eleven-by-fifteen-foot storage space two miles from LAX.

I have never been much of a collector. In the dozens of moves I have made in my life, I have always found it easier just to start over than to take the detritus of my last stop with me. Last August, when I split with my girlfriend before returning to Iraq for the fifth time, I rented a small truck to bring the stuff I wanted. Aside from a small couch and table, it would have all fit in my car.

I brought it all here to this storage center and unpacked it neatly, hanging up my clothes on an overhead pipe, putting my surfboard in a protected niche, the couch and the table arranged almost as if it were my living room.

When I finished, I sat down on the couch and thought how easy it would be for me to live here—if only there were some electricity. I had spent enough time roughing it in such places as Kosovo, Afghanistan and Iraq that an L.A. storage locker didn't seem like much of a stretch.

Now that I'm back, I realize that I won't be able to just keep my things in tidy little boxes. I'll have to start my life again. But I'm a forty-two-year-old man with the contents of this locker, a car—and little else. I sleep at night on a couch in the middle of my sister Shawn's living room.

My siblings have been a humbling part of my career trajectory, and they're used to my "stopovers." I'm grateful to them for taking me in. I have only one complaint: there is not a single comfortable piece of furniture in my sister's whole house.

THE MEETING

I'm on the fifth floor at 30 Rock in New York City. It's the management offices of NBC News. I've put off coming here as long as I could. Since the mosque shooting, I've been able to fit in a month's vacation in Asia and another three weeks covering the tsunami, and spent several weeks catching up with friends and family back in Los Angeles.

But finally I had to board a flight to the East Coast for what I only imagine will be a strange meeting with Bill Wheatley, David Verdi and Danny Noa—the same NBC triumvirate who "managed" me through the mosque shooting.

I have a feeling it will be a combination of congratulations and interrogation, but one that will end, I hope, with them letting me try out for a staff reporter opening in Hong Kong.

Immediately following the mosque shooting, NBC distanced itself from me by publicly emphasizing my freelance status. Now, after I have been acknowledged for my reporting and journalistic ethics with two national awards, the network seems more eager to bring me back into the fold.

While I am waiting outside Wheatley's office, Noa arrives. He and Verdi both work from the MSNBC building across the river in Secaucus, New Jersey.

After shaking my hand and making some small talk, Danny pauses for a second.

"You know, Kevin," he says, "if I were that guy's lawyer . . ."

"What guy's lawyer?"

"That Marine's lawyer," he answers. "I bet—I know I could get that guy off, convince them it was self-defense."

I'm a bit stunned by his remark. It illustrates to me just how difficult my ongoing task is going to be when even some of my own bosses still don't understand that, where my actions are concerned, the mosque shooting was about being loyal to the truth, not just about catching someone in a war crime.

Inside Wheatley's office we are joined by David Verdi, vice president of Foreign News, and things begin just as I thought they would. Wheatley congratulates me on making it out of Iraq alive—then asks me what I've been doing since my return.

Verdi jumps in and the conversation goes in the direction I anticipated. "What is it," he asks, "that you want to do next?"

I tell them I've had inquiries from two other networks, but my desire is to stay with NBC, if I can evolve as a reporter beyond the perpetual rotation into and out of Iraq.

"What do you want?" Wheatley asks.

"I know Ned Colt is leaving Hong Kong to join the London Bureau," I say, without hesitation. "I want you to give me a chance at that correspondent slot. China is the biggest foreign story going, and I can bring the same kind of aggressive approach to covering China that I bring to Iraq."

"Kevin," Noa jumps in, "we've all been talking and we think that we need to play to your strengths—and those strengths are in covering Iraq. We could make you staff and have you base out of London, but we'd really want you there primarily for Iraq rotation."

This was not what I want to hear—but it is what I thought would be offered first and is the last thing I would consider. If I was going to continue going back to Iraq, I would prefer to stay freelance living in California— where I could at least surf and see the sunshine during my breaks home.

In my time in network news, I have learned that news managers rarely make efforts to accomodate low-level correspondents like me. We are disposable, dispensable and lining up in the hallway with smiles and the word *yes* on our lips. But I have spent too much time in war zones, risking too much, to be easily assuaged with the same offers tossed to the young and eager.

They are happy to send me to places like Afghanistan, Iraq and the tsunami region, places where viewers will accept someone who doesn't look like a clean-cut network news correspondent, but I am not on anyone's short list for an established bureau slot.

FROM MARS

I remember meeting with Wheatley once before, prior to my last tour of Iraq. I knew I was not a favorite of his, and somehow we got into a discussion of how I look on air, with my longish hair and goatee.

"I think viewers expect freelance war correspondents to look a little different," I had defended myself by saying. "We're in war zones—we don't have time to shave every day and run a comb through our hair."

"Yes, they expect you to look different," Wheatley had said, "but not like you're from Mars."

At that point, I had a very clear idea, regardless of my reporting skills, of where the network saw me in its hierarchy. I was not on the same planet.

But in this instance, Verdi is willing to let me make my case, partly, I believe, because he thinks I deserve at least a hearing—but, just as importantly, it will allow him to ask me the question they have really invited me here to answer. And so it comes.

OVER THE FENCE

"To be a bureau correspondent for the network, we have to know that you're with us one hundred percent all the time," Verdi says, setting it up. "When we tell you we need something from you in the field, you're not an independent contractor, you're not in a position to say no and you can't go AWOL." Here it comes, I think.

"In Falluja, you went AWOL on us when you said you weren't going to feed that tape." I nod. "As a staff correspondent, that can't happen. Why did you go over the wall on us in Falluja?"

I think for a moment before answering them, trying to collect my thoughts without getting defensive or angry. It's not normally easy for me, but this is a moment to be calm and deliberate.

"I didn't go AWOL on you in Falluja," I state, politely but firmly. "When I first captured that shooting on videotape, I had the desk contact all three of you immediately. Knowing how conflicted I was about the whole thing, I wanted to create a kind of safety net—so that I wouldn't be able to destroy the tape or ignore it—as long as you knew I had it." They look at me, nodding in recollection.

"But this was an incredibly volatile situation made even more precarious by the fact we were a part of the network pool. I felt NBC would be responsible with the tape, reporting it in context, but I had no idea what everyone else would do." I pause. "But while I'm struggling with all the ramifications of this videotape on the ground, what I'm getting from you guys is pressure to release it so we don't violate the rules of the pool. Honestly, I couldn't care less about the pool during that time. You all know that since I was the one that shot it, I would also be the one to take the brunt of whatever resulted from its release—not NBC or the pool." They are all silent, waiting for me to go on.

"I've taken all the fallout for that tape, and while it's tapered off, it hasn't stopped. I still get hundreds of hate emails and death threats every day. When I told you in Falluja I wasn't going to feed that video, it was the one certain way I knew to get a dialogue started again, which is what I needed more than just pressure to feed it."

They remain quiet while I make my close. "I'm a good journalist. I'm aggressive, but I'm ethical—I had very real moral concerns about whether I could live with the results of releasing the video—I had to come to my own rightful conclusions, not be bullied into them."

"Well," says Wheatley, after another long pause, "it was a situation that I've never encountered before. I don't think any of us ever have."

The meeting lasts only ten minutes more, no time for other explanations or other offers.

A STRANGE OFFER

A week after our meeting, NBC calls and makes me an offer I never saw coming. Instead of sending me back to Iraq or giving me a shot at Hong Kong, they want to see if I'm interested in staying in the United States and working as a domestic correspondent. But the offer has, as I suspect, some strings attached.

"You'd have to get a haircut," Verdi tells me over the phone, "and you'd have to shave the goatee. Also, we'd send you to correspondent 'boot camp' in Atlanta for a few months to work with Charlie Ryan."

I know Charlie. He is a top-notch senior producer who is also responsible for training the new guys. We worked together when I was a staff producer, during the Olympic Park bombing in 1996. I have also seen him during his stints at the Baghdad Bureau in Iraq.

I don't know what to say to Verdi, other than that I need some time to think about it. I had done some domestic reporting when I was at CNN, but I didn't care for the hard focus on ratings generators—stories on kidnappings, missing children and serial killers, such as the Washington, D.C., area snipers.

I also feel a little slighted. I have been a professional journalist for fifteen years, including a sabbatical as a college-level lecturer, and have been reporting and risking my life in war zones for network news since 1999, but now that I might appear on air in America, I need to learn how to do the job—and how to look like everyone else.

THE HOT ZONE

Back in Los Angeles, I'm having dinner at the house of Joel and Trudi Behr, the connected couple who helped me through the mosque shooting aftermath.

Joel tells me he has a proposition for me. Over dessert he asks me if I've ever considered working outside of network news.

"After the year I've had, I'd consider almost anything but the networks," I joke.

Joel smiles. "Good," he says, with his even tone betraying little. "I have a friend named Lloyd Braun who's just been hired by Yahoo! to head their new media group. He told me that there's so much potential there he feels like he's at CBS at the dawn of the television era."

I nod, not sure where he's going with this. "He's considering all kinds of programming ideas, so I pitched one, 'Kevin Sites in the Hot Zone.' Within thirty seconds he said, 'I love it.' "

I must look a little confused. "It would be you on the Internet doing multimedia reporting, video, text stories and even live, online discussions with readers. And the 'Hot Zone' is any topic you decide to cover."

"Mostly conflict stuff?" I ask.

"It can be conflict or anything you consider a hot zone—drugs, the environment . . . Does that sound like something you'd be interested in?"

"Yeah," I say, thinking about the possibilities, "very much so."

A few weeks after the dinner, Joel calls me on the phone and asks me to write a proposal for the Hot Zone that he can send to Lloyd.

Surprisingly, even though I'm putting it together from scratch, writing the pitch is incredibly easy for me. In fact, the first paragraph of the proposal has such a swagger of "new media" picking a fight with "old" that it comes off almost arrogant:

> *Yahoo! outmaneuvers its Internet competitors and the dinosaur television networks by deploying veteran combat correspondent and pioneering SoJo (solo journalist) Kevin Sites into global hot zones for live, interactive news reports using video, text and still imagery to tell*

the stories the world isn't seeing and providing them in a way they haven't seen before.

But in this emerging new dynamic, arrogance, at least in the start-up phase, may be necessary to overcome the obstacles in actually getting the Hot Zone up and running.

After I meet with Lloyd Braun, Joel calls to tell me that we have a deal. It's a confirmation of the idea's power as well as a frightening realization for me that now I have to make it work.

I know Lloyd is a genius at spotting innovative ideas that others don't have the vision to see or the stomach to make real. He is, after all, the ABC executive who green-lighted the most expensive pilot in the history of television, *Lost*. That decision cost him his job there, but he would be vindicated when it became a smash hit—for a few seasons, the biggest show on television.

THE TURNING POINT

For me, the opportunity is a professional crossroads. Could I give up a career as a TV war correspondent after sacrificing so much to get there? The Internet is a notoriously fickle and unforgiving place. The late '90s dot-com bomb proved that. There are a lot of bloggers out there—but no solid, independent news business model in place yet. Additionally, I know that in the cyberworld, the time allocated to make something work is notoriously short.

"We'll know within a few months of launching," Joel said to me, "whether it's working or not."

If it doesn't, I wonder, will I be able to go back to network TV?

I hadn't called NBC back about its domestic correspondent offer but was fairly certain I wasn't interested. I am, however, still interested in China, even though I am doubtful NBC will give me a shot at it.

In some ways, I feel I owe something to the Internet. Using my own personal blog after the mosque shooting, I was able to clarify the facts, to provide depth, details, nuance and personal emotion to the story and still reach an audience in the millions without going through a television network or a publication. Its power and impact are obvious to me.

After talking it over with friends and colleagues, I decide I will make the leap into cyberspace and sign a letter of intent with Yahoo! Two weeks later, Danny Noa from NBC calls me on my mobile phone.

"How would you like the chance to give us a month in Hong Kong at the same day rate as you get in Iraq?" he asks me.

I am caught off guard by the call and somewhat incredulous at the timing.

"Danny—I begged for a shot at Hong Kong and you guys were silent for months. Now you're going to give me a shot?" I shake my head in disbelief, but I know the time has come to cut my network ties finally and officially. I hope it will not be forever, but I understand that it might be.

"It's too late, Danny," I say. "I took another offer."

PURPLE AND GOLD

It's June, my first week in Yahoo!'s offices in Santa Monica, California— and I'm mortified. All the furniture is purple and gold and there is a big gold stars on each cubicle with the name of the employee who sits there.

Since the Yahoo! Media Group is just being formed, many of the cubicles are empty. They seem to me like rows of unplanted fields. While I look out over my new domain, I realize that I have left the world of Brokaw, Jennings and Rather, the medium of such luminaries as Edward R. Murrow and David Brinkley, and I have joined the realm of companies whose names sound more like baby noises than words. And as if the point were not definite enough, my new company spells its official name with an exclamation point.

But the décor is the smallest of my problems. I have three months to hire a staff, purchase gear, create the actual site and specifically define what the actual mission of the Hot Zone should be.

It is, at first, a paralyzing set of challenges. As the biggest Internet portal in the world, with four hundred million unique users every month, Yahoo! has made its mark both as a search engine and an online community. Its successful business model has been about aggregating information, not creating it. I am nothing if not an anomaly here.

Yahoo! News, the Web's most popular news site (twenty-two million users a week), does not write a single word of original copy but compiles information from the wire services and other media outlets and puts it all in one easy-to-find place. It has been a no-brainer recipe for success—and now, with me as its first news correspondent, that strategy is about to change.

Lloyd Braun's vision for the media group is to assemble a production powerhouse of original programming for the Internet—not just to repurpose TV programming and dump it onto a Web site, but to create news and entertainment as unique as the medium itself. It's a vision that will very quickly run into opposition from the man who hired him, Yahoo!'s CEO, former Warner Bros. studio chief Terry Semel.

HIRING THE TEAM

The plan is for me to travel and report solo from the hot zones, but I will need a team to help get me from place to place, to provide research, editorial oversight and even to post the stories to the Web site.

My first hire is researcher Lisa Liu, born in China and now an American citizen. Lisa is an Internet wiz and has previously worked for Radio Free Asia, but, more poignantly, she has a direct and unfortunate connection to conflict. Her father, a Chinese academic, was one of the estimated half million killed during Mao Tse-tung's murderous ten-year "Cultural Revolution" from 1966 to 1976.

For senior producer, I hire someone I worked with at both CNN and NBC but have never before met face-to-face; a tall, lanky rock 'n' roll drummer named Robert Padavick, who also happens to be a top news desk pro-

ducer. He has impressed me by being able to reach anyone, anywhere in the
world, by phone.

During the invasion of Iraq, when I was working for CNN, my team and
I were camped out in the tiny smuggler's town of Chamchamal, waiting for
Kirkuk to fall to coalition forces.

Annoyingly, Robert would find me when I didn't want to be found, calling my Thuraya satellite phone at 4:00 or 5:00 A.M. to wake me up for live
shots anytime someone in Atlanta needed to fill air.

He did the same thing during the Battle of Falluja, when we both worked
for NBC. I know that his perseverance and unmatched ability to dial into
any remote goat-pen location in the world where I might be could come in
very handy for the Hot Zone project.

Together the three of us begin honing our concept and our approach. I
eventually hire a fourth team member, Erin Green, who has worked as a
desk assistant for NBC in its Washington Bureau but who was also a journalism student of mine when I took a two-year teaching sabbatical at California Polytechnic State University in San Luis Obispo.

Erin had always stood out as someone willing to ask the difficult questions—something she did to me when I first met a group of students during
a preliminary interview at Cal Poly.

She had asked me flatly, with no sugarcoated preface: "You're a network
producer working at NBC—why would you come here?"

I stumbled to answer, since part of the reason I decided to take the teaching slot was personal difficulties in my former marriage, some of it caused
by incessant work travel.

Erin is the kind of person who has no problem saying the emperor has
no clothes. I'm the kind of person who needs frequent reality checks to keep
from veering too far off course. I need her on my team, and after some cajol-
ing to get her to leave Washington and a brand-new producer job with
CSPAN, she comes on board.

ALL CONFLICT, ALL THE TIME

Shortly after we begin planning, I realize that despite Yahoo!'s millions of viewers, our own microsite within it will face a huge amount of competition for eyeballs.

All of the research that I have seen concerning successful Internet sites seems to point in one direction—niche markets.

Like the magazine and cable television world, everything has become specialized.

The potpourri days of *Life* and *Look* and *The Ed Sullivan Show* are over. We are living in a time of the Food Network, *Runner's World* and *Cat Fancy*. To succeed, the Hot Zone will also have to to be very specific about what we are going to cover and who our audience will be.

An idea comes to me, appropriately enough while I am online researching conflicts. The London-based International Institute of Strategic Studies (IISS) has a site that serves as a clearinghouse for information on armed conflicts raging around the world.

Aside from Afghanistan and Iraq, it is information that much of the world probably knows little about: a Maoist insurgency in Nepal; Tamil Tiger rebels in Sri Lanka; multinational and ethnic tribal fights in the Congo.

All these conflicts, despite how remote they might seem from daily life in America, have an impact on us, whether through the consumer goods we use from those regions, such as African diamonds, or through the growing terror alliances, such as the Al Qaeda–linked Abu Sayyaf in the Philippines.

The Hot Zone, I decide, will have the ambitious but narrowly defined goal of covering every armed-conflict zone in the world within one year. It will, I hope, be the most important journalistic endeavor of my life so far. Simultaneously, the idea scares me shitless.

Focusing on conflicts will create an unmistakable mission and identity for the Web site in the minds of its viewers. On a loftier plane, it will fulfill a sense of civic and moral responsibility I feel in providing more coverage to the world's nameless and voiceless conflict victims.

THE WAY WAR IS COVERED

The way wars are being covered by some media outlets bothers me. Time limitations for television news programming usually mean that only the news of the day is getting reported.

In Iraq and Afghanistan, news of the day means body counts from the latest bombing. These stories are essential—but fall short in helping educate an audience about the changing dimensions and nuances of the conflicts, which are necessary for people to truly understand them.

As the world's last remaining superpower, the American public's ambivalence about world affairs is not just regrettable but irritating and unacceptable.

Obviously, our little project is not going to change all of that, but it does seem like a way to shoot a flare into the night sky.

According to the IISS, at present there are twenty to thirty active global conflict zones in various degrees of violence. With that number, I will only be able to spend a week to ten days in each place to complete the project in a year.

That means I won't be able to report in depth on each conflict's full chronology or its geopolitical dimensions; there will be no "War Zone 101" on the Hot Zone. Instead I will have to focus on the small stories, in front of and behind the conflicts, which when strung together might help tell the larger story.

What I can accomplish in limited time on the ground is to tell the personal profile stories, to put a human face on global conflict. My model will be the kind of journalism found every Sunday in the *New York Times Magazine,* strong character-driven narratives about people you might not know but whom you learn to care about once you are taken into their worlds.

We won't ignore the larger context of the conflicts, but the Hot Zone will have to find different ways to address them besides my own original reporting. One option is by using the strengths of our new medium, the ability to hyperlink to other information sources.

For example, I'll report about the people I meet on the ground but we will link to BBC country profiles or other reputable information sources for historical background.

The goal is to get our viewers interested through the personal narratives while enticing them to learn even more from additional outside sources. I don't want the Hot Zone to be the last word on any conflict, but for many people, I know it may be the first.

HOW IT WILL WORK

My plan is to use a small Sony high-definition digital video camera, an Apple PowerBook laptop and an RBGAN satellite modem to report almost every day, from around the world, at least one 800-to-1,200-word text dispatch, a still photograph slide show and a couple of video clips—all posted on the Internet by my team back in California.

At the end of the week, they will also compile all the video clips I have transmitted into a narrated network-news-style packaged story that summarizes the issues and challenges faced by people of a specific region.

It's a simple but powerful concept in which story characters can be brought to life multidimensionally using the strengths of all the mediums: the text story providing nuance, the video story recording the inherent drama of movement and the still photograph capturing the human spirit revealed in people's faces.

I'll soon learn, though, that I have vastly underestimated the overwhelming donkey work it takes to report so many dimensions while also having to write and transmit the material at the end of my day—when I am both physically and mentally exhausted.

When we announce our plans for the Hot Zone, I'm criticized by some members of the media for creating a one-year deadline for the project. Some say it's gimmicky, like an online reality TV show about a war correspondent trying to survive a year in the world's most dangerous places. They're wrong, but at the time I can't tell them why. Here now is the reason: I knew that if I didn't complete the project in one year there was a good chance Yahoo!

might cancel it before I finished. (My expectations will be on target. We had only one paid advertiser for our entire year run, one in which our content was not a problem: the film *Syriana*, starring George Clooney and Matt Damon and based loosely on the Middle East experiences of CIA field agent Robert Baer.)

THE FIRST HOT ZONE

While the concept of focusing specifically on armed-conflict zones made sense both journalistically and from a marketing standpoint, I know that commercially it could be a disaster. War coverage draws sizable audiences, but advertisers usually shun it.

Companies wouldn't be clamoring to buy space on the Hot Zone when what we had to offer them was going to be the reporting of violence and tragedy day after day. This would make us very vulnerable in the volatile world of the Internet.

That vulnerability is reinforced shortly before our official launch date, when Lloyd Braun asks me to do a short "explanatory" presentation of the Hot Zone project to Yahoo! CEO Terry Semel. I am under the impression that Semel already knows the details of our plan and has signed off on it; this is simply a courtesy briefing.

I am wrong.

In a large conference room in Yahoo! Media Group's Santa Monica offices, I lay out my goal of covering every armed-conflict zone in the world in one year to Terry and several other executives. While I'm talking, I can see that his jaw is dropping, lower and lower, in apparent disbelief.

And while I watch his reaction, my mouth becomes the Whitney cotton gin. My tongue is as dry as a three-thousand-year-old mummy and just as stiff. I stutter and stumble over my words, realizing that my first Hot Zone as a Yahoo! correspondent will not be in some faraway land but right here, right now—trying to tell my boss's boss why I think a controversial combat reporter and his project is a good fit for a company that brands itself with yodelers.

When I'm finished, I look nervously at Lloyd Braun, who knows he's going to have to dive in and do some damage control. After a few moments of silence, Semel finally speaks.

"And what will I say at the hearing," he says dramatically, "when I'm called before Congress to testify about one of your stories in which a soldier purposely flushed an inmate's Koran down a toilet?"

It's not exactly the start I had hoped for.

PART II

INTO THE ARMS OF MAMA *AFRICA*

Rebels, Rape Victims
and the Children of War

CHAPTER 4

SOMALIA
Chew on This!

MOGADISHU, SOMALIA | SEPTEMBER 18, 2005

BANDIT AIR?

The flight into Somalia hardly meets my colorfully imagined "Bandit Air" flight scenario of a khat-chewing pilot at the controls, assisted by a three-legged goat, zigzagging through antiaircraft fire and coming down for a hard landing on a debris-strewn landing strip just long enough to drop me off, pick up some contraband and take to the air again without even shutting down the engine.

In reality, my plane is a Kenya-based African Express Airways DC-9, and while the runway is dirt—and a full hundred miles away from the capital, Mogadishu—it's graded smooth with hardly any debris.

But with no functioning central government for fourteen years, Mogadishu—and Somalia at large—is still the land of the gun, a nation held captive by warlords and their armies of thin, expressionless men wrapped in bandoliers of 7.62 rounds and riding in modified pickup trucks called "technicals" with antiaircraft and machine guns bolted to their beds.

I'm hyper with anticipation of the wildly unfamiliar that is about to unfold before me. Will it be, as colleagues described it, "Mad Max meets East Africa"?

I felt this same way when entering the small sliver of Northern Alliance–controlled territory in Afghanistan in September 2001, when I crossed the swiftly flowing Amu Darya River on a pontoon raft in the dead of night. Then as now, I'm painfully aware that my local hosts view me as an unfathomably rich Western journalist who has just placed his trust, safety, fortune and fate into their hands—hands gripping AK-47s and RPK machine guns.

YOU CAN KILL ME

For some reason I pick this moment to think of a story told to me by a close friend and international aid worker named Dennis Walto. Walto, who is now the country director of Save the Children in Jordan and Lebanon, worked for CARE in Somalia in the early '90s during the peak of the country's famine and violence.

He nearly lost his life on two occasions to gun-wielding militiamen. On the first, the man pointed his rifle at Dennis and pulled the trigger, but the gun jammed. Walto says his bodyguard then shot the attacker.

In the second case, another gunman was about to dispatch him with an AK-47 round to the head, but before he could do it, Walto repeated a Somali proverb he had memorized.

"You can kill me," Dennis said in Somali, pronouncing each word correctly despite the pressure of the moment, "but you have to have a reason."

Walto said the gunman was so surprised that he bent over laughing.

MY OWN PERSONAL ARMY

When the hatch of the DC-9 opens to let us out, the brightness and heat outside envelop me. Duguf, my fixer (an interpreter and local guide), is there to meet me. I found him through a colleague. Duguf has worked with foreign journalists in Somalia for more than a dozen years, starting out as a driver. Now he's a freelancer for Associated Press Television News and also guides reporters through Somalia's danger zones.

I get into the back of Duguf's new green Toyota pickup truck while he sits in the front passenger seat and a man named Jamal waits behind the wheel. We drive away from the airstrip and stop near a shack on the roadside, where eight heavily armed men hop in the bed of the truck.

"These are your security," Duguf tells me. I think, More like my own personal army.

Two of them have Russian-made RPK machine guns and ammo crisscrossed over their bodies. The others are armed with the most popular assault rifle in the world, the AK-47, and wear olive green web harnesses holding magazine pouches filled with thirty-round banana clips. They are dressed in a mix of Gulf War–era American "chocolate chip" camo fatigues, t-shirts and counterfeit Adidas tracksuits made in China.

In Somalia, Duguf tells me, a show of force is the only way to get from one block to another without getting shaken down for cash by other heavily armed gunmen at ad hoc roadblocks every half mile or so.

One warlord, Duguf says, bragged that he was making the equivalent of thousands of U.S. dollars every day by operating dozens of roadblocks throughout the region. Even empty passenger buses must pay between four and six dollars at each blockade—a fortune in poverty-stricken Somalia.

Duguf tells me that the men in my security team are from different clans. He chose them that way so we could pass through any roadblock manned by any clan without getting shot. Duguf pays his men with money, but some warlords pay their fighters only in khat—a leafy bush that Somali men chew almost continuously for its slightly narcotic effect. Shipped in by plane from Kenya, it has become an integral and sometimes debilitating part of the Somali economy and culture. Some say there is nothing so unnerving as the glazed stare of a Somali fighter with a cheek full of khat, a loaded AK-47 and nothing much to lose.

As we drive toward Mogadishu, I watch from the back of the pickup as a world of green scrub and red sand whizzes by. The driver, Jamal, uses his horn as much as his gas pedal, beeping incessantly if anything as big as a scorpion tries to share the road with us.

BRAKING FOR CAMELS

Duguf makes him hit the brakes for one spectacle—a large herd of camels passing on the right side of the road. I get out of the truck and video a long panning shot of the beasts, who regard me as just another annoyance on their trip to nowhere in particular. For the rest of the ride, I shoot video of my security team as we roll across the African plain.

When we arrive in Mogadishu I feel a twinge of déjà vu. The city has the familiar patina of third-world poverty with dirt streets covered in garbage and corrugated metal shacks on each side where vendors sell anything they can get their hands on, from meat to khat to brightly colored pillows.

From a nearby minaret, the sound of afternoon prayers is broadcast over a battered public address system. Somalia's population of nearly eight million, two and a half million of it in Mogadishu, is predominantly Muslim.

TEAS AND SAMOSAS

Outside a tin-and-iron gate, Jamal beeps the horn. A man peeks around the corner, pulls open the gate, then quickly closes it behind us.

Like the plane ride, the Shamo Hotel defies my expectations. The three-story building is newer than the others in this Mogadishu neighborhood and so isn't pockmarked by bullet holes and damage from rocket-propelled grenades (RPGs).

Once we are inside the gate, six men meet me at the pickup to help me with my two bags of gear and small backpack of clothes. Inside I notice that one wall of the lobby is covered with the business cards of journalists from all over the world: reporters and producers from Japan's NHK, Britain's BBC, America's CNN, as well as Turkish, Italian and Russian media.

My new entourage leads me up to the second floor, where they show me to a clean, spacious and comfortable-looking room with a private bath. But before unpacking, I take a compass reading inside and discover the windows face north. I know that from here I won't be able to get a signal with my modem, which needs to beam south to connect with a communications satellite so that I can transmit my stories, video and pictures via the Internet back to Santa Monica and my team.

I tell them my problem, which it seems they have heard before because of all the journalists that have stayed here. They shrug, grab my bags and take me up another flight of stairs to a similar-sized room in the back of the building. This one has a small balcony. I step out and shoot a compass reading.

"This is perfect," I tell them. Then a balding, middle-aged Somali man, who I later learn is the owner of the hotel, pulls me aside.

"My friend," he says, in very good English, "it is not safe to sit out there exposed to the street; please keep your head down. We have had other guests who have been shot at out there."

A quick glance below and I can already see that the people down there are noticing us. "Hello," some boys shout up to me, "how are you?" I say nothing, wave at them and go back inside.

The owner and his staff leave while I unpack and test my gear. At 4 P.M. there is a knock at the door. One of the hotel workers has brought me a plate with two spicy samosas and some black tea. Again I am pleasantly surprised but realize that in addition to Islam's tradition of treating guests with unparalleled hospitality, I'm a rare commodity these days in Somalia—a foreigner with money to spend.

In fact, at first I feel like I'm the only guest at the hotel, but at dinnertime I meet two members of the International Committee of the Red Cross who have come to Mogadishu to support a local humanitarian group. There are also six employees of a Chinese telecom company that is helping to supply Somalia with cell phones and remarkably affordable service plans. Commerce, I will learn over the course of my time here, is attempting to meet Somali consumer demands whether there is a government or not.

For our meal, we are served yams, green beans and brown, stringy meat—which I am told is camel. It will be a staple at nearly every meal for the next ten days.

OFF THE GRID

Despite the surprising comforts of Mogadishu so far, I begin to realize just how far off the grid I have come. Most of the international aid agencies left the city after two humanitarian workers were recently killed. Mogadishu is so dangerous that even its interim government meets mostly outside the country, in Kenya. Duguf tells me that we can move around only in daylight hours; at dusk we need to be back in the compound and behind the gates.

BLACK HAWK GROUND

I tell Duguf that the first story I want to report is from the neighborhood where one of the two American Black Hawk helicopters was shot down by militia loyal to Somalia's then most famous warlord, Mohammed Farrah Aidid.

I'm anticipating that the Hot Zone's viewership will be primarily American and that the only knowledge many will have of Somalia is from Mark Bowden's book *Black Hawk Down* and the film it inspired.

HOMEMADE BARBED WIRE

I get into the truck with my eight bodyguards and we drive a couple of miles away from the hotel and stop in a narrow alleyway in a neighborhood called Halwad. It's nearly dusk, so we won't have a lot of time on the ground.

Duguf walks me over to a place he says is the exact spot where the chopper crashed, a mound of dirt covered with a dense thicket of cactus plants. Over the years, most of the wreckage has been snatched up by the locals as souvenirs, but there's still a small bit of the helicopter left.

Through my viewfinder I can just make out some twisted fuselage. Duguf tells me that clan leaders had the cactus planted as homemade barbed wire to keep people from carrying away every last bit of the Black Hawk. He says the clan leaders want to retain some evidence for a time when they might bring legal charges against America for the deaths and injuries suffered by civilians during the battle.

Many people in this poor neighborhood are connected to the clan of Mohammed Farrah Aidid. Aidid became the most hunted man in Somalia when his fighters were blamed for killing twenty-four Pakistani United Nations peacekeepers here.

American troops, who had come to Somalia on a humanitarian mission code-named Operation Restore Hope, soon found themselves at war with

Aidid's militia. On October 3, 1993, Aidid's militia scored huge symbolic victories by shooting down two U.S. Black Hawk helicopters during a botched American raid that eventually became known as the Battle of Mogadishu.

CRUSHED

A woman named Maria Osman approaches us by the cactus plants to tell us that the helicopter's hulking wreckage fell on top of her three-year-old daughter, Hani.

"There was not enough of her left to bury," she says, repeatedly covering her mouth with the end of her hijab. Osman says that she was also hit in the cross fire between the American troops and Aidid's militia. She pulls back the material covering her right arm to show me a brown, leathery road map of scar tissue that runs from above her wrist to below her shoulder. The arm hangs by her side, nearly useless for anything, she says, but as a reminder of that day.

"I HATE THE AMERICANS"

"I hate the Americans," she says but begins to laugh when she continues. "If I saw one I would cut them up in so many pieces." The crowd that has gathered around us also laughs, but some begin to eye me suspiciously.

Another woman in the crowd shouts that she lost four family members in the fighting that day—including a child.

This seems to agitate the crowd of fifty or so people.

"Why did you bring a white man here?" one of them demands of Duguf. While I continue to videotape, he taps me on the shoulder and nods toward the truck. We make haste just as fingers begin to point and voices grow louder and angrier.

THE MOVIE AND THE GAME

When the film *Black Hawk Down* premiered in Mogadishu in 2002, thousands went to see it. Even the poorest of the poor can usually pay the penny it costs to see a movie here.

The reviews were not good. Many were angered by the paper-thin portrayal of the Somalis, who appeared as little more than targets, while the film fixated on the struggles of the eighteen Americans killed and seventy-three wounded in the fifteen-hour battle. An estimated one thousand Somalis were also killed.

In Halwad, before we left, one of the people says they have heard the battle has also been turned into a video game (for Xbox and PlayStation 2). It mocks the tragedy of the event, she tells me.

SON OF AIDID

I have been invited to a *shabna,* or ceremony of remembrance, for Aidid, the deceased warlord who was America's all-time Somali nemesis.

There I will meet the man who succeeded him in one of the strangest political twists that Somalia has had to offer.

When I arrive, Hussein Mohammed Aidid is wearing a gray business suit and tie, yet the sleeves of his jacket are pushed up to his elbows—and he is barefoot. We enter a small building that contains the white-ceramic-tiled tomb of his father, while the men surrounding it inside begin a rhythmic, guttural chant that grows in loudness and fervor.

Hussein, now forty-three, was chosen to lead his father's Habr Gedir clan after the infamous warlord was killed in a 1996 gun battle with a breakaway faction within the clan. He also became the Somali interim government's minister of the interior, a position with responsibility for ending the strife and chaos of the country's warlord rule.

It is a heavy responsibility for a man who only two years earlier had been a planning department clerk for the city of West Covina, California—as well as a former U.S. Marine.

Hussein actually came to America with his mother as a political refugee when he was fourteen because his father was part of a rebellion seeking to overthrow Somali dictator Mohammed Siad Barre.

The family settled in southern California. Hussein quickly took to his new home. He made friends easily, ate ice cream, studied martial arts, went to dances, attended school. In 1987 he enlisted in the Marines, and he became a U.S. citizen four years later.

Aidid, who went by Hussein Farrah at that time, his grandfather's last name, even returned to Somalia as an interpreter for the initial phase of Operation Restore Hope. He was the only Marine in the region who spoke Somali.

He says he was open about his family connections and, with the permission of his commanding officer, even met with his father on several occasions. After his tour with Marine Reserves ended, he took a job as an urban planning engineer in the city of West Covina. Now married, he settled into suburban life.

But all that changed at the end of summer in 1996, when his father was killed and Hussein returned to take control of the clan.

"When I was a boy," Hussein says, "I made a promise to my father to serve the people of Somalia in whatever way I could. When he died, it was time to honor that promise."

But it's hard to understand such divided loyalties. During our meeting I ask him how he felt back home in California (his Marine unit left Somalia before the Black Hawk incident) watching television footage of his native countrymen, his clan even, dragging the dead body of a soldier from his adopted nation through the streets during the Battle of Mogadishu.

He responds without hesitation. "It was the most difficult thing I have ever experienced in my life," he says, "and every year I've worked to reconcile this part."

But that is different from the rhetoric he first used when he returned to Somalia in 1996 and, at a gathering at a local stadium, called the Battle of Mogadishu a "gloomy day for the aggressors" and "a victorious day for the Somalis."

One of the criticisms of Hussein in Somalia is that he is an opportunist, ready to switch sides whenever politically convenient.

Others say he lacks his father's intellect and leadership.

Indeed, after the shabna ritual and a feast where the men sit under a shade tree, eating large chunks of camel meat and rice from a communal platter with their hands, Hussein confides to me that he faces challenges within the clan—partly because of his American background.

"My values in some ways are U.S. values," he says. "A nation of immigrants in less than two hundred years becomes better than Europe, better than China, better than Russia, better than Africa, better than any country. A nation who allowed people who have been abused in different countries to come together and form in Philadelphia a constitution and making the machine to survive and become a superpower."

This connection to the United States has some wondering whether Hussein will, ironically, be the back door that brings American political and military influence into Somalia again—after his father helped usher them out. For now, he has put his clan militia and his energy into supporting the U.S.-backed interim government. He's made no secret of his desire to one day be president of Somalia, a goal that could get a boost from his current loyalty.

But first, Hussein must survive the rumblings of his own clan. At this moment, as we talk, he seems circumspect, this Somali turned American Marine, turned East African warlord; perhaps he is wondering what his father would do in this situation, as both personal and political crises brew.

One of the principal reasons I wanted to begin the Hot Zone coverage in Somalia was because, like Afghanistan, it illustrates the consequences of ignoring a failed state.

Afghanistan's two decades of civil strife following the withdrawal of the Soviet Union allowed the rise of the tyrannical fundamentalism of the Taliban, which in turn allowed the rise of Al Qaeda, which used Afghanistan as a terror training ground and safe haven for its top leadership, including Osama bin Laden.

In Somalia, fundamentalists were also making gains by providing some stability amid the corruption and chaos of modern-day fiefdoms controlled by warlords and their militias.

UNION OF ISLAMIC COURTS

A consortium of these groups called the Union of Islamic Courts has attempted to win over Somalis by providing humanitarian relief, schools and even security in some parts of the country, while at the same time spreading fundamentalist ideology, one that is linked, the United States claims, to Al Qaeda through guns, money and training.

The U.S. State Department says the group and one of its primary leaders, Sheik Hassan Dahir Aweys, once a colonel in the Somali army, may have ties to the 1998 U.S. embassy bombings in Kenya and Tanzania. Aweys denies any Al Qaeda connections but does say he wants Somalia to become a theocracy. Duguf takes me to meet him at his compound on the outskirts of the city. When we enter, we are met with cold stares and thoroughly searched.

We're taken to a second-floor office, where I see Aweys for the first time. He has penetrating eyes and a red-henna-tipped beard. He's notoriously suspicious of Western journalists. I'm only the second to interview him in the last six months.

"ARE YOU AN AMERICAN . . . A JEW?"

As I set up my camera and tripod he asks me if I am an American . . . and a Jew. He looks at me askance, as if I were a spy, but consents to the interview anyway.

"The only reason Western powers say that Al Qaeda is in Somalia is because they are afraid that Somalia will become an Islamic state and they will do everything they can to stop that," Aweys says. "I believe there's not even one person in Somalia connected to Al Qaeda. We are one clan, one color, one language. We would not accept foreigners [Al Qaeda] here."

Aweys says he is, however, sympathetic to "jihads" being waged against Western forces around the world.

"If you lock a cat in a room all the time," Aweys says, "what do you think it will do? It's going to fight back."

He says he also supports Somalis who have gone to Iraq to fight against the Americans there.

"Islam is one body. If you're wounded in one place, you feel it everywhere. We all feel it when Americans kill Muslims," says Aweys. "I know in my heart I cannot accept when they say we must stay outside. Western countries fight to take what they want from us. We won't accept those conditions."

After thirty minutes Aweys ends the interview and we're shown out. We're both happy, I believe, to be done with each other.

THE MARKET

Our cold reception continues when we walk through the nearby Bakara Market. There have been reports by terror watchdog agencies such as the International Crisis Group that American commandos, with the help of anti–Islamic Union warlords, have been kidnapping off the streets Somalis suspected of having ties to Al Qaeda.

Whether true or not, its effect on the local psyche is obvious. As I walk by with my security team, trying in vain to engage people and shoot some video, many shake their fingers and shout at me.

"Why did you bring a white man with a camera to the market?" they ask Duguf.

"They think you're going to show their pictures to the Americans," he says to me, "and they will be snatched up."

One older man, speaking in English, stands up when he sees me in the crowd.

"Tell Bush we're ready," he says. "Tell him we're ready to fight."

"Ready to fight, why?" I ask.

"Because he's attacking Muslims in Iraq, he'll come here, too," he says, knowingly.

A YEAR LATER

Almost exactly a year after my interview with Sheik Hassan Dahir Aweys, his Union of Islamic Courts takes control of Mogadishu after defeating the forces of the American-backed interim government, including the militia of Hussein Mohammed Aidid. The fighting leaves hundreds dead.

But the Union of Islamic Courts only holds the capital for three months before regrouped Somali interim government forces and U.S.-trained Ethiopian army troops push them out, back into their strongholds in the south.

Later, in January 2007, the American military will use AC-130 "Spooky" gunships, mounted with airborne howitzers and miniguns, to attack the retreating Islamists and attempt to kill Al Qaeda–linked leaders who they say were responsible for the U.S. embassy bombings in Africa. It's the first public U.S. offensive in Somalia since the Battle of Mogadishu in 1993.

INTERMISSION

Khat Tales

_____

SOMALIA

I tell Duguf I want to try khat, the East African shrub that has been chewed here for centuries because of its stimulant effect. Khat is like currency in Somalia, and although Somalia's market stalls are full of the stuff, nearly a million dollars' worth is flown in from Kenya every day. It's not cheap. A bundle of khat, or mira, as the Somalis call it, costs about 120,000 Somali shillings or $8.50.

It's late afternoon and our work is done for the day. I meet Duguf on the roof of my hotel, where he's sitting beside a glass table piled high with khat. He shows me how to find the fresh ones and break the stems and we begin chewing. To me, it seems slow and arduous. Our cheeks bulge like chipmunks as we store the leaves, letting our saliva release the cathinone into the linings of our mouths and stomachs.

A boy from the hotel brings us two bottles of Sprite and a large bottle of water, which I'm desperately thankful for—since this bush has made my mouth feel as dry as the ground it grows in. After a while, I'm wondering what all the fuss is about. I'm not experiencing any of the so-called mild euphoria you're supposed to get from chewing khat. In fact, I'm thinking I've had a better caffeine buzz from a Starbucks venti drip with an added shot.

Khat got quite the bad rap during the early '90s when scores of journalists came to Somalia to cover Operation Restore Hope, the humanitarian relief project that turned into a war. True or not, most dispatches from the region nearly always began with a sentence about a Somali fighter high on khat with his hands on the controls of an antiaircraft gun mounted to the back of a pickup truck.

There is a refreshing breeze blowing in from the Indian Ocean, and I begin telling Duguf how much I want to report what is really happening in Somalia, that the shifting alliances, chaos and perpetual fighting are central to the narrative but there's so much subtext—Chinese businessmen setting up cellular service, stories about American secret ops kidnapping people from the streets, piracy off the coast . . . and then I realize I'm talking very fast, very excitedly. I want to write it all down so I don't forget a word of the wisdom that is coming out of my mouth nearly as fast as the thoughts are forming. Duguf smiles at me, kicks back in his chair and chews. He looks up, his thoughts drifting away from my patter and into the blue Somali sky.

At the end of the week I will pay $100 for a ride out of Somalia and back to Kenya, fittingly enough, in the cargo hold of an empty khat plane.

CHAPTER 5

DEMOCRATIC REPUBLIC OF THE CONGO

Worse Than the Guns

KINSHASA, DRC | SEPTEMBER 28, 2005

RUMBLE IN THE JUNGLE

When I began planning the Hot Zone mission with my team, I knew that without some kind of on-the-ground support system in these conflict zones, I could find myself in plenty of trouble with no way out.

When I worked for CNN and NBC, I had news bureaus around the world that could supply me with gear, cash, vehicles or even a helicopter evacuation if I needed it. Yahoo! had sales offices in many international locations, but not the kind of operations a dirty, unshaven, DEET-covered backpack journalist could count on.

The Hot Zone needed strategic partners that could help me identify stories quickly—and also physically reach them. The solution we decided on was inspired in part by the U.S. military's embedding program, but instead of always attaching myself to war zone combatants, I would embed with politically neutral humanitarian organizations when possible.

In the Democratic Republic of the Congo (DRC), I'll work with the International Rescue Committee (IRC), a nongovernmental organization known for a low-key but effective approach to humanitarian relief and development. My producer, Robert, has made arrangements for me to meet with them in Congo's capital, Kinshasa.

On the ride from the airport to the offices of the IRC, I see women in brightly covered dresses carrying heavy bundles of wood on their heads. While I watch them, I wonder if I will make the same mistake of so many travelers who encounter the new and unfamiliar: being so overwhelmed by differences that I see only what's on the surface and not beneath.

Will these *National Geographic* images, now alive before me, seduce me into only chronicling what I sense, rather than doing the work it will take to understand? The DRC has the power, I know, to symbolize Africa for me on so many levels, including the poverty and desperation of people abused both by colonial masters and then by corrupt dictatorships, the incessant and complex violence, the exotica of its nature.

The IRC staff can almost smell this on me, wondering aloud, only half-jokingly, if I can report on the Congo without referring to Joseph Conrad's classic novel *Heart of Darkness*—or the famous Muhammad Ali comeback fight with George Foreman in 1974 here called the Rumble in the Jungle. Well, the answer is obviously no.

Those are certainly Congo touchstones for outsiders—but this is a country as rich in stories as it is in diamonds, gold and mystery. When I leave the capital for the northeast city of Kisangani, nothing helps me focus on that more than a ride I take down the mighty Congo River in a canoe hewn out of the trunk of a cypress tree. While cruising down the chocolate brown waters, I don't just see the spirit of the Congo, I feel for a moment as if I've become part of its winding current.

BRIEF HISTORY OF THE CONGO

Unfortunately, a big part of that current is the legacy of war. After its independence from Belgium in 1960, the new nation was placed (with the help of Belgium and the United States) firmly in the hands of army chief Joseph-Désiré Mobutu, who renamed it Zaïre.

Mobutu systematically plundered the nation for more than thirty years in a dictatorship that did much to define corruption in Africa. The rebel leader Laurent-Désiré Kabila finally overthrew Mobutu in 1997 with the help of troops from Uganda and Rwanda. But a year later, those countries decided Kabila was not their man after all and sent troops and money to topple him.

In response, Zimbabwe, Namibia and Angola all sent troops to support Kabila. The conflict became known as Africa's first world war.

An alphabet soup of rebel groups, ethnic militias and foreign fighters—primarily motivated by access to the DRC's diamond, gold and coltan resources—clashed in eastern Congo.

Kabila was assassinated in 2001 and succeeded as president by his son Joseph. A power-sharing agreement was signed with the rebel groups a year later, creating a transitional government and an intermittent peace pending the Congo's first democratic elections.

Joseph Kabila won the presidency after a runoff contest with the former rebel leader Jean-Pierre Bemba in October 2006.

BECOMING A KILLER

But the repercussions of the DRC's violent history are still being felt across the country, and some of the most unfortunate victims have been children forced or recruited by all sides to support their armies or become actual fighters. Some estimates have their numbers as high as thirty thousand.

They are not faceless monsters but real boys, like "Claude" (not his real name), whom I meet through the help of the IRC. "Claude" was only eleven when he was forced to join Laurent Kabila's rebel uprising against the Mobutu government.

"I never accepted it," he says. "I never believed in what I was being told to do. I'm not a killer. But once others are shooting at you, you have to shoot back."

He may not have been a killer, but he became one; a very good one.

He's only nineteen now, but his face is tired and drawn. He says he has killed five men.

"But when I killed it was because of the drugs," he says. The drugs, he tells me, were a concoction of hashish, khat and a small amount of gunpowder that they used to smoke.

"It takes away your fear," he says, "and once you decide to hurt someone, you hurt them. Once you decide to kill someone, you kill them."

There's one killing that stays in his mind and that he can't escape. It wasn't during a firefight—it was simply murder.

"As soldiers, we often didn't get paid," he says, "so my friends and I would use our guns to rob people. One night we robbed a very rich man. We took his money, his watch, his jewelry. Everything we wanted. Then we shot and killed him."

"Claude" says the man now haunts his sleep.

"It's that one I see at night, I see his face, he comes to me in my dreams— asking for his things back."

Now he spends his nights sleeping in the church, because it's only there, he believes, that the dead man can't reach him.

WORSE THAN THE GUNS

The other segment of the population that has been brutalized by the Congo's perpetual violence is women.

A local women's support organization organizes a meeting for me in eastern Congo where 170 women have gathered in a church with a dirt floor. The women carry infants, swaddled tightly against their backs with colorful scarves called kitambalas. Many of these children, I'm later told, are the offspring of rapes.

I talk with some of the women in private afterward but point my camera away from them and at myself during the interviews to protect their identities.

A thirty-three-year-old woman named "Marie" (not her real name) tells me that in 1997, three members of the Hutu Interahamwe militia killed her husband, then raped her. The Interahamwe is the same group responsible for much of the 1994 genocide against ethnic Tutsis in Rwanda, but it fled Rwanda after the killings and now occupies parts of eastern Congo.

"They use rape as a weapon of war," she says. "They have guns, but this is worse than the guns."

Other women say the terror continues nightly. They're afraid to sleep in their homes, so instead they hide among the banana trees while rebels carrying torches come down from the hillsides looking for them.

These assaults also leave legacies beyond the children. In a nation where an estimated three million people are infected with the HIV virus, women and their families are concerned that their rapes might actually be a slow and painful form of murder.

"The actual aim of these soldiers," says the leader of one of the women's groups, angrily, "is to exterminate their victims by giving them AIDS."

SERAPINA'S STORY

For twenty-five-year-old "Serapina" (not her real name), the tragic moments of her life lay on top of one another like bricks, each one heavier than the last, slowly building into a crushing weight of unthinkable misery.

It began for her, too, in 1997, when Rwandan soldiers supporting the Congolese revolt led by Laurent Kabila came to her home in the mountains of eastern Congo.

"They forced the door open," she says in a sure and steady voice. She has shared this story before. "They tied my husband to a tree. Then they made me lie down—and the first one got on top of me, then the second, then the third, then the fourth . . . all six of them. They had sex with me."

When they were finished, she says, they shoved a piece of cloth far into her vagina.

"Then they took me outside," she continues, "they beat my husband. Then . . ." She pauses. "They killed my two children in front of me."

She says they looted everything from the house and then torched it. They left her standing naked in front of the flames. In one night, nearly everything in her life was murdered, destroyed or humiliated. It was too much; mind and body shut down, she says, and she fainted.

That story would be more than enough tragedy for anyone to bear in a lifetime, but "Serapina" would have to relive the horror again seven years later. This time, she says, rebel soldiers connected to another Congolese rebel leader, Laurent Nkunda, came to the IDP (internally displaced persons) camp where she and her husband were living after losing their home and land.

"They killed my husband," she says. "Then this time, they tied me to a tree and raped me. I was three months pregnant."

Two days after the rape, she says, she had a miscarriage.

"They mutilated my husband's body. Cut off his arms." And then she says, in an unfathomably calm tone, "They forced me to eat my husband's flesh. They said they would kill me if I refused."

I look at her nearly dazed by the gravity of pain she's endured in her life. It's the most horrific story of personal tragedy that I've heard in my career as a journalist.

"Serapina" says she wishes she had died then. The only thing that has given her any hope in the aftermath of these assaults is the comfort of hundreds of others like her, women also victimized by the armed groups camping near their communities.

Local Congolese nonprofit groups, supported with funds from larger organizations such as the International Rescue Committee (IRC), are organizing the women of these villages to create a network of support and empowerment.

GOODNESS

"Barwana's" (not her real name) husband divorced her after she was raped by Laurent Nkunda's forces last year. The twenty-six-year-old woman's eyes begin to well up with tears as she cradles a tiny baby in her arms.

"I've experience only suffering," she says. "Sometimes I feel I have no reason to go on living."

But then she says it is the other women in the group who give her hope. "Without them," she says, "I would already be dead."

"Barwana" says she doesn't know if her child is from her former husband or from one of the men who raped her.

She holds the baby tenderly, still seeing the beauty even beyond the possibly darker story. And in a quiet defiance to the crime against her, she has named her child Binja, which, in her Kihavu language, means "goodness."

MISERY INDEX

At the end of my reporting in the DRC, I realize that with the stories of the child soldiers, the rapes, the poverty, I had constructed an edifice of misery that could easily overwhelm Hot Zone viewers.

Indeed, some of them wrote that they felt paralyzed with sadness, unable to even react, after reading about the lives of people like "Claude" and "Serapina." I had at times felt the same thing myself.

It became imperative to me that these tragic tales somehow be put into perspective. While their tragedies were real, these individuals were also more than the sum of their suffering.

On October 12, 2005, I posted a personal essay, much different from my daily reporting, which we ran under the banner "Reflections from the Hot Zone." I titled it "There is Laughter Too."

THERE IS LAUGHTER TOO

We are sitting in the back jumpseats of the International Rescue Committee's white Toyota Land Cruiser and with every bump and rut in what passes for a road here, I feel like the vehicle's entire rear wheel base is going to lodge irrevocably up my ass.

I'm in a mood. Petulant, even. And it's not just the ride. Sharzad, the IRC's 22-year-old intern, freshly graduated from Princeton, has just told me for the fourteenth time that I cannot take a frontal photo— even a very wide one—of the women that I'm covering for a story on sexual violence. I've been pushing the issue but I'm not sure why.

They have been victimized enough and I want to protect their privacy, dignity and most importantly their lives against possible repercussions from the armed groups who have raped and terrorized them.

But I know that stories are ultimately in people's faces. While I can't, and shouldn't, show them in this circumstance, I worry that it may be difficult for readers to invest in them when all they can see is the back of their heads or their hands.

They become objects, concepts rather than people. I just want one photo, even from a distance, that allows their collective faces to show what they've suffered.

But here's the thing—when they are together like this, it isn't just about collective suffering. There is laughter, too. Lots of it.

For one—they look at me and laugh. In these dirt-poor villages when I hop out of the vehicle with my high definition camera and backpack bulging with video and computer peripherals, I might as well be dressed in a bunny suit and carrying an Easter basket . . . or wearing a neoprene wet suit, mask, fins and snorkel and walking backwards. I'm not exactly passing for one of the locals.

I marvel at these strong women who have dressed in their best, most colorful clothes to meet us. Some carry large golf umbrellas to shield them and their babies from the intense sun.

These same women, welcoming us with broad smiles and their rolling tongue chants, are forced to hide in the banana groves at night in fear of men bearing torches and guns who search them out.

They look at me, I think, as a man from another planet, who could, with all of his ridiculous trappings, bring some relief—even if it's just comic.

I find myself reeling a bit from the responsibility. Worried that once we all get back in the Land Cruiser that we've left them again with nothing—except their fear. I want to stay and protect them, fantasize about turning their predators into prey, but I'm armed with a camera not a gun. It seems to me at the moment, a poor substitution.

It makes me feel both angry and impotent. Where are the FARDC (the Armed Forces of the Democratic Republic of Congo) that are supposed to be protecting them?

"They are hungry too," one woman tells me. "They don't get paid so sometimes they are the ones doing the looting—and the raping."

When I sit down to interview some of the women about their spe-

cific stories I am humbled. They bear their pain heroically—the physical and mental trauma and its aftermath, even loving infants that were forced upon them in the most cruel and unloving ways.

When I listen to them, I sometimes feel ashamed. The worse the story, the less emotion I show—hardening myself against the waters of pain which threaten to destroy the levee I've built for my own protection.

I also worry that my reporting will become this deluge of tragedy for people, who like myself, unable or uncertain of what to do, let it wash over them. Some African journalists call it poverty porn—stories or images of intense suffering designed solely for emotional impact, but often have the effect of shutting people down rather than helping them step up.

How do we get beyond that? I'm not sure. I guess by truly empathizing—not just with their tears, but their laughter as well.

In another village a few days earlier, I was surrounded by 1,600 people waiting for relief supplies from the IRC. Their names would be called and they would receive a coupon for cooking pots, soap and some other essentials. Many of these people hadn't eaten in days—and they were certainly suffering.

But some, who like one old man whose name was called, had no problem sharing the joy of the moment by performing a little impromptu dance for my camera, making this crowd of people laugh with abandon. Everything had been taken from them—but their humanity.

As the day went on I began to get hungry and was unsettled by my own needs. I knew at some point, later in the evening, back in town I would be able to eat.

Yet so many around me would go hungry again this evening—probably hungry enough to make a meal out of the press credentials that hung around my neck if I offered them.

Again, I wondered if I would be more useful holding something else, a loaf of bread maybe, rather than this camera.

I know in my heart that this is not just an exercise in navel-gazing. People read these stories and respond. So many have posted responses on the site saying their eyes have been opened to people and issues they never knew about.

Others, however, perhaps overwhelmed by what they read, say Africa should be written off, that it's beyond repair. My experiences so far say we should put it in perspective.

For instance, a new nation that has just won its independence from a colonial power struggles with internal graft and corruption, civil war and economic turbulence—more developed nations see it as a basketcase. Yet 200+ years later it emerges as the world's sole superpower. Yes, America.

Most African nations have only had their independence for 10 to 40 years. They're struggling not just with the legacies of colonialism, but also the cold war in which the U.S. and former Soviet Union propped up opposing proxies on the continent to protect and promote their own strategic interests.

There are many challenges here, endemic corruption, a rapidly expanding AIDS epidemic, simmering armed conflicts, the struggle for democracy. At moments it can seem insurmountable. But there is also, as I've seen and heard, in the most unexpected places, laughter too, and with that, hope.

INTERMISSION

Hammering Rocks

I'm so tired that I've shut down any brain functions unnecessary for keeping my body alive. I'm a vegetable in the passenger seat, a giant squash just staring out the window as we drive through Bukavu, eastern Congo.

On the side of the road I see groups of men sitting on piles of large granite boulders. Nothing really registers at first, but then I see they have hammers in their hands. I look again. Unbelievably to me, they're using those small, handheld hammers to turn those big boulders into gravel.

There's an obvious metaphor here, and I'm hoping that if I can just shift some blood flow back into the cognitive areas of my brain, by the end of the drive I'll grasp it just as firmly as the men grasp their hammers.

But at the moment, I'm still slightly dazzled by the absurdity of it all. In an age of cloning, can this still be the way some people make little rocks from big ones?

TOO AMBITIOUS?

I'm less than a month into this journey, yet it seems so much longer. When this was just a concept, I understood there would be difficult moments, but now I'm wondering if we were too ambitious with the project, that we're trying to do too much multimedia storytelling on a daily basis.

To work from remote and hostile territory for a full year is a daunting thought, especially when I've just started. It doesn't help that I've had trouble finding a rhythm to the workflow.

When I'm reporting in the field I sometimes get confused about which camera I should grab first. Am I shooting still photos for the text story or video for the narrated television-style report? Should I conduct interviews with just my pen and notepad or record them on videotape?

And at the end of the daily news gathering, my day is far from over. I still have to write my stories, edit my photos and video, then transmit everything. Depending on how tired I am, the writing can take hours; trying to digest all the research I read, the notes I've taken, the interviews I've done—trying to stay focused and not nod off. Usually it's late in the evening, eleven or twelve, before I'm ready to transmit on my portable satellite modem.

If there are no technical glitches, the transmissions can take an hour or two, but there are always problems: weak satellite signals, hardware bugs. Sometimes everything crashes right in the middle, forcing me to start all over. It's always a game of catch-up and I've just begun.

It can be frustrating and exhausting rarely getting to bed before 2:00 A.M. each night, then starting all over again at 7:00. It's just as hard on my team back in California, who try to keep the same hours I do.

THE METAPHOR

Toward the end of my ride, I'm able to shake my daze long enough to get the metaphor of the men hammering the rocks. It's a metaphor, I know, constructed for me at this particular moment.

There is a large and overwhelming pile of boulders in front of them; a backbreaking daily task that could defeat them before they even start. But then, each day with purpose, they begin; they hammer and hammer.

Eventually, the big immobile boulders become smaller boulders, the smaller boulders become rocks, the rocks become pebbles, the pebbles become gravel; the mountain of rock becomes gravel—manageable, movable gravel. The boulders have not crushed them; they have crushed the boulders. They sit on the gravel now, like kings on their thrones.

It must be the same for me. I need to begin each day hammering and hammering until the world becomes countries, the countries become people, the people become stories, the stories become understanding. The world of stories small enough for me to move them on my laptop and around the world.

CHAPTER 6

UGANDA

An Army of Children

KITGUM, UGANDA | OCTOBER 10, 2005

LORD'S RESISTANCE ARMY

I can think of few things more cruel than a society forced to hunt down and kill its own children, but that has become the twenty-year legacy of Uganda's war with one of Africa's strangest and most brutal rebel groups, the Lord's Resistance Army, or LRA.

Its leader and self-declared prophet, Joseph Kony, is considered a brilliant battlefield tactician but also bizarre. He wants a government based on the Christian Ten Commandments, but Kony's movement seems to be spiritual in name only.

The LRA is accused of committing a whole litany of atrocities from murder to mutilation, but its main stock in trade has been the widespread kidnapping of children—as many as twenty-five thousand over two decades—who are then turned into fighters, servants or "wives" for LRA rebels.

Of that number, 7,500 have been girls. One thousand of those have been returned to their families—pregnant and forever stigmatized by their abductions.

Kony uses this strategy, former abductees say, because he knows he can brainwash children more easily than adults; by replacing their family with his, he makes them both vulnerable and obedient. He has often tested their loyalty by sending them on missions to kill their own parents and brothers and sisters.

In one particularly brutal incident, the LRA kidnapped fifty men, women and children that they say had betrayed them to the government. They cut off the nose, ears, lips and arms of each one.

Christopher Arwai was a young seminary student when he was captured by the LRA in 1998.

"They try to indoctrinate you," Arwai says to me. "Every day teaching you that any community outside the LRA was immoral; that only those living in the bush were good. It was a blend of spiritual and cult persuasion."

Arwai is now the manager of a Kitgum reception center that tries to reintegrate former LRA abductees with their families and their communities. It is difficult on many levels.

"He's very charismatic," Arwai says of Kony. "I met him during my abduction. He's very literate and convincing and he has a talent with children. He's had plenty of practice, with at least forty wives of his own and probably dozens of children by them."

Arwai was able to escape after two months with the LRA, but he knows the hold Kony and the LRA have over the children.

"They have a special fear of him," he says. "He tells you that once you've been captured, once you're part of the LRA—you always will be."

At its peak strength in the mid to late '90s, the LRA was estimated to have as many as thirty thousand troops divided into three divisions: the Father, the Son and the Holy Spirit.

According to the Uganda People's Defense Force, the LRA's numbers have now dwindled to a few hundred, but their actions have created societal repercussions that will likely be felt for decades.

NIGHT COMMUTERS

The most destructive result of the war has been the phenomenon of night commuting, in which rural families, out of fear of LRA abductions, leave their homes each night and walk miles to protected urban areas, where they spend the night, then return to their homes the next day.

An estimated fifty thousand Ugandans make this journey every day, and it has wreaked havoc on their communities by disrupting their planting and harvesting cycles, children's education and family cohesion.

Some experts even believe it has contributed to Uganda's HIV/AIDS crisis by creating an environment where unsupervised night-commuting teens and young adults are more likely to engage in high-risk, unprotected sex.

Nancy Akwon tells me she has been coming to the shelter of this girl's school in Kitgum, northern Uganda, every night for the last fifteen years. She has nine children now. Before darkness falls they all walk the two miles here for nothing more comfortable than a cold, concrete floor—and peace of mind.

But she has good reason to make the nightly journey. In 1991, the LRA abducted her seven-year-old son, and she has never seen or heard from him again.

"I think he's dead," she says, rocking her youngest child in her arms. "I told myself I would never let that happen to any of my other children, which is why we come here every night."

And she says she will likely continue to do so, for some time to come.

"I'm not sure when things will really get better," she says, "or when we'll feel safe again."

UPDF

I ride on the back of Lieutenant Deo Akiki's red Honda 250 motorcycle to an IDP camp called Amida, a couple of miles outside Kitgum. Akiki is an officer in the Uganda People's Defense Force, or UPDF.

He is in his early twenties and was once in a Catholic seminary studying to be a priest but quit to join the army.

"They are both callings," Akiki says, "just different types of service."

He has received a report that seven Lord's Resistance Army fighters were seen in the area around the camp, which has been a target of the LRA, looking for food, money and new recruits.

We join up with a patrol of veteran UPDF Mobile Forces soldiers, an elite commando unit whose only assignment is to hunt down and attack the

LRA. I talk with members of the patrol as we weave through the thick elephant grass leading up to the dense bush.

Private Joey Ongala says he has been in so many clashes with the LRA that he cannot remember them all. But he does say there is a pattern.

"They're always young, they're always in tatters," he says. "They also seem very hungry, but they still try to fight us."

Ongala is waiting to lead his squad into a thickly forested area about a mile and a quarter away from Amida.

"I've had to kill many of them," Ongala says, "unless they surrender. I sometimes feel bad, but these children are firing at us."

But Ongala says things have quieted down recently, that they haven't had any contact with the LRA for weeks.

In fact, many UPDF commanders say the LRA is finished, that their numbers have been so depleted that the rebels are all but irrelevant.

But why, many people here are asking, has it taken the Ugandan government twenty years to stop an insurgency that some experts say is more of a child-snatching cult than an army? Regardless of the answer, the cost has been brutally high, with as many as one hundred thousand dead and a million displaced.

INNOCENT

Inside a small mud-and-grass hut called a thuckle, I watch twenty-year-old "Regina" (not her real name) bounce her seven-month-old son on her knee.

Despite the fact the child is the offspring of one of her LRA captors, Regina has appropriately named him "Innocent." She was just twelve years old when she was abducted. Most of her village had fled from the LRA to a refugee camp, but she stayed behind to cook for her father, who was still working in the area.

The rebels took her to their camps in southern Sudan, where she says they taught her to shoot a gun and to farm. After two years, she was given to one of the LRA commanders as a house servant.

"I never accepted my life in captivity," she says. "I thought about my parents and my home all of the time."

Eventually, the commander gave her to another rebel soldier as a "wife." She bore him a daughter, now four years old, and then a son.

Her freedom came at a high price. She says UPDF forces attacked their camps in Sudan. Her daughter was hit by a bullet and her rebel "husband" wanted to leave the girl behind and flee.

"Regina" refused and tried to carry both her wounded daughter and newborn son to safety while her husband fled in a different direction. During the fighting, she was shot in the leg by the UPDF and captured.

Now she is going through a reintegration program at this northern Uganda reception center called the Kitgum Concerned Women's Association, which helps to deprogram the children and help them rejoin their families and communities.

She's happy, she tells me, to finally be going home after eight years and grateful to learn that her family and village will accept her without hesitation; that is not always the case with formerly abducted children. Many of them are rejected because of atrocities they were forced to commit by the LRA against their own villages.

"THAT SHOT SAVED ME"

Fifteen-year-old "Deo" (not his real name) was held by the LRA for less than two months, but it was a hard time and it shows. He says he was beaten nearly every day, and now I can see he is a Swiss army knife of nervous tics; his face, his hands, feet, are all constantly moving, shifting, rearranging.

He feels more peaceful when he has something in his hands, he says. I watch the smile spread across his face as he beats the drums outside one of the thuckles at the center.

"Deo" tells me a bullet was the key to his freedom as well when the UPDF's elite Mobile Forces starting firing at his camp. A round struck him above his right hip.

"That shot saved me," "Deo" says. "I thought the Mobile Forces were going to kill me, but instead they carried me off the field and treated me."

Some human rights organizations have questioned the Ugandan military's use of helicopters and artillery in attacking the LRA. These weapons can be indiscriminate, and they say children, already traumatized by their abductions, should not be further endangered by violent assaults.

But Lieutenant Akiki tells me that with the LRA it is almost impossible to tell who is a combatant and who is not, since many of those shooting at them are indeed children.

POETIC JUSTICE

At the center is also a girl I'll call "Anne" (not her real name), fifteen, who is very quiet, but I can feel the the swirl of her emotions just as plainly as I can see the swell of her belly.

There is anger, sadness, silence; the confusion of just how the bones of fortune were shaken and thrown in her particular case. She is, at this tender age, both victim and defiant, captive and free, wronged and avenged, child and mother.

There is also an enviable grace of acceptance firmly saddled to these feelings that dart and bound beyond her slumped pose.

"Anne" tells me she was only twelve when she was abducted by the LRA.

After two years as a house girl, she was given as a wife to a rebel unit leader. Despite her youth she is strong and independent; she tells me she refused him. But that didn't stop him. He raped her, repeatedly, until she became pregnant. He was killed when a Ugandan army helicopter dropped a bomb on their camp.

The bomb alone didn't break the grip of the LRA, "Anne" tells me. She had to do that herself.

She told the senior LRA commander that now that her "husband" was dead, she would be a burden to the group, pregnant with no one to take care of her. He agreed. She walked away.

She is confident she can rebuild on the rubble of the past three years, but there is something she knows she can't walk away from: the baby she has carried for five months.

She tells me candidly that she will accept the child but isn't yet sure if she can love it. There is the sound of both wisdom and justice in her words. I am, for a moment, enriched by the power of her story.

Only later will I realize that "Anne's" story has helped me find the answer to the dilemma I've been struggling with since coming to Africa: how to report on the misery and misfortunes here without paralyzing myself and my readers with the overwhelming magnitude of it all.

Instead of fretting about the immediate need to do something for her when I hear the tragic aspects of her story, I realize how she is also helping me. Her story, with all its epic tragedy, is also a tale of grace and perseverance. When open to that idea, I'm not just angered by the injustices she's suffered but also inspired by the courage and intelligence with which she has dealt with them. I am better just for knowing about her.

She's a victim, like the subject of so many of my stories, but also defiant; the very things that confuse her also infuse her with strength. She is learning to see and accept these roles, while I'm learning to see and accept my own role as a witness to powerful and instructive lives like hers.

CHAPTER 7

SUDAN
The Longest War

REMBEK, SOUTH SUDAN | OCTOBER 25, 2005

LAND OF GIANTS

I am in the land of giants. At nearly six feet two, I'm reasonably tall, but here, walking through the marketplace in Rembek, south Sudan, I find myself tilting up to take photographs.

South Sudan is the land of the Dinkas, a group of pastoral tribes known for cattle herding and legendary height. Though anthropological research on the Dinkas states there is no scientific proof of their vertical dominance, my eyes tell me differently.

RITUAL SCARS

The faces of both men and women are covered by ritual scarification. The men have mostly a halo of welts circling their heads, made by dragging sharpened cow bones across the skin; the women a pattern of tiny raised dots, like braille, covering their cheekbones or foreheads.

The look, combined with their size, makes them seem fearsome, although at the moment they are much more interested in preening for my camera. They tap me on the shoulder, then motion with an open palm, curling their fingers toward themselves as if they are trying to draw in the scent of something, telling me, wordlessly, to take their picture.

For many of these young men in south Sudan, it is finally a time for posing rather than fighting. The region is just emerging from a twenty-one-year civil war, the longest and bloodiest on the continent. The conflict in this part of Sudan ended in January 2005. Now there is a complicated, power-sharing peace agreement between northern Arab Muslims who dominate the government and southern Christians and animists who rebelled in 1983 after the government tried to impose Islamic sharia law on the entire country.

THE TOLL

The civil war took the lives of more than two million people (mostly through famine and disease) and created a small nation of four million internally displaced people.

The "black" southern Sudanese say they have always been marginalized and discriminated against by what they call the northern Arab "elite." All across the south you see the remnants of the war—buildings bombed into standing jigsaw puzzles—and almost everyone here has a story of loss to tell.

Sudan is the largest nation in Africa, larger than all the countries of western Europe. Because of the war, it is also the least visited by outsiders. Sudan is underdeveloped in the way the moon might be considered underdeveloped—vast and empty. It is underdeveloped in a way difficult to comprehend in the twenty-first century.

In south Sudan, one in nine women dies during pregnancy or childbirth, one in four children never see their fifth birthday and more than 80 percent of the population is illiterate.

I notice two things on my arrival: (1) there are virtually no cars, only bicycles (vehicles and fuel are much too expensive for everyone but the international aid agencies working here); (2) most of the children wear a shirt or pants, but rarely both.

CURRENCY OF COWS

They are dirty because here water is more precious than gold, and though their bellies are swollen from malnutrition and worms, they laugh and play like any children anywhere in the world. This, I soon learn, is part of an indomitable spirit that deals with its suffering and happiness in the same way, moment by moment.

"I'm constantly amazed by what people can do without here," one aid worker tells me. "We have to fly in everything we need: fuel, a sheet of paper, everything. They live without any of these things."

It is a society of physical hardship; people live in clusters of thuckles. They plant subsistence gardens and pound their own flour for flatbread with mortar and pestle, made of a rounded log that is thrust into a hollow stump.

In south Sudan, wealth is measured in one type of hard currency—cows. This includes everything of any value, even women.

Here a woman who is to be married is purchased from her family with a bride's price of cows.

In the past a woman who was kept close to home and uneducated was worth more cows. She was considered purer, less exposed to detrimental concepts and ideas.

But the war has decimated the cattle economy, and now educated women, according to local officials, draw a higher price because they have more potential to help the family earn in other ways.

SUDAN PEOPLE'S LIBERATION ARMY

In a field in another part of Rembek, a sergeant from the Sudan People's Liberation Army (SPLA) blows a whistle and soldiers begin to form up into squads under giant cypress trees.

Some have uniforms, a mix of camouflage from any number of world army castoffs. Others are in street clothes: sports jerseys, t-shirts with the image of Sean Paul or other Western music artists. Some tote battered AK-47s while others just have sticks. A few wear boots, but most march in nothing more than plastic sandals.

What they seem to lack in military style, the rebel SPLA has made up for in determination.

Their revolt, led by former Sudan army chief John Garang (who died in a helicopter crash in July 2005), forced the northern Arab-dominated government into the power-sharing agreement that is beginning to take shape, but in which there is also great suspicion and mistrust, especially among the former rebel combatants.

"I defected [from the Sudan army] when Commander Garang defected," SPLA Colonel William Kersid Makuac tells me during an interview near a dilapidated barracks. "During that period the struggle was very hard. We had difficulty finding food, feeding our soldiers, getting ammunition. And we never had any vehicles. Our soldiers mostly deployed on foot, sometimes walking for days."

JANJAWEED

In a circle of twenty SPLA fighters, I ask them to raise their hands if they have lost an immediate family member in the fighting. Every hand goes up.

"Sometimes they would bomb four or five times a day," Colonel Makuac says, "and then into the night. We didn't have any antiaircraft guns, so we shot at them with our AK-47s and RPGs. We brought a lot of them down," he says of the Russian Antonov planes the government used against them.

Most of the men here say they joined the SPLA because of atrocities committed against them by Arab tribal militias known as Janjaweed. The SPLA claims the militias are sponsored by the government, a charge the Janjaweed denies.

SPLA Sergeant Tihong Garang says that ten of his family members were killed when the Janjaweed attacked his village, including six children. "They looted everything," he says, "raped the women and shot the children. After— they burned it all down."

In 1999 the Janjaweed also attacked the village of SPLA Sergeant Guot Kueth while he was away.

"They killed many people," he says, "and also burned the village—and they took my wife and two children."

He hasn't seen them since, not his wife nor his three-year-old daughter, Piol, nor his two-year-old son, Guot.

"I can remember their faces," he says, "but I've tried to forget them. It's easier since I don't know if they're alive or dead."

The Comprehensive Peace Agreement is supposed to set these longtime animosities aside and integrate forty thousand of the SPLA into the Sudanese army. However, the agreement mandates that after six years there will be a national referendum in which the country can vote to decide whether it will remain one united Sudan or become two different entities, north and south. Regardless of the outcome, most here agree that six years without war will be even more precious than food dropped from the sky.

The western Sudan region of Darfur has also been decimated by Janjaweed killings, to the point that humanitarian organizations are calling it genocide. However, it is not covered by this agreement because different rebel groups, not associated with the SPLA, are fighting there.

ALWAYS OUR ENEMY

Most of the SPLA men here scoff when I ask them about combining military forces with the Arab north.

"We laugh," one says, "because the Arabs have always been our enemy. They still have the upper hand and used the Janjaweed to attack us."

Another says, "We've been fighting them for so many years. We don't trust them. We should have our own country."

But staying together, at least in the short run, could be profitable for Sudan, which has untapped oil reserves and hundreds of thousands of acres of land that could be cultivated, if the fighting stopped long enough.

There is also international aid—about $4.5 billion pledged—if both sides can adhere to the agreement.

But already things are off to a shaky start, with criticisms from the south that the north is reneging on a host of items, including promised ministry slots in the new government.

Lieutenant Johnson Marur Awou is a grizzled SPLA veteran who has been around for all twenty-one years of the conflict.

"We haven't had anything," Johnson says. "The northern Arab elite have treated the blacks [southern Sudanese] as slaves."

The lieutenant says it will take pressure from the international community to make the idea of one Sudan work.

"The northern Arabs are like foxes," he says, "the international community will have to monitor very carefully if there is going to be peace."

And if not? He and others say they have fought for twenty-one years for an independent south Sudan. If they have to, they can wait for another six.

KHAWAJA

In south Sudan, as in most of the Africa I have traveled so far, it is difficult to forget that I am a foreigner—and white.

As I walk down the dirt paths that wind through the village of Maluwalkon with International Rescue Committee staffers Julie Steiger and Richard Haselwood, children follow after us—waving and shouting, *"Khawaja."*

"What are they saying?" I ask.

"There go the rich white guys," Haselwood laughs.

In Liberia it was *toobabu,* says Haselwood, *poumouy* in Sierra Leone. *Mzungu* in Kenya, adds Steiger.

They don't see them as insults or slurs, just words, both know, that emphasize difference here, not just in color but in place.

"I miss being a normal human being sometimes," says Haselwood. "I miss being anonymous like I am in the U.S."

Steiger nods.

I tell them that since I've been reporting in Africa, there have been more than a few reader responses on the Hot Zone from people who believe that tribal and religious conflict is inherent in black Africa and that Western nations should just wash their hands of them.

"I hear a lot of talk about how race or tribe plays into these conflicts, but really when you examine it closely—it's economics," says Haselwood. "The people who are conducting these wars, whether they're governments, companies or armed groups, use tribes, race and religion as tools of those wars. They're not the causes. The diamonds in Sierre Leone are a perfect example. Same for DRC."

NO MERCY

It's nighttime in the IRC compound in Malualkon where I'm staying, and a few solar lights plus the glow of my computer screen have drawn insects the size of birds. They dart around our eyes, mouths and nostrils—anything with moisture. And despite the thick glaze of DEET we have covered ourselves with, the mosquitoes show no mercy.

I am full of respect for Steiger and Haselwood, who have just left dangerous postings in Chechnya and Liberia, respectively, to come to work here in war-ravaged south Sudan.

"UNKNOWN SOLDIERS"

It bothers me that in some U.S. circles, international aid workers are smugly derided as bleeding hearts, dismissed as misfits who can't get "real jobs," attention deficit disorder adventure seekers, or spiritual dilettantes with little to offer the world but kind thoughts and good intentions.

In reality, international aid agencies are highly selective in whom they hire as expatriate staffs. It's too costly to hire people who don't have the language abilities or skill sets to make aggressive contributions to overseas relief and development projects. Many, including Haselwood and Steiger, have advanced degrees in international studies from top-notch universities.

They are individuals willing to endure the dangers of armed conflict and hostile environments, including exposure to bullets, bombs, malaria, land mines, isolation and long separation from family and loved ones. They are the real "unknown soldiers."

And perhaps most surprising is that they do it with almost no public thanks and scant acknowledgment of their contributions.

"Some people might not value the work we're doing here," says Haselwood with a shrug, "but that's okay. I never see those people. I'm here with people who are grateful—a mother whose baby was horribly scalded was able to get her child to a medical facility that my organization built and staffed and that child's life was saved. She sees the value in what I'm doing."

At the end of a long day their only comfort is a hot meal and a chance to turn the gas-powered generator on for a few hours to watch a DVD or use their computers.

While they have committed themselves to this challenging and uncomfortable environment for a full year, I know I will be glad to leave at the end of the week, though I won't say it aloud, even if my next stop means going back to Iraq.

INTERMISSION

Young Woman and a Log

SOUTH SUDAN

I'm wandering through Malualkon by myself, as conspicuous and perhaps as silly looking as a walking snowman, when I see a young woman pounding corn next to her hut.

With two hands she is raising a heavy log as high as her head and bringing the rounded tip down into a concave wooden stump filled with corn kernels. With each lift and downward heave, there is a dull, rhythmic thump as she turns the kernels into powdery meal flour.

She stops for a second and wipes the dripping sweat from her forehead as she sees me walking toward her. She is in her early to mid-twenties with high cheekbones and smooth skin the color of eggplant.

She smiles, laughs as I say something ridiculous to her in English, maybe commenting on how hard she's working, even though she does not understand a word coming out of my mouth.

She returns to her work, again laughing, while I tape her from various angles: overhead as the log comes down on the stump, a close-up of her face as beads of perspiration cling to her cheeks, from the side as her body undulates like a wave, working with gravity and against it in this strangely beautiful dance of survival.

Just as the rest of this south Sudan village, she has virtually nothing, only the tattered clothes on her body, her grinding tools and some corn kernels— she is not worried about how her hut is furnished, her breast size or where she will holiday in the summer.

She is just pounding corn and laughing at me—and I am almost certain it is the truest laugh I've ever heard.

PART III

PHANTOMS OF FALLUJA, BROWN

SUGAR JUNKIES, MARTYRS' MOMS

AND OTHER *MIDDLE EAST*

NIGHTMARES

CHAPTER 8

IRAQ

What Cannot Be Left Behind

AMMAN, JORDAN | NOVEMBER 7, 2005

GATE 6

At Gate 6 at Queen Alia International Airport in Amman, Jordan, there is a glass partition that separates those who have just arrived from Iraq from those who are going there.

Five times already, I've made that return walk—and each time I peered inside the glass for a moment or two to see the anxiety, bravado or circumspection on the faces of those about to make the trip.

Usually they are hired American or British security men decked out in khaki cargo pants and baseball caps with tactical day packs, or journalists toting laptops, flak jackets and bottles of whisky or vodka in plastic bags from the duty-free, or Arab businessmen in brown suits and well worn shoes.

BEHIND THE GLASS

Those behind the glass, in my experience, tend to look at those on the outside with a combination of relief and envy; relief at the tangible proof that people do return from Iraq alive and envy that, at this moment, those outside are walking away from a war zone rather than toward one.

Today, I'm one of those behind the glass. Today, I'm the circumspect face.

Since the invasion of Iraq in 2003, I've accumulated about fifteen months total in the country—usually three to four months at a stretch working for CNN, NBC and now for Yahoo! News.

I've embedded with ten different U.S. military units, as well as Kurdish Peshmerga militia, in nearly every different region of the country. I've survived roadside bomb attacks, sniper fire, ferocious combat, capture by the Fedayeen militia, and one of the most controversial video clips of the war.

Now, after six weeks of reporting in Africa, I'm still exhausted, even though I took a couple of days to see friends in Amman and sleep in a hotel bed with clean sheets. And while the Sudan "jungle" rash that covered my right arm is disappearing (I've been taking an antibacterial drug prescribed for me by a tropical medicine clinic prior to leaving the United States), I have now contracted some kind of upper respiratory tract infection that I can pinpoint to the moment a fellow passenger coughed uncontrollably into my "airspace" for a frightening twenty minutes straight.

SIN OF OMISSION

Regardless of these minor irritations, I need to return to Iraq. There is unfinished business for me there, although I'm not sure how I will resolve it—or even if it can be resolved.

DOG TAG

In Uganda, digging through my backpack, I feel a flat oval inside a dark crevice. I pull it out and realize I haven't seen it for over a year. It's a military dog tag threaded with a piece of parachute cord.

This is how it came into my possession: I was reporting for CNN in 2003 during the initial invasion of Iraq, and while attempting to be the first journalists into Tikrit, which had not yet fallen to coalition forces, my crew and I were captured at a checkpoint manned by Saddam Hussein's Fedayeen militia, just eighteen miles outside the city.

The Fedayeen leader, an overweight, unshaven, middle-aged man in a dirty raincoat, armed with a locked and loaded AK-47, called me a spy. He immediately fired a shot at the asphalt between my legs as I stepped out of the car.

He had my attention; in a moment we were surrounded by other armed men. The four of us were forced to the ground with AK-47 muzzles pointed at the base of our skulls.

They beat my Kurdish translator, Tofiq, and they kicked and punched my CNN colleague Bill Skinner and our security advisor, Mitch. For some reason, they didn't hit me but instead tied me up, binding my arms from wrist to elbow tightly behind my back with nylon rope.

While my translator negotiated for our lives, I saw a glimmer of silver partially buried in the sand. I bent beside it, lifted it from the sand and slipped it into my back pocket.

Eventually, Tofiq got the Fedayeen to release us to the local tribal chieftain, who eventually let us go—but only after Tofiq bluffed that killing us would mean the chief's village being bombed back to the Stone Age by co-alition forces.

Only after we were released did I discover what the silver metal was: tiny dots and dashes tapped into an oval metal plate—a dog tag of an Iraqi soldier. He had most likely discarded it along with the rest of his uniform as American soldiers and Marines advanced toward Tikrit; an attempt to disappear, blend into the countryside like so many other unwilling conscripts in Saddam's army.

Since that time I've worn it around my neck on successive trips to Iraq; it's a good luck charm of sorts, and one that I'm happy to have found in time for this journey.

THE ROUTINE

Queen Alia Airport in Amman has become such a busy transit point for those coming and going that there's a Starbucks at the entrance to the gate. It's a familiar place for me now. I check in my large duffel, which contains two changes of clothes, a cold weather parka for the desert night, rain gear, extra battery chargers, sleeping bag, bivvy sack, toiletries, tripod, videotape stock and usually some gifts for Iraqi friends.

I carry on my camera, laptop, satellite modem and phones. My strategy here is that if my personal gear is lost, I'll still have the tools to do my job. So far I've been separated from my bags twice on this trip; six days total, most recently on my flight from Nairobi to Amman. Fortunately, the bags were recovered the day before my departure to Baghdad.

After checking in and passing through immigration, remarkably easy because of the flow of Westerners coming and going to Iraq, I go to the airport's well-stocked duty-free shop and buy a music CD, since I won't have anything new to listen to for a while. Then, if I have calculated correctly, I'll use up my last few Jordanian dinars for a coffee at Starbucks and a large bottle of mineral water for the plane flight.

FELLOW PASSENGERS

I know that on the Fokker F28-4000, which carries around eighty people, the brave and cheerful flight attendants will pass out plastic containers containing two dry sandwiches on tiny French rolls, one cheese and one bologna. They will also serve juice and water but, prudently, no booze.

Today I'm sitting next to an Iraqi man who tells me he has had to leave the country to work.

"If I work with you," he taps my shoulder, indicating that I'm symbolic of Westerners in Iraq, "I am in danger. If I work on my own, I am in danger. There is no place safe, but to work out of the country."

He hasn't seen his family in six months and is understandably concerned about their safety. Two American security contractors are seated in front of me, one who looks like a double for the bearded and ponytailed former SEAL Team Six leader and *Rogue Warrior* author, Richard Marcinko, the other like a Pennsylvania state trooper with a buzz cut, glasses and a gray T-shirt with "K-9" in big black letters on the back.

Behind me, two Brits discuss the possibility of Turkey joining the European Union.

THE SPIN-DOWN

But the most memorable aspect of this flight to Baghdad comes at the end: the "spin-down." Instead of the gradual descent most planes execute, this flight begins a series of hard-banking left turns from its cruising altitude. The sun passes through the windows on the right, then on the left, then on the right again and so on—as the plane spins down like a falling maple leaf until it reaches the hard deck of Baghdad International.

The maneuver is both dramatic and necessary to make the plane a more difficult target for insurgents armed with shoulder-fired missiles or RPGs. One shooter already proved his marksmanship a year and a half ago with a hit on a DHL cargo plane, which was luckily able to land safely.

Most on board seem to consider it a fun ride, as long as no one is shooting at you. Once on the ground, I get an Iraqi visa at the airport for eighty-one U.S. dollars and letters from my employer and the U.S. embassy. The price is double what I paid a year ago, which could be considered a little unfair since the security situation seems to worsen with each trip I make.

UPSIDE DOWN

Outside the heavily fortified airport terminal, I wait for my pickup. A fifteen-year-old boy named Ahmed, a baggage handler at the airport, strikes up a conversation with me in his limited English and my very limited Arabic.

I ask him why he is not in school, and he pulls out a wallet filled with Iraqi and Jordanian dinars—as well as U.S. dollars.

"Baksheesh," I say, motioning to the contents of his wallet, his tips. He nods. "You can make more baksheesh if you go to school and study," I say automatically, but without conviction.

I give him a Hot Zone t-shirt and a few stickers used to identify my gear cases. From all my time in places like this I've learned that "swag" with some kind of English script is often more prized than cash. Ahmed peels the back off one of the Hot Zone stickers and places it on his chest—upside down. Somehow it seems appropriate, so I don't bother to correct him.

Soon, a Marine lieutenant from the joint public affairs command arrives and takes me to a staging area where I will wait for another ride to the Coalition Press Information Center. There I will be credentialed and wait for an eventual helicopter to fly me to my embed with a Marine unit—in Falluja.

PHANTOM FURY

It is November 7, 2004. I'm too tired to feel the butterflies in my stomach, but I know this will be the biggest combat action that I've witnessed in my career. Operation Phantom Fury, as it is code-named, will include ten thousand U.S. troops and another two thousand from the Iraqi army.

After being up all night, waiting to deploy with the Marine unit I'm embedded with, we are now prepositioned in the desert scrub on the northern outskirts of the city.

I listen to the prebattle chatter, as members of the 3.1 Marines' CAAT team and India Company dig in for the night. The voices are filled with both introspection and bravado.

In the Humvee in which I've been riding, Lance Corporal Brandon Burns sits in the canvas sling of his Mark 19 turret (a weapon that launches 40 mm grenades like a machine gun). Burns is scanning ahead and discussing the Old Testament with Corporal Steven Wolf, the squad leader.

While reading his Bible, Wolf marvels at what a strong warrior and leader King David was. But Burns reminds him of David's sins—sending Bathsheba's husband into battle to be killed so he could take her as his wife.

"It was pride," Burns says, from inside his steel perch. "His pride made him turn away from God."

Their talk is interrupted for a moment by explosions, followed by black and white smoke plumes drifting up from the horizon a couple of miles in front of us. Artillery units are registering their mortars in the late afternoon, using both explosive and controversial white phosphorus rounds that leave an arcing white streak in the sky.

The train station at the northern border of the city is to be the first target. And in the deep darkness of this overcast night, we watch as air strikes and artillery rain down on the position.

On a satellite phone, I describe to television audiences watching MSNBC News the bright orange blasts and thundering explosions in the distance, thousand- and two-thousand-pound bombs being dropped, the whining of the "Spooky" AC-130 gunship as its miniguns and onboard howitzer level football-field-sized swaths with each pass.

ONE YEAR LATER

Now, on the anniversary of that battle, a full year later, I am at the same Falluja train station where it all started. The place is currently serving as the headquarters for Echo Company of the 2.6 Marines.

Tonight, I'll patrol the same streets that became a supercharged combat zone last November, but I'll do it with Marines who were not here then, who only know the stories.

Back in Iraq, until this moment, I haven't let myself think about it much, but on this clear and cold night as I follow the squads across the tracks, through the bombed-out depot and back into the city, I consider my year-long journey and all of the burdens I gathered up here and that I continue to carry.

AFTER THE SOFTENING

Dawn is breaking, but you can barely tell. The skies are still overcast and a chilling drizzle does little to diffuse the smell of cordite in the air. The air strikes have stopped and we've advanced into the outskirts of the city. Falluja seems abandoned, residents apparently heeding the warning of coalition forces to evacuate the city before the offensive.

Forces begin to pour in from all sides, moving south, block by block. Tanks and Bradleys rumble by, stopping, pivoting and firing their main guns down each alleyway at cars parked on the street; a precaution in case they've been rigged with explosives.

The concussions of the Abrams M1A1 tanks ripple through my body as I push down the street on foot, videotaping the advance. Around the corner on the left-hand side of the street I see the body of an insurgent, my first of the bat-

tle. He's on his back, dressed in all black with the exception of a pair of white
sneakers.

His ammunition pouches crisscross his chest, with rounds spilling out onto
the street where he fell. Beside him is a Russian Dragunov sniper rifle. Weirdly,
his hands are positioned underneath his head and make it seem almost as if he
is relaxing—but for the pool of black blood that surrounds his body.

The advance through the city seems like it will be quick, with most of the
resistance already broken by air strikes and devastatingly precise Marine
sniper teams on rooftops around Falluja. But when we pass through the mar-
ketplace near Jolan Park, everything changes.

BARKING DOGS

Tonight, in the same area, there's no movement, no sound except a few bark-
ing dogs. There's been a curfew in Falluja for the last year, from 10:00 P.M.
until 5:00 A.M. Of the 150,000 residents estimated to have returned after the
battle, no one, it seems tonight, is willing to stir outside past the legal hours.

The Echo Company squads, led by a young first lieutenant named John
Bradenham, search an empty office building whose lights are still on. There
is nothing in the rooms but a few chairs, desks and papers. The search seems
like a tiresome exercise to me, and I stand on the roof and look out over the
marketplace, trying to imagine it a year before.

JOLAN MARKET

Back then the air strikes had turned the fruit and vegetable stalls into a twisted
maze of wood and metal. It was there, navigating through the passageways of
the Jolan Market, that the first RPG round struck.

A young Marine caught shrapnel in the head and was pulled by squad
members into a protective enclosure. A Navy corpsman bandaged him while
another Marine propped him up from behind. Through my viewfinder I saw
maroon rosary beads dangling from the wounded man's pants pocket.

From that point, the "cakewalk" through Falluja turned into a frantic fight for survival. We rounded the corner onto a main east-west route through Falluja that military planners had named Elizabeth Street.

It's the same street that leads to the infamous bridge on which an Iraqi mob hung the charred bodies of American Blackwater security contractors after killing them in April 2004.

On Elizabeth, more RPG rounds exploded against a wall behind us.

The Marines believed the firing came from a nearby building and unleashed a massive barrage of small-arms fire, AT4 missiles, .50-caliber machine guns and even 120 mm tank rounds to their rear.

KILLING BOX

When the Marines finished firing, the building was a smoking ruin. But almost as soon as they resumed their advance the other way, more RPG rounds were fired at them from behind. Then insurgent snipers began firing rifle shots in front of them as well, picking off Marines and creating a killing box on Elizabeth Street.

Lance Corporal Brandon Burns was one of the victims. The tip of an AK-47 round penetrated his Kevlar helmet just enough to pierce his skull. His blood was splattered near the picture of his girlfriend taped to the inside of the Mark 19 turret. Burns survived the incident but suffered permanent disabilities.

STOP AND STARE

As the Echo squads moved from the empty office building onto Elizabeth Street, I stopped for a moment in the darkness and just stared down the street. It is so different, yet so much the same. Many of the buildings destroyed in the battle remain as crumbling ruins.

There are piles of rubble everywhere, but tonight there is no gunfire, only silence. There is also evidence that people once again live and work on this battle-scarred street; that would have been impossible to imagine last year.

The fight down Elizabeth Street was just the first day of a battle that would go on for several more weeks. In that time period I would see much that will linger in my mind, likely for the rest of my life.

THE MOSQUE SHOOTING

The mosque shooting, a week into the battle, was just one of those incidents, but one I've had to spend an enormous amount of time writing and talking about. I've been called both traitor and hero for reporting it. I know I am neither. I simply witnessed the complex truths of war.

The video tells the story of an unjustified killing. Anyone who has ever seen the entire tape knows that. But airing the story was not about prosecuting that Marine. The story is about being loyal to the truth as a nation, that citizens of a democracy are collectively responsible for what their troops do in war, good or bad. It's my job to make sure they see all of it.

OWNING UP TO THE TRUTH

Supporting the troops, I've learned from my time with them, means trying to understand what they actually go through during their deployment. Many tell me they cringe when they come home and people thank them in that hollow way for "fighting for our country." What they've been through is so much more than that—some of it they're proud of, some of it they're not.

One young soldier sadly wrote to tell me about the guys in his unit who, perhaps like their fathers in Vietnam or grandfathers in Korea, routinely pose for snapshots with the bodies of their dead enemies.

As a society, do we want to just say thank you to those soldiers—or do we need to try to understand that asking them to kill for us may also kill something inside of them?

That is what brutally honest reporting helps us to do.

Not owning up to the truth, regardless of consequences, makes us hypocrites, mocks our principles and kills trust.

During this most recent embed in Falluja, I saw a sign at the headquarters of a Golf Company that read, "If you don't correct a Marine when he is wrong you weaken him, the entire unit and lower our standards."

I believe the same applies to citizens of a democracy. We have to be strong enough to own up to our mistakes, even when they happen at difficult times.

Although as a war reporter my job is not to pull a trigger, my choices in doing my job can still be wrought with moral dilemmas. My personal burden from the war in Iraq is no longer about the mosque shooting. I'm confident that, despite my internal struggle, I did do the right thing in that situation.

MY STRUGGLE

My burden comes from the first day of the fighting in Falluja, just as I was about to turn onto Elizabeth Street with the 3.1 Marines.

My truth is that in the heat of battle I forgot or ignored my own humanity . . . and that is the memory I now must live with.

Here's how it happened: walking down the street with the Marines, I saw an old Iraqi man lying on his back near the curb. He was wearing a white t-shirt that highlighted the stream of crimson blood flowing behind him.

At first I couldn't see his wound, but as I came closer, peering over him—I was shocked for a moment. I had seen plenty of gunshot wounds before, but the right half of this man's skull had been blown away, revealing portions of his brain. It was a sniper shot, clean through his eye. What disturbed me most, however, was that he was still breathing; the man's chest was rising and falling. He was alive. There was no weapon nearby.

A Marine in a Humvee saw the man and yelled at the two Marines I was walking with, "Somebody put a bullet in that guy." I assumed he was talking about a mercy killing. The man was definitely going to die. The trauma of the injury was too great—he was already bleeding to death.

One of the Marines looked at my camera and asked me if I was going to videotape it if he shot the old man. I nodded yes, that I had to. He said that he wasn't going to do it then and walked off to join the other Marines—leaving me there alone with the old man.

I looked at him for a long moment, wondering what I should do. Should I try to bandage him up, even though he was dying? Should I hold his hand for a second, a small comfort from one human being to another during his last moments?

Ultimately, I couldn't bring myself to do either. Bandaging him, I thought, was futile—and holding his hand might make me seem weak or sympathetic in front of the Marines.

Instead I left him there and caught up with my unit—looking back once but soon forgetting about the old man for the next six hours as the battle on Elizabeth Street raged.

I made a choice to do nothing for that man, not even a reassuring touch, yet a little while later, I didn't think twice about picking up the end of a stretcher with five other Marines to transport wounded Lance Corporal Brandon Burns to a military ambulance.

Helping Burns was easy; there was an empty handle, other people involved, a need, a reason, a goal, little cost to the effort. Helping the old man was fraught with peril; I was alone, what would I accomplish? There would be a cost for my action. Now I know there was also a cost for my inaction. To do the difficult thing required strength; to do the easy thing didn't. Looking back, I wish I could have found the strength to do them both.

PLUMES OF SMOKE

These are the realities of war, the choices before us like black and white plumes of smoke turning into furious phantoms ready to haunt us until we accept their truths.

On this quiet night back on Elizabeth Street a year later, the Marines in my viewfinder are painted green by my camera's infrared light. Moving tactically from corner to corner, they, too, look like phantoms to me. Here I have become one as well; a phantom chasing phantoms, which maybe only the dogs can see.

CHAPTER 9

LEBANON
Hanging with Hezbollah

BEIRUT, LEBANON | DECEMBER 20, 2005

MY AFTERNOON WITH HEZBOLLAH

I'm at the Hezbollah media relations office in its stronghold of south Beirut. If I didn't know where I was, the sign behind the bearded male receptionist would set me straight. It features the yellow-and-green Hezbollah logo with a raised AK-47. It says, in both Arabic and English, MEDIA RELATIONS—HIZBOLLAH.

My driver, Henry, a Christian from East Beirut, dropped me off here and is waiting by his taxi. He told me he had never been in this part of town. I can tell he's a little nervous, perhaps with good reason; men on different street corners pointed out our vehicle almost as soon as we entered the neighborhood. The cell phones came out and we were immediately stopped and questioned about why we were here.

I'm waiting to talk with Hussein Naboulsi, the foreign media liaison for this Shia Islamic political and military organization, whose name means "party of God."

POLITICAL POWER

In Lebanon's fractious political spectrum, it's one of two main political parties representing Shia interests; it gained not just political legitimacy but actual power by winning 14 out of 128 seats in parliamentary elections.

With the other Shia party, Amal, it controls almost 30 percent of the legislature.

It's an impressive evolution for an organization initially created in 1982 to fight Israel. (Israel first invaded southern Lebanon in 1978 in pursuit of Yasser Arafat's Palestine Liberation Organization, which was launching attacks against it from Lebanon.)

Now there is pressure from Christian and Sunni blocs in the Lebanese government and the international community for Hezbollah to disarm its militia under United Nations Resolution 1559.

But Hezbollah is reputedly funded and supported by both Syria and Iran and is better armed and trained than the Lebanese army—which is also 60 percent Shia and would probably not move to disarm Hezbollah even if it were able to.

"ARE YOU JUST A BLOG?"

I'm waiting for fifteen minutes before Naboulsi comes out to meet me. He's young, early thirties, and at first I'm not even sure he's the man I've come here to meet. When I shake his hand, I notice a jagged scar on his neck and the large turquoise ring he is wearing. He seems annoyed that I am here and does little to hide his sizing me up on the media-importance scale.

He takes me to his small, Spartan office. There is a computer on his fiberboard desk and a message framed in English on the wall that says, "Special friends are like one of the close family." I know at this moment I am neither.

I give him a card and tell him about the Hot Zone project. He shakes his head.

"Are you just a blog?" he asks me dismissively—and in perfect English.

I quickly try to explain the value of my presence to him, both in terms of the number of unique users each month on the site, which at this point has been building steadily to almost two hundred thousand a day, and how the site is amplified when our stories are picked up by the Scripps Howard News Service and reprinted in small newspapers around the United States.

He is still not convinced that I am worth his time, so I tell him to go to the site itself. He tries several times, typing the address into the computer, then clicking over a leopard-print mousepad, but the site will not come up. I begin to think he may believe I'm lying. Finally, I see that he typed the address incorrectly. I redirect him and the site comes up.

Then I realize it was not such a good idea. My last posting had been about Iraq, where I was embedded with American Marines and army soldiers. Their photographs and stories are spread across the screen. Regardless of the editorial angle of the stories, the coverage could seem pro-American to someone considered by the American government to be working for a terrorist organization.

THE INTERVIEW

To my relief, Naboulsi waves it off and signals for me to begin the interview. I ask him first to clarify what Hezbollah actually is.

"Hezbollah is Hezbollah," he says. "There's no change in its definition. It's a political, religious party created as a reaction to Israel's invasion of 1982. Politically, it's represented in both cabinet and Parliament—and considered by all to be a legitimate party. But if you're against Israel, the U.S. administration labels you as they want."

LITANY OF TERROR

The U.S. government blames Hezbollah for an entire litany of acts that nearly defined Middle East terrorism in the mid-'80s, including the April 1983 U.S. embassy bombing in Beirut that killed sixty-three people, the Beirut truck bombing in October 1983 that killed two hundred forty-one U.S. Marines; a second bombing of the U.S. embassy that killed twenty-two people in September 1984; as well as the 1985 hijacking of Rome-to-Athens TWA Flight 847, in which a U.S. Navy diver on the plane was killed (the man convicted for the murder was released earlier in December 2005 by German authorities after serving nineteen years in prison).

Hezbollah denies involvement in any of these attacks.

The United States also claims the group carried out a series of kidnappings of Westerners from 1982 to 1992, including the torture and killings of CIA station chief William Buckley and U.S. Army Colonel William Higgins, and the abductions of the American journalist Terry Anderson and the Archbishop of Canterbury's special envoy, Terry Waite.

LIBERATORS?

Despite the terrorism allegations, many in Lebanon, especially among the majority Shia community, an estimated 40 percent of the population, consider Hezbollah a resistance movement, even liberators, since it forced Israel to retreat from southern Lebanon in 2000.

"This organization should be considered the most patriotic in Lebanon," Naboulsi tells me. "We fought the Israelis and forced them to leave. Hezbollah sacrificed 1,800 martyrs and thousands of wounded soldiers for the sake of this country—for the sake of the dignity and honor of this country."

Because of that perception, Hezbollah is the only faction in the country that has been allowed to keep its weapons, ostensibly as a buffer against Israeli incursions, but realistically because the Lebanese army is too weak to disarm them. Naboulsi says they've earned the right to be armed.

"Fighting the Israelis is not a picnic, it's blood split. It's not a reward in a festival," he says, his voice rising with emphasis—to the point that he seems to be performing now. "No one can take that mission . . . no one can take that mission unless he has faith, extreme faith and loyalty to this country."

THEOCRACY

Hezbollah has said in the past that it would like to see Lebanon become a theocratic state in the model of one of its primary funders and supporters, Iran. But it has backed off a bit from those statements recently, perhaps in the hopes of appearing more conciliatory.

It may need that new tone to offset a potentially costly political position these days—its full-throated support of its other primary financial supporter, Syria. Hezbollah actively opposed the so-called Cedar Revolution, the outcry following the February 2005 assassination of former Lebanese prime minister Rafik Hariri—which, along with international pressure, led to the withdrawal of Syrian troops after thirty years in Lebanon.

"The Syrians played a key role in the stability of Lebanon," says Naboulsi, "putting an end to the civil war. And Syria really supported the resistance, which ended up forcing the Israeli enemy out of Lebanon."

But being that outspoken has a price. Some Christian parties are pushing even harder to force Hezbollah to disarm.

KEY PLAYER

Naboulsi tells me that Hezbollah can withstand the pressure both inside and outside of Lebanon.

"Hezbollah is an essential part of Lebanon which no one can ignore," says Naboulsi. "It's the biggest party of the biggest sector of the population and because of consensus democracy no one can form a government without our contribution."

For its own political base, Hezbollah's anti-Israeli, anti-American rhetoric is part of the appeal. Hezbollah has called for the destruction of Israel and even offered to open up a second front against the Israelis during the Palestinian intifada. As for the United States designating Hezbollah as a terrorist organization, Naboulsi is matter-of-fact: any future dialogue is doubtful.

"The American government has labeled us as terrorists. They say they don't negotiate with terrorists . . . and neither do we."

ONE-DIMENSIONAL

By the end of the interview he has warmed a bit—but I still realize that the portrait I have of both the organization and the man is very one-dimensional. I try to get him to put away his talking points and at least reveal why he was drawn to join Hezbollah.

The answer I get reminds me of a job seeker's overly earnest response when asked by a potential employer to describe a personal weakness: a disingenuous "I am a workaholic."

"Islam pushed me toward this organization," Naboulsi says. "It's good to form yourself within an organization because Islam is not about rituals, it's about helping people, it's about politics, it's about caring about others. Islam is so much more than acting alone."

I don't know it now, but the next time I see Naboulsi will be on television eight months later, escorting the CNN reporter Nick Robertson around the rubble of that same south Beirut neighborhood following Israeli air strikes during the thirty-four days of fighting in August.

"We must go now! We must go now," Naboulsi tells Robertson in a voice bordering on urgency and panic. "They could strike here again at any moment."

INTERMISSION

Defendant "198964"

It's morning in Nairobi, Kenya, my "base camp" in eastern Africa. I'm just back from Uganda and recharging before my next movement, a trip into south Sudan. I'm having coffee at my hotel and reading my email.

At this point "it" is just another message in my inbox, a note from my sister Shawn. She has frequently sent me messages of encouragement during my past war zone deployments and I have no reason to believe this is anything else. But what I will soon read will change everything—and nothing.

She has sent me a link to a story about a Chinese business journalist named Shi Tao, or defendant "198964."

TIANANMEN SQUARE

The article says Shi was accused of sending an email that summarized an internal Communist Party directive, warning Chinese journalists not to fan the flames of dissent during the fifteenth anniversary of the Tiananmen Square massacre. Shi's electronic user name, 198964, represents the actually date of the event—6/4/89, or June 4, 1989.

Chinese authorities labeled the Tiananmen directive a state secret and sentenced Shi to ten years in prison for divulging it.

But here is where the article clips me in the knees. It says the Chinese authorities were able to track the email back to Shi's computer at his newspaper, *Contemporary Business News,* through the help of his Internet service provider—Yahoo!

I have to read it three times before the full gravity of the article sinks in. If true, not only was I working for a company that had helped to jail a fellow journalist but it would also seem that the integrity of our mission would be compromised by the association.

THE CALL

I immediately email my team and ask them to set up a conference call with Yahoo!'s legal and corporate communications reps who can explain the entire case to me.

Instead what I get is a mid-level public relations manager who, at the moment, is the media point person on the issue. She is perfectly nice but does not realize that I'm sensing an earthquake that she thinks is a thunderstorm.

She tells me that Yahoo! didn't know at the time why Chinese authorities were asking for the information, but that it is a routine occurrence, even in America. But when she trots out a version of the same line I had read in the article, something about Yahoo! having to abide by the laws of the countries it operates in, I lose it.*

"That's the most cavalier and insufficient explanation you could possibly give," I say, anger in my voice rising. "You will get eaten up alive if you keep trying to dish out that kind of crap."

My outburst has set off alarm bells in the Yahoo! Media Group—as it should. And now I have to make my own decision: do I resign over the issue or complete the Hot Zone project?

ANOTHER ONE?

It is a decision I struggle with daily over the course of several months. In the meantime, the journalist advocacy group Reporters Without Borders claims that Chinese authorities have jailed another man, a blogger named Li Zhi, also with the help of information provided by Yahoo!.

As a journalist who has been in the center of the maelstrom over the free and uncensored distribution of information, I wonder how I can continue to accept a paycheck from an organization that could do this, unwittingly or not.

Established news organizations that I had worked for in the past, such as

---

* At the time of this book's publishing, congressional investigators say they will look into the allegations that Yahoo! *did* actually know the nature of the Chinese authorities investigation into Shi Tao when they provided information to them. Yahoo! denies any misrepresentation.

NBC and CNN, I believed, would not make this kind of error. The rules of journalism were embedded in the business model there—you don't give up your sources.

But this is new territory for Yahoo!—which had only aggregated news before I joined them, never gathered it. Still, in the effort to get a foothold into China's explosive Internet market, is Yahoo! being callously calculated or just willfully ignorant?

Questions from the other side of the argument are equally unsettling. Were the underreported stories I was covering for the Hot Zone important enough to keep going despite this dilemma? Could a company, like a human being, be capable of possessing competing belief systems that allow it to pursue good and bad things at the same time? If so, in this case, did the good—reporting the causes and true costs of global conflict—surpass Yahoo!'s alleged complicity in helping to jail these men?

PUBLIC SERVICE

From all my years in journalism, I know conclusively that no other news organization at this moment would fund such an uncommercial project as the Hot Zone. The idea of covering the faceless and the voiceless in some of the world's most obscure places doesn't make financial sense at the bottom of any business's balance sheet. This is journalism at its core—public service.

We are only halfway into the project but our readership is building to several hundred thousand unique users a day, as many as two million page views a month. From the reader responses, I feel that we were having an impact in making people more aware. I have to think very carefully whether ending the project in protest will accomplish anything, let alone honor Shi Tao's and Li Zhi's sacrifice for free expression.

After discussing it with my direct team, Robert, Erin and Lisa, we decide to complete the project—but to post an item on our site about the case and call for the immediate release of Shi Tao and Li Zhi.

FIREWALL

Yahoo!'s vice president of news, Neil Budde, himself a veteran of the *Wall Street Journal,* has the delicate task of explaining to Yahoo!'s top brass that our actions are consistent with how real news divisions are supposed to operate—behind a firewall that allows them to report independently, even critically, about their own parent companies.

But the posting does little to ease my continuing concerns. When I'm back in the United States the issue comes up again when the wife of another Chinese Internet activist named Wang Xiaoning sues Yahoo! in U.S. federal court for allegedly aiding Chinese authorities in identifying her imprisoned husband, too. Shi Tao has since joined in the suit.

It's obviously not good news for Yahoo!, which is battling bad press about underperforming stock prices and an overpaid chief executive officer, Terry Semel.

Yahoo! has undoubtedly been generous with me—underwriting a journalist's dream project—but as it has always been in my career, my primary loyalty lies with the ideals of my profession, not my employer.

MY EMAIL

Sitting at my desk at 9:00 P.M. in the empty Media Group offices one night, I can't help myself from sending an email to Terry Semel and Yahoo! co-founders Jerry Yang and David Filo about the China situation.*

In it I ask them to do a number of things; most drastically, to set a deadline to withdraw Yahoo!'s business investment in China (Yahoo! operates in China through a 40 percent share in the Chinese corporation Alibaba.com) if Chinese authorities do not release the dissidents allegedly jailed with Yahoo!'s help.

I read it over, hesitate, and then hit send. I'm not sure exactly what I've done—but for the moment I feel better.

Early the next morning, when I check my inbox before going to work there's an email response . . . from Jerry Yang.

* Entire text of email can be found in Appendix B.

It reads:

> *Kevin, I'd be more than happy to talk to you about this in person. As you can imagine, we've had a long and intensive discussion around all the alternatives you've suggested. Happy to walk through this with you next time you are in town.*
> *Jerry*

I'm floored, especially since I sent the note so late. But it's not just a wink and a pat on the back. When a week goes by and I haven't made an appointment to see him, he emails me again to remind me.

With all that is going on in the company, Yang, one of *Forbes'* 500 richest people in the world, has found the time to ping me twice over an issue he can't possibly be eager to talk about—but is willing to do so.

JERRY YANG

Yang himself is Chinese, born in Taipei, Taiwan, and when he came to America at age ten with his mother and brother (his father died when he was two) he knew almost no English. But within three years, he mastered it. Then years later, as a doctoral student in electrical engineering at Stanford, he turned the directory of Web sites that he and fellow student David Filo devised in a campus trailer into what would become the largest Internet portal in the world.

The name Yahoo!, the company's PR info relates, was an acronym for "Yet Another Hierarchical Officious Oracle," but the two founders insist they were drawn to the dictionary definition of a yahoo as "rude and uncouth." Thirteen years later it is a giant of the industry, albeit a wounded one.

After I make an appointment to see Jerry Yang at Yahoo!'s headquarters in Sunnyvale, California, the news breaks that embattled CEO Terry Semel is resigning—and Yang will actually take over, a position he hasn't held since the mid-90s.

Surprisingly, he keeps his previously scheduled appointment with me despite his new responsibilities.

THE INTERVIEW

He looks tired and a little frazzled from the endless internal and external questions that have come with the management shakeup—but still spends one and a half hours with me talking about China in a conference room named "Jerry Garcia" (most are named after movie and music legends).

"David and I didn't found this company to see people put in prison," he says earnestly.

I take notes as he explains to me how the Internet landscape was so different in 1999 when Yahoo! first started operating in China. He admits that mistakes were made in that transitional period and that things would be done differently today, both from a technological and a business perspective.

He tells me, as Yahoo! has stated before, that when the Chinese government makes requests for information concerning criminal investigations, they don't provide reasons for the requests. (Neither do U.S. law enforcement agencies, which make hundreds of inquiries a month, Yang says.)

He says Yahoo! has formed a task force with other Internet competitors, such as Google and MSN (who have also been criticized for acceding to Chinese censorship laws) about how they can help maintain the integrity of human rights when entering emerging markets in places like Indonesia, Myanmar and Vietnam—where principles of democracy are ignored or even suppressed.

"But what about the people in jail in China now?" I ask him.

Yang nods. He gives me numerous background details, but because of the recent lawsuit and other confidential concerns, he says, it's almost impossible for him to speak openly and on-the-record about Yahoo!'s efforts on their behalf.

I tell him the company line about abiding by Chinese law comes off as opportunistic and insensitive.

"It's incredibly frustrating," he says, "not being able to say more."

Yang does say, however, that the company is actively working with human rights organizations in China, as well as developing global standards for protecting privacy and free expression on the Internet.

He also says there are more safeguards in place now in China—including warnings to users that Yahoo! China email is subject to Chinese law.

CHINA'S APPEAL

What does not have to be said, however, is that China's business appeal for Internet companies seems irresistible. With an estimated 150 to 200 million Internet users and a recent study cited in *Forbes* magazine claiming the Chinese spend more time online than even American users, a whopping 1.7 billion hours per week compared to 129 million hours a week for Americans, Yahoo!, Google and MSN won't likely be pulling up stakes anytime soon.

"The Internet is changing China," Yang tells me near the end of our meeting. "People have so much more access to information than they ever have had before. It's created dialogue about the environment, corruption and communities. My friends who live there say things have changed so much— even in just the past few years."

"Is the Internet changing China," I ask him, "or is China changing the Internet? If no one stands up to their demands on privacy issues and censorship they won't have any reason to stop making them."

"This issue isn't just a storm for us to weather and forget about. As a person I couldn't live with that," Yang tells me. "But remaining engaged with China is the best leverage we have—otherwise, we won't have anything."

ENGAGEMENT?

In a speech Yang gave at the Yahoo! stockholders meeting in June 2007 he stated, "We the employees and executive team at Yahoo! are dismayed and distressed by the impact of people imprisoned in China and around the world. We have been and will continue to be actively engaged for the long term."*

Reading the quote, it's not lost on me that the decision Yahoo! has made on China, a policy of engagement—change from within—is the same choice I have made about continuing my relationship with Yahoo! I'm far from certain, but, for the sake of Defendant 198964 and the others, I hope we have both chosen wisely.

---

* At that same shareholders meeting, two proposals to change Yahoo!'s policy on China were overwhelmingly voted down; the first asked the company to avoid hosting user data in "Internet-restricted" countries like China, the second sought to establish a human rights committee to help avoid "corporate complicity in the violation of human rights."

CHAPTER 10

IRAN
Under the Hijab

MAHMOUDI

I am waiting in the immigration line at Imam Khomeini International Airport. Opened in 2004, it is all gleaming marble floors and soaring glass walls, sleek and modern, the face Iran wants to project to the world first.

Out of my jacket, I pull a red passport embossed with a golden harp and imprinted with Gaelic and English letters that spell *Ireland*.

As an American journalist with Irish heritage, my access to George Bush's "axis of evil" nations is much easier as an Irish citizen than as an American one. While it took my team nearly two months to get me the visa, within minutes I have passed through passport control and into Tehran.

I have been here twice before, both times on my way to war. The first was in 2001, when I was trying to get into Afghanistan through Iran's eastern border. Unsuccessful. But I had other things on my mind then. Neither time did I give Iran much thought, beyond its use to me as a transit point. This time will be different; now I am here to cover Iran.

Coming here is a clear and intentional departure from the Hot Zone's stated mission of covering only armed-conflict zones. Iran is currently not at war, although by the heated rhetoric it is exchanging with the West, it sometimes seems on the brink.

Iran's president, Mahmoud Ahmadinejad, has been effectively pushing all the wrong buttons with the West by denying the Holocaust and saying Israel "must be wiped off the map." But beyond the words, it's his actions that have raised the most concern. Ahmadinejad is insisting on restarting Iran's uranium enrichment program, which he says is for peaceful energy production, but which the United States and the United Nations fear could be used to make nuclear bombs.

While almost all the recent coverage of Iran has been about these issues, I believe American viewers need to get a deeper and more penetrating view of Iran, beyond the headlines. I can achieve that here by trying to peel back Iran's public face to see the more private one underneath, by telling smaller, more personal stories—not just the official ones.

Iranian friends and sources have told me about the internal opposition to Ahmadinejad, both because of repressive measures he has reintroduced to the country following the attempted reforms of his predecessor, Mohammad Khatami, and his failure to restart the country's faltering economy. I hope to hear some of these voices and speak to some of these people.

Near the luggage carousels, I see a man holding up a homemade sign with my name, sort of, on a sheet of white paper. It says, Kavein Sites. But while the sign is misspelled, I recognize the man holding it up.

Ibrahim Mahmoudi was my driver when I had first come to Iran in 2001 with NBC. I hadn't realized that we would be working together again, but it is a comforting surprise in a not-so-familiar place.

Mahmoudi gives me a big hug and kisses me on both cheeks repeatedly.

"Mr. Kevin, Mr. Kevin," he says, "I am so happy to see you."

To see a friendly face, someone genuinely happy to see me at this point in the journey, buoys my spirits, especially when I'm starting to feel the cumulative exhaustion of my travels and the difficulty of having to report almost every single day from a different place.

Mahmoudi has been driving foreign correspondents around Iran for nearly thirty years. He has seen it all, from the days of the shah to the takeover of the American embassy. He knows Tehran better than the secret police do.

Over the roller-coaster ride of the next week, he'll make me laugh and give me gifts like a ten-pound bag of pistachios, drawings made by his daughter and a beautiful ornamental dagger, all without reason—and then top it off with a bundle of roses on New Year's. I joke with my fixer, Darius, that with all the gifts from Mahmoudi, I feel like we're dating. Darius laughs but tells me that in Iran men typically give flowers to other men as a sign of thanks or congratulations.

FLEA MARKET

It is early Friday morning and Darius asks me if I want to check out a Tehran flea market held every Friday in a downtown parking garage. Five floors of trinkets, carpets, art, books and musical instruments, it's a trash-or-treasure trove more similar to a weekend American garage sale than shopping at a Middle Eastern souk.

Near one stretch of vendors' stalls, Farhad Nayati bangs out the theme to *Dr. Zhivago* on a toy dulcimer. He's a rock star, as far as parking garage musicians go. Both children and adults gather round as he plays with confidence and virtuosity, making sales and handing out cards for lessons at the end of the performance.

But if there were an award for most popular vendor at the Tehran flea market, it would almost certainly go to record seller Ali Aughar Moosavi. His stall has the cool, dingy ambience of a Seattle coffee shop on a cold day. An ancient hi-fi spins some old-school jazz while customers flip through his stacks. Ali says he makes about a hundred dollars every Friday selling all kinds of vinyl, while also giving away priceless music lore in reverential tones.

"I used to work in a record shop," he tells me while I videotape him. "It was called Beethoven's. It was one of the most popular, but the government shut it down in 1978."

He says he has over ten thousand albums at home, all vinyl, but only brings a small sampling here every weekend to sell. He shows me an electric mix that's impressive, although not very current, including the Monkees, Simon and Garfunkel, Cat Stevens, Iron Butterfly and Milt Jackson.

Ali says he got into music when his father died. He was just twelve years old and took refuge in rock 'n' roll. He says there are records in his collection he would never sell.

"I have five thousand just for me, from Pink Floyd, Eric Clapton, B. B. King, Eagles, Dire Straits, Beatles," he tells me in English.

"You won't part with these?" I ask.

"No, no, no—no sale, no sale!"

"Why not?"

"Music is my life," he says, pointing to his heart and unveiling a small smile that seems to have shaken off ten thousand disappointments in his lifetime.

BROWN SUGAR JUNKIES

We are in a bad part of town—the junkies' part of town. For Iran, being so close to the world's largest poppy producer, Afghanistan, has its price. By official government estimates, there are at least two million drug users in a nation of seventy-eight million; two hundred thousand shoot drugs intravenously, and of those, fifty thousand are infected with HIV. Unofficially, experts concede those numbers are low, but the truth is, any way you count them, the Islamic Republic of Iran has more than just a huge drug problem—it also has a serious health care crisis.

Forty-three-year-old Ali is a part of that crisis—and now, perhaps a part of its solution. In the world of IV drug use, Ali could be considered a model of self-restraint. Anybody who is still alive after doing smack for twenty-two years, an endless cycle of searching, scoring, shooting, must know how to hold back a little.

"Most of my friends are already dead," he tells me inside the Persepolis Harm Reduction Center, a pioneering drug treatment clinic in Tehran. "But since I was also working, I didn't overdose."

But Ali was hardly a poster child for clean living, either. At the peak of his addiction, he was pumping four and a half to five grams of Afghani brown sugar into his veins; a twenty-dollar-a-day habit and a fortune in Iran, where the average worker only makes about one hundred dollars a month.

Ali started stealing and tells me he was arrested fifteen times in the last thirty years, but that didn't stop him from scoring. Iranian junkies say it is easier to get drugs in prison than it is on the street. But the danger also increases, too; shared needles help to spread HIV in Iranian jails like the common cold.

Ali's wife left him five years ago because of his habit. Then, after he spent more than two decades as a human pincushion, shooting up everywhere he could find a vein that hadn't dried up like straw, the needle took its toll.

"My whole body became infected," he says, pulling up a pant leg to show a weepy wound that he says still won't heal after two years.

What saved him he says, is this place, the Persepolis Center, and its unorthodox founder, Dr. Bijan Nassirimanesh, who convinced government officials, in an ultraconservative Islamic country like Iran, to let him start a needle exchange and methadone treatment for Iranian drug addicts, controversial even in some Western nations.

But Nassirimanesh took it a step further. He put the needle exchange and the methadone treatment programs under the same roof at his center. He believes doing so helps the addicts, such as Ali, in their evolution toward recovery.

"The guy on the methadone program comes into the center," he says to me, "and sees the guy on the needle exchange program all hunched over and dirty, probably hasn't bathed in weeks, and it reinforces the idea that he doesn't want to go back to that. While the guy on the needle exchange looks at the guy taking methadone who is clean, maybe even has a job, and he thinks, Why don't I try that?"

Ali says he first came to the center for needle exchange but then tried methadone and finally kicked the habit completely. Now he works at the center helping others try to do the same.

Nassirimanesh gives me a tour around the clinic, a three-story building on loan from the city. The top two floors house administration and counselors as well as hundreds of boxes of 3 cc and 5 cc syringes.

On the first floor is the drop-in center, where addicts wait in line for methadone or to exchange needles. The walls are dirty and the place has no furniture, with the exception of a table for the doses of methadone, ground with a mortar and pestle and placed in plastic cups. Space is at a premium here, so in a cramped stairwell a bearded man in a white coat stirs a giant vat of bean soup, ladling it out into disposable bowls for the men in line.

Nassirimanesh shows me the kit they give to addicts when they first join the needle exchange program, which, aside from the cautionary guidebooks on HIV, might seem like a heroin shooter's dream come true. It contains a collection of syringes, alcohol pads, foil for smoking opium and a large metal spoon to cook heroin.

"The list of why people start drugs is similar all over the world," he says. "It starts with curiosity and ends with pain. It can be everything from a kidney stone to, as one client told me, the day he accidentally backed over his child with his car. The mind can't afford to tolerate this kind of suffering."

He now has three clinics like this one in Tehran, all treating about five hundred addicts a day, but he tells me he needs at least ten more in Tehran alone to even begin having a real impact on addiction and the spread of HIV.

That there is even one here seems to me a remarkable accomplishment in a country where many women still wear full-coverage black chadors in public and talking about drugs and sex is strictly taboo.

Nassirimanesh says that while there is a lot of support for the clinic, he does have enemies. There has been talk of a possible eviction, something he's desperately trying to head off in talks with municipal and Ministry of Health officials.

MY FIXER

I hired my fixer/interpreter Darius from one of two Iranian agencies officially cleared by the government's Ministry of Culture and Islamic Guidance to work with foreign journalists.

I like Darius. He lived in both the United States and Canada for a fifteen-year stretch; his English is excellent and he understands the demands of Western media. But it's well known among the journalists who use them that these same fixers must also act as "minders" and will have to file a report on us with the ministry accounting for our activities after we leave.

I'm almost halfway through my coverage, and while I've gathered some fascinating material, I still need someone from the government to answer sensitive questions about Iran's nuclear program, as well as address President Ahmadinejad's remarks about wiping Israel off the map.

Ahmadinejad has already declined our invitation, and other government officials seem to be ducking the controversy. I'm getting nervous and pushing Darius harder and harder to find someone to speak to me. I'm sure he's doing all he can, but no one is cooperating. If we don't get an interview, I tell him, then we might as well be doing a travelogue on Iran. I feel I have one more option.

Late at night, after talking to my team in California, I call Darius. I'm fairly confident that Iranian authorities have tapped the line. I tell him very slowly and clearly that if we don't get an interview by Wednesday, I'll pack up and leave Iran without filing any reports, except one in which I point out that no one in the government would speak to me about the nuclear issue.

It may only be circumstantial, but two days later Darius tells me he's landed an interview with Dr. Kazem Jalali, an Iranian member of Parliament and spokesman for the foreign affairs and national security committee.

In the interview Jalali defends Iran's right to enrich uranium and calls allegations of Iranian aid to Iraqi insurgents "just rumors." Mostly standard answers, but when I ask him about Ahmadinejad's remarks, he is more circumspect, intimating that if America had been more receptive to the attempts at reform by Iran's past government, it might not be dealing with this one now.

HOTEL GYM

In the basement of my hotel there is a small pool and an old pulley-and-plate-type weight machine and a couple of sticky treadmills. The "fitness center" is reserved for women during the day and men at night. After a frustrating day, still with no political interview, I decide to work off the stress. I expect to have the gym to myself, but I am quickly disappointed. The pool is packed with Iranian men and there are even a few working out. I am focused and don't really want to talk. I've turned the sound up on my iPod all the way.

Traveling around the world, I've become used to getting stared at. It's a natural reaction anywhere in the world to those who obviously look different from the locals. It is usually just surprise, then simple curiosity. Rarely is it hostile, even in countries where anti-Western feelings might be expected.

But today I feel like I'm getting the vibe. There are two men working out on the machines; they have come straight from the pool and are still wearing their bathing suits. The weight benches and the floor are wet from their dripping all over them. It pisses me off and maybe that shows. One of them, a stern-looking guy with a very full beard, sometimes characteristic of more religiously conservative Muslims, gives me a disapproving look.

My normal approach as a traveler is to try to engage people right away, take away their fear, suspicion or even their curiosity by breaking down the barriers and saying hello in their language with a full and unapologetic American accent.

But today I am having none of it. I'm going about my business and I find myself becoming very judgmental, the stereotypical, suspicious provincial American traveler. In my mind the bearded guy is a jihadist. In my imagination, I see him wearing a yellow Hezbollah headband that says "Allah Akbar" and waving an AK-47. In reality, he is just lifting weights, not even paying attention to me anymore.

I try to do the same but continue this strange and unspoken buildup of animosity toward him and others who filter into the room. I begin running on the treadmill, but my only thought is how much I hate being here at this moment. Not even the exercise is breaking down my stress; in fact, it seems to be feeding it. I run faster and faster.

After a few minutes, another man comes into the weight room on crutches. At first I think he must have sprained an ankle, but then I look more closely. From below his right knee, his calf slides into what seems more flipper than foot—a deformity from birth.

Yet the man puts his crutches aside and works out beside the others, who seem to know and like him quite a bit. He talks with the bearded one, who, with easy kindness, helps him adjust the lat bar. They laugh and the man begins the exercise, raising and lowering a stack of plates while the bearded one holds down his shoulders.

At that moment I'm ashamed of my own thoughts, for feeding my emotional ignorance rather than working to dispel it. I leave the room with a silent apology, more humble than when I had entered.

ALL MY FATHERS, ALL MY SONS

Even though I'm making an effort to seek out the unfamiliar here, I know I can't ignore the large conservative sector of the Iranian population, which since the 1979 Islamic Revolution has become the more public face of Iran. It is not difficult to find.

In Iranian society, there are few more revered than the martyrs, defined as anyone killed during war or violent struggle in support of Iran and Islam.

"Martyrdom for us is our school, our ideology, our heart and our prayer," says Mullah Hassan Ali Ahangaran, a religious consultant to the Martyrs Museum in downtown Tehran. "It allows the continuation of Islam. The blood of the martyr revitalizes our religion."

Inside the Martyrs Museum, guide Morteza Alizadeh, twenty-seven, takes me on a tour of the exhibits.

Alizadeh says his father is one of those still missing from the bloody, ten-year war with Iraq. Alizadeh says his father left for the war when he was just a baby, so he never knew him.

"But working here," he says as we walk through the museum, "I feel like all of these men are my fathers."

The exhibits are a combination of the macabre and the mundane. There are always photographs and usually some of the martyr's military gear, boots, a canteen, a worn-out sweater, an ammo belt.

But there are also items representing hobbies and interests—a karate robe, the ribbons and trophies of an equestrian champion, a picture of another riding a motorcycle. In some ways the exhibits remind me of the kind of shrine a family creates when it preserves its dead child's bedroom: books just the way they left them, photos and ribbons pinned to a bulletin board, a toy on a shelf covered with dust.

The museum, however, is also filled with lots of letters, like one from a fifteen-year-old boy named Gholam Reza Rezaei, who wrote these words to his parents before he left for the front lines in the war with Iraq: "If I am to reach the high level of martyrdom, please don't cry for me and don't wear anything black for me. Please just pray and give praise to Imam Khomeini."

There are also displays for so-called foreign martyrs, including those who have become suicide bombers in attacks against Israel. In another part of the city, near the airport, the significance of martyrdom in Iranian society represents itself in the ritualized grieving of mothers.

It's Thursday afternoon on the sprawling grounds of Beheshte Zahra Cemetery—and as on any other Thursday, Iran Allahkarami plans to spend the day with her sons.

To fight off the winter chill she has brought a large silver samovar filled with hot water for tea, and on her blanket there are plates of cookies, dates and oranges that others have given her as they make their rounds. She invites me to sit down and eat a cookie.

"We come here on this day every week," says Iran, "from morning until night—and when darkness falls we say, 'How quickly the night has come.' "

Every row is alike here, long stone slabs laid side by side with the name of the martyr, an etching of his face, and the date and name of the place he was killed, if known. A rectangular glass display case at the head of each grave is often filled with the martyr's Koran, prayer beads, an Iranian flag and a color photograph.

Allahkarami lost two sons in the Iran-Iraq War, but makes a sweeping gesture across the rows of graves that have no names or photographs, the unknown martyrs.

"These are all my sons," she says, which sounds to me like a very familiar sentiment.

PARTY

In an upper-middle-class neighborhood in north Tehran, a group of artists and academics gather for a Friday luncheon. They are dressed as if they could be gathering in a living room in London or San Francisco. There are no headscarves here. Most have spent time in the West, either working or at university or both. Abstract artwork adorns the walls and the conversation is spirited and open.

While alcohol is forbidden in Iran, with some exceptions for religious minorities, partygoers here sip homemade red wine or drink a punch made with Absolut Citron.

"Oh, it's easy to get," one man tells me. "You just make a phone call and they deliver it to your door."

I ask a university professor at the party if his students are afraid to speak out politically in class, for fear of retribution.

"No, no, they say whatever they want," he says. "These guys are smart enough to know they can't crack down on every kid. The shah did that—and look what happened."

But while a little middle-class lawbreaking may be ignored, the government does seem to be cracking down in other areas—areas that offer tougher challenges to their authority.

Every day there are small court items about Iranian journalists being charged with "contributing to the distortion of public opinion" or editorial cartoonists charged with creating images that ridicule public figures.

Some of that cultural crackdown is felt more indirectly by young people, who just want to express themselves but can't because of a decree by President Ahmadinejad banning the performance of Western music.

ROCK 'N' ROLL FANTASY

Twenty-five-year-old Amir Tehrani and his friends formed a heavy metal band six years ago called Mine, as in land mine. But legally the only place they can play is in Amir's cramped bedroom in fashionable north Tehran, which is jammed with a drum set, keyboard, guitars and amps.

They've tried to perform legally but couldn't get a permit from the Ministry of Culture and Islamic Guidance, so now they perform underground concerts. They've even gone so far as to hire a female singer.

"If they're going to make us go underground," says Amir, "we thought let's go really underground then."

He says the first performance was everything he could have imagined it would be.

"The first time we played we were not alone in that moment," Amir tells me. "When we're playing it's usually just the band or five or six guys here, but in that place there were about one hundred people and we were not alone. They were supporting us and we liked it."

In between our conversations, he and the rest of the band perform a couple of songs. They're skilled musicians, and metal fans anywhere would likely be headbanging to their sound.

Amir and the others were all born around 1980, at the start of the Iran-Iraq War, which lasted eight years.

"I feel like we lost the best years of our lives," he tells me. "We weren't able to have any fun then [because of the war], and now today in Iran, what can we do? We just want to play our music. I mean, Madonna says time goes so slowly. But here in Iran time goes so fast. I mean, I'm being totally honest here, we're running out of time."

"Why are you running out of time?" I ask.

"Because," he says, "we're getting old."

Driving back to my hotel after interviewing the band, I think about the different aspects of Iran that I've been exposed to so far. There's the traditional image of a fiercely conservative Islamic nation, still angry at the West for supporting its oppression under the shah.

But also, underlying that anger, there's an enlightened middle class, still fiercely Iranian and not yearning so much for Western culture as for the ideals of Western freedom.

Iran is a nation that lives in two worlds, one reader emailed me after my reporting there. *The way we live outside our homes is very different from the way we live inside.*

INTERMISSION

Persians Can Jump

IRAN

This is how much I love my driver Mahmoudi—I don't even have to tell him to stop when he sees a group of young men playing basketball in the downtown Tehran neighborhood known as "Flowers"; he just hits the brakes.

"Mr. Kevin, you want to film." It's more a statement than a question.

I do, of course, but I'd rather play more.

I give my camera to my fixer, Darius, and jump into a three-on-three game with some twenty-something guys who quickly proceed to hand me my ass.

They're college students and guys just starting their careers, but every Friday you won't find them at their local mosque—you'll find them here playing hard-core street ball.

A twenty-one-year-old named Ali wears an L.A. Lakers jersey with "Bryant" on the back, after his favorite player, Kobe. Although he's only about five feet nine, Ali can jam. In fact, the rim is bent from his hanging off it after executing his two-handed dunks.

"Why play soccer?" he says to me. "Basketball is everything."

During our game I'm panting and wheezing trying to guard a twenty-five-year-old surveyor named Mujtaba, who's landing three-point jump shots. I want to blame my breathing on the heavily polluted air in downtown Tehran, but that wouldn't be honest. In truth, I haven't been on a basketball court in years and I haven't had a workout like this since I started my trip four months ago.

After some hideous bricks, I finally land a shot or two by following up my own misses. Probably because of my sandbag performance, my team loses, but it still feels good to put the camera down and participate, rather than just watching other people's lives through the viewfinder.

As I get ready to leave, I ask them why they don't have a net.

"We did," says twenty-three-year-old Sarmad, "but somebody keeps stealing it."

Yeah, I smile to myself, that would never happen in America.

CHAPTER 11

SYRIA

Without Mouths

DAMASCUS, SYRIA | JANUARY 18, 2006

BUMP AND GRIND

For a place branded by the West as a rogue nation, crowded with terrorists, I think Syria has a decent club scene.

I'm at the Mar Mar in Damascus's old quarter—watching young couples sip cocktails and bump and grind on the dance floor to a techno beat.

Damascus bills itself as the oldest continuously inhabited city in the world, with people living here as long ago as 5000 B.C., and in this section of town, ancient Arab walls form a maze of twisting passageways so narrow that pedestrians sometimes have to push their backs up against the cold stone to avoid being kneecapped by cars.

If the bumpers don't pin you, the sound systems will. A black Mazda weaves through the alley, forcing back pedestrians with its mass . . . and the heavy bass thump of American rapper 50 Cent popping from its sound system.

Inside the Mar Mar, I talk to twenty-two-year-old Johnny Kharouf and twenty-one-year-old Rand Sabbagh, two university students taking a break from their studies.

Like others here, they feel Syria gets a bad rap.

"I'm like anyone else who cares about Syria," says Sabbagh. "They don't understand us in the West—they think we're all terrorists or we all wear the hijab [modest dress]."

In another room at Mar Mar, two women, Nibas and Zeina, drink mugs of beer rimmed with salt. They are both married with children, but they say that doesn't stop them from going out and partying.

Lately, though, things have changed.

"It's because of the political situation," says Zeina. "We just don't feel very comfortable coming out. We feel a little guilty having fun when everything is so bad right now."

SQUEEZE

At this moment, the Syrian government is feeling the squeeze of international pressure both from the United Nations, which claims Syria was involved in the assassination of former Lebanese prime minister Rafik Hariri, and from the United States for letting Iraqi insurgents and foreign jihadists use Syria as an entry point to Iraq to attack American and Iraqi forces and civilians.

Syrian officials say they have beefed up their border security—putting as many as seven thousand soldiers along the nearly four-hundred-mile border with Iraq in response to U.S. and Iraqi complaints. The government also recently released five key political prisoners in a gesture it says shows a move toward democratic reform.

"It is an example of the enlightened policy of openness," says Fayez Al Sayegh, a spokesman from the Syrian Ministry of Information. "From time to time, people will be released."

But that openness has its limits. Earlier in the day, while videotaping in the Hamedieh souk, I was tailed by the Mukhabarat, the Syrian secret police. When I talked with a group of students in a local teahouse, another man, likely working for the Mukhabarat, craned his neck in a painfully obvious attempt to listen to every word of our hour-long conversation.

TOY SOLDIERS

After a lot of wrangling with the Ministry of Information, my fixer, Nawara, has arranged an opportunity for us to drive to Syria's border crossing with

Iraq. We have to take a minder with us from the ministry—a woman named Muna.

The ministry has also faxed the army outpost we are visiting at Tanef so that by the time we get there they are already in place. Like toy soldiers in plastic poses, frozen in space, they point their weapons in the direction of Iraq. It's not that I doubt their intentions, it just seems, well, a bit staged.

There are at least a dozen Syrian soldiers, spaced about twenty feet apart along a sand berm. They are armed with AK-47s, Russian DShK "Dushka" machine guns and RPG launchers (though the launchers are empty of grenades).

They are silent and still, looking straight ahead like the stoic guards at Buckingham Palace, even while I crawl around them trying to get the perfect shot in the rose-gold tones of dusk. About a mile away, across an expanse of demilitarized, featureless desert, is Iraq's Al Waleed border crossing. We can't see them, but a Syrian officer tells me that that is where the American and Iraqi troops are. He pantomimes an American or Iraqi soldier holding a weapon and carefully stepping backward while looking ahead.

"They never give us their backs," he says. "Never."

While they are a bit overprepared for my visit, I can hardly blame them. This is a sensitive spot. Since the American-led invasion of Iraq, this long border has become one of the most contentious pieces of real estate in the world.

Tensions between the United States and Syria about the border reached their peak in July 2004, when several Syrians were killed in a gun battle with U.S. Army Rangers. The Syrian government lodged a protest at the U.S. embassy in Damascus over the incident.

The Syrians say they've repeatedly asked the Americans and the Iraqis to form a joint security command to help avoid future problems—but so far, they say, their offers have been refused.

It is dark by the time I finish videotaping and photographing the Syrian soldiers at Tanef. It is getting cold and the local commander invites us to have some Turkish coffee and warm ourselves by a stove in a small guard shack.

He and the two other officers there have been told not to give any interviews, so instead we chat about their families and the long separations they endure in their duties. We speak in generalities about the uncertainty of this place and time.

One by one, the "toy soldiers" come off their posts on the sand berm to smoke cigarettes and peer inside the shack, where we are sitting, warm and comfortable, wondering what news we might bring.

GETTING LATE

It's getting late in Damascus. Not rave-party late—just reporter late, as in, I have an 8:00 A.M. flight leaving Syria, which means a 5:00 A.M. wake-up call. It's already after 11:00 P.M.

But this is important—very important. At least I think so. My fixer, Nawara, has contacted a well-known Syrian artist named Ismail Nazir and we are going to meet him at his small studio off one of the winding alleyways of the old city in Damascus.

MINISTRY OF INFORMATION

It's an appointment I'm looking forward to, especially after just finishing an interview with Fayez Al Sayegh, the chief of state-run Syrian Television and government spokesman. The interview began to go downhill shortly after my first question.

I asked him to respond to claims by the chief U.N. investigator that Syrian intelligence officials were involved in the murder of former Lebanese prime minister Rafik Hariri. He answered this question, I'm sure, dozens of times in the last few weeks, but at that moment, he really wasn't in the mood.

He lit his pipe and told Nawara that his time was very limited. We rushed through as many other questions as I could ask and actually get translated within the fifteen-minute window we had been granted. As I packed up my tripod and camera gear, he asked me, rhetorically I learned, why I don't write a story about rendition of terrorist suspects and "Bush's secret black prisons" in Europe. When I started to answer, he told me, "I don't want you to answer, I just want you to write it."

PASSAGES

Ismail Nazir meets us at our car. His eyes are kind and there is an easy calm behind them. He is short and stocky with long gray hair, looking like the missing fifth member of Crosby, Stills, Nash & Young.

We begin the ten-minute walk through the narrow passages to his studio in what's known as the "Jews' " neighborhood. Ismail says it was once home to a large Syrian Jewish population, before they began emigrating to the West and Israel.

He likes to make this walk early in the morning or late at night, when it is quiet and gives him time to think. There is obviously much to ponder here. The history we brush against is as thick and dense as the layers of stone walls that have crumbled, been replaced, crumbled and again been replaced—carrying forward their sections of time until they stretch into the moments of this night.

In some dark corners there is loose garbage piling up, waiting for someone to come by with a shovel and bucket, but until then the calico cats enjoy a feast.

Ismail's studio is no more than a rectangular room of about four hundred square feet. There are several worktables fitted into a U with a rocking chair in the middle. The tables are covered with works in progress. A small electric heater warms the room.

"In the past," Ismail says, pulling out stacks of completed pieces for us to look at, "artists made all of their materials themselves, their paper, their pants, even their brushes."

Ismail says he does the same, trying to maintain that historical link to the artists of the past. On his desk are plastic jars filled with pigments that he has devised from household products such as turpentine, dyes and detergents. Some of his brushes are constructed from wood and frayed leather;

his canvases are anything from old newspapers to pieces of cardboard, all treated with acid tints and sealers.

But while the craftsmanship is impressive, it is the art he makes with his homemade tools that is so intriguing. His muse, it seems, is the human head, depicted in various states of abstraction and emotion with harsh-edged scratch marks all the way to soft-bleeding watercolors.

WITHOUT MOUTHS

Like a deck of cards in a game of solitaire, one by one I place a pile of smaller works on Ismail's tables, displaying them side by side in long rows. As I look over this body of work I notice a pattern. Though not literal representations of the head, they do seem to be lacking a common anatomical trait.

"So many of them," I say, "are without mouths."

After Nawara translates, Ismail just nods his head in agreement but does nothing to alleviate the mystery. Unable to resist the vacuum, I fill it as I so often do—clumsily.

"Does it have something to do with the pain of not being able to express something?" I ask tentatively, trying not to imply too much.

"It's whatever you see," says Ismail. "Whatever it says to you—that's what it is."

Nawara is intrigued by his answer. "I like that," she says to me, "I believe that anything, a story, a novel or a piece of art, has a place for you in it. A place that is yours to decide."

It's a thought that, like the stone walls outside, transcends this moment and makes me wonder if that is too generous a concept for most people. Many choose their place as quickly as they can without trying to understand, seeing only the garbage on the streets rather than the art inside.

CHAPTER 12

ISRAEL AND GAZA
Burned, Blind and Reborn

TEL AVIV, ISRAEL AND GAZA (OCCUPIED TERRITORY) | FEBRUARY 1, 2006

KINNERET

At her apartment in a hip and artsy Tel Aviv neighborhood, Kinneret Boosany tells me the story.

She was working a Saturday shift at "My Coffee Shop," in Tel Aviv. Because it was the Sabbath—and fairly late, about 9:30 P.M.—the restaurant wasn't very crowded.

She says she was tired and a little hungover after celebrating Passover the night before, smoking and drinking with friends. Then a young guy came into the place and asked for a cup of coffee. When she turned around to get it, he detonated explosives taped around his body. When Kinneret regained consciousness, it was July, four months later.

AMANI

In their Gaza home just a block away from the gently lapping waves of the Mediterranean, the Al Hissi family offers me a cookie and some tea. My fixer, Sami, a Palestinian journalist, had written about their daughter Amani last year—so as they get reacquainted, I take out my notebook and jot down some questions, without breaking eye contact.

They tell me the story as a family—everyone knowing their parts.

It was 1987, during the first intifada, and Palestinian boys were spray-painting anti-Israeli slogans on the walls near their home. When the boys were confronted by Israel Defense Forces, they scrambled over the wall and hid inside the Al Hissis' house.

When seven-year-old Amani Al Hissi opened the gate and looked into the alley to see if the coast was clear, there was, her father, Kamil, says, the distinctive thump of a tear-gas grenade being fired. It struck Amani just over her left eyebrow.

"It was very, very painful," says Amani, now twenty-seven, "but then I passed out."

Kamil says he scooped up the body of his little girl and rushed her to the local hospital.

BURNED

The coffee shop attack killed one woman. Kinneret survived, but just barely. She had burns on 70 percent of her body; her dominant left arm was damaged the most. She lost the sight in her right eye and half the capacity of her lungs.

Despite the severity of her injuries, Kinneret tells me that there was never a time when she wished she had been killed instead.

"Never," she says. "For the whole time I was in a coma I was struggling to live. It's kind of like you're fighting your own demons."

In fact, she tells me, she believed that the threshold between death and life was a holy place for her—because that was where she feels she discovered a critical truth about her existence.

"The first time you wake up you say, 'Thank God I'm alive and I'm alive at cost but I don't care what's going on with my body.' That's all that matters. But the farther you get from the danger of death—you get more confused because the pressure of the material world begins to affect you again," she says, sitting on a couch and petting her dog.

"You've been in a place much more holy because you only survived to live. You don't care if you have no legs, no eyes, no skin, you don't care—as long as I'm alive, that's what matters. But when you start coming back to reality, which unfortunately is worship the money, worship the body, it becomes more confusing. You start asking yourself questions: How will I manage the house, how will I find a partner?"

BLIND

Amani's father, Kamil, tells me that after he took Amani to the local hospital, the doctors in Gaza told him her internal injuries were too severe, that she needed to be taken to a special eye clinic in Jerusalem.

Kamil becomes angry in the telling, as he says it took a whole day before he could convince the Israelis to let him pass through a roadblock to Jerusalem. He tells me they tried to leverage a father's desperation against him, trying to turn him into an informant in exchange for letting him go. He says he refused, and when he finally was able to reach the clinic in Jerusalem, it was too late.

Amani had already lost the sight in her left eye because of retina damage and hemorrhaging. The news got worse. The doctors said that eventually, because of the trauma, Amani could lose the sight in her other eye as well.

Amani picks up the story. She says it took four years, but as the doctors predicted, by the age of eleven, she was completely blind.

"It was so difficult, I was miserable," she says, at her parents' home, where she lives, just a few hundred yards from the Mediterranean shore. "But there was also something positive. It created the soul of challenge in me—my blindness helped me to focus on other things, politics, culture and literature. I only lost my sight for Palestine, not my life or my soul—like others."

She says she used that drive to pursue a broad range of interests. She learned to read and write in Braille and studied Arabic literature. She plays the accordion and hosts several different programs on the Voice of Youth Radio station, including one that deals with creative writing.

"I've adapted to my blindness," Amani says, "but nothing can replace sight. The other things I've gained from this are only compensation, not replacement."

SKIN DEEP

For Kinneret, recovery from the bombing meant years of surgery and reha-bilitation. She has needed skin grafts, repairs and cosmetic work—requiring no less than fourteen operations so far.

A photograph of her before the bombing shows a smooth-skinned beauty with an uncertain smile and searching eyes. Her smile today seems more confident, possessed. She jokes about her neighborhood, a kind of Soho bohemian spot where, she says, "I'm not the only weirdo."

Kinneret's face shows the scars of her surgeries. There is discoloration from the patching and grafting. But it isn't hard for me to see the beauty that was there before. She wears long sleeves to cover and protect her arms and a glove on her left hand. I imagine that the burns have made her flesh as sensi-tive as rice paper.

Though she suffered through intense pain, she says the physical chal-lenges were not as much an issue as the psychological ones. She found a way to channel some of that anger by videotaping herself in her apartment.

"There is more peace, more calm. There's less need to look around for stuff elsewhere. Now if I feel a lack of something, I know I need to go into me, it's all inside. A lot of problems that I used to have then, I don't have them anymore. You know that you can get through anything."

BIGGER THAN THE SEA

Amani says the loss of her sight has given her the gift of imagination. In fact, when she speaks it sounds like poetry. She tells me that when she sits on the beach near her home, she can see everything in her mind.

"With every wave that hits the shore," she says, "my imagination be-comes bigger and bigger. I see all the waves, all the sea, all the horizon, all the sunset—my imagination is as limitless as the sea."

But while her mind may have no limits, her body does. When she wants to teach her younger brother, Kamal, how to write his name, it takes her many attempts to feel where the notebook cover ends and where the actual paper begins.

While I sit with her, she laughs easily and often, making funny remarks. When I ask her to tell me about the day she was shot with the tear-gas canister, she quips sarcastically, "Don't remind me of that day, I love it so much."

But while she talks, she nervously and incessantly plays with bracelets or her hands, an underlying restlessness of one who must now see with her fingers. She has difficulty talking about her loss in personal terms but instead frames it, like so many people in the occupied territories do, in the larger context of a Palestinian struggle.

"It's impossible to put my anger aside," she says, referring to the shooting. "We are the innocents here; all this could be avoided by ending the occupation. If we get them [Israelis] out of Gaza, there will be no more victims."

KINNERET REBORN

Kinneret says she doesn't harbor any anger toward the suicide bomber, who, she learned, was her same age, twenty-three, at the time of the incident.

She does, however, think about the bomber's mother every once in a while. She was told the mother did a television interview after the bombing, saying how proud she was of her son.

"I don't believe she really felt that way. I think she definitely misses him," Kinneret says, "regardless of what she said during the interview."

She says her own mother was the key to her recovery.

"My mother essentially gave up her life for me," she says, "quitting her job and putting all her efforts into my recovery. I say she gave me life twice."

She tells me that despite the hardships, she is happier with the person she is today than she was before the bombing.

"This is my lesson that God sent me," she says. "It has nothing to do with the Israeli-Palestinian conflict. Kinneret got burned, Kinneret died, I was reborn—now Kinneret lives."

GIVE ME MY CHILDHOOD

On a bench in the courtyard of her house, Amani feels through a sheaf of papers for a poem she has written. When she finds it, her fingers move across the raised dots on the page.

"Give me my childhood," she reads, "don't leave me alone, don't shoot me in the head, I have a lot of sadness, I am a child in the age of flowers, they stepped on my head, I'm a child in the age of flowers, they have no mercy on me or my childhood, please brothers don't leave me alone."

Around her neck Amani wears a gold heart with the letter R. It is, she tells me, the initial of her fiancé's first name. He is an intelligence officer with the Palestinian Authority. She tells me he sought her out at the radio station after hearing one of her programs. They will marry in the coming year.

Amani is confident she will have a full life, maybe fuller than most. She may be physically blind, but not within her mind's eye. She has an imagination, it seems, big enough to encompass both the past and present, anger and hope.

"There's a saying we have in Arabic," she tells me as I am preparing to leave her. "Some people have eyes but their hearts are blind."

INTERMISSION

Sami

_____

GAZA

Sami grabs my arm and leads me down an alley. We're in the midst of a funeral procession for two militants killed while firing rockets into Israel.

I follow Sami as he veers left and right down the narrow maze of buildings until we come out just ahead of the procession. He helps me climb up on a telephone box so I can get a high shot. I hit record as the thousand-plus crowd, many of them firing weapons in the air, carry the bodies of two slain members of the al-Aqsa Martyrs' Brigade toward an already overcrowded cemetery.

In the cemetery, Sami stops for a moment to wipe the dirt off a flat, white stone.

"This is the grave of my brother," he says, "the one killed during the intifada." He told me earlier that his brother was shot in a confrontation with Israeli soldiers after spray painting graffiti on a wall.

He says a small prayer over the grave as the cemetery fills with hundreds of armed young men, their faces covered by checkered kaffiyehs or black hoods.

One man taps me on the shoulder and glares at me. I've mistakenly stood on the edge of a martyr's grave, although in a place so crowded with headstones it seems impossible to know where one begins and another ends.

After the burial, Sami and I stop at a small café to have coffee. He is a reporter for the Palestinian News Agency, which acts as the information arm for the Palestinian News Authority. Despite what we've just witnessed, he tells me he tries to get the reporters at the agency to write about things other than just the violence.

"I tell them to write stories about music and art—it's not just about the guns in everyone's hands," he says. And in the face of the violence that surrounds him, Sami is impossibly calm. The night before, I lay awake in my sleeping bag, while I watched him sleep like a baby during Israeli air strikes that shook his entire apartment building.

Sami doesn't use the angry rhetoric that so many Palestinians use when speaking of Israel. In fact, he seems more curious than hateful. As a student he spent school holidays there as an agricultural worker but says he wasn't exposed to anyone in Israeli society. Something he dreams of now.

"I want to go to Israel, I want to meet the people," he says. "I want to experience that society and see for myself what it's really like. I see Israeli journalists come to Gaza sometimes and I'm jealous of them. I want to be able to do the same, but I can't."

I wonder exactly how many voices like Sami's are left in Gaza.

PART IV

THE CHILD BRIDE, ENDLESS GRIEF

AND MUSIC TO DISARM TO

Lives and Lessons from *Europe*,
Central Asia and the *Americas*

CHAPTER 13

CHECHNYA
Art Amid the Ruins

GROZNY, CHECHNYA, RUSSIAN FEDERATION | FEBRUARY 26, 2006

LIFE LESSONS

When CNN hired me in the fall of 2002, they put me through a course called Hostile Environment Training, which, depending on your experience, was either a primer or continuing education for war correspondents.

The course was taught by a former British Special Air Service commando, and during the three-day session I learned just how many safety mistakes I had made in covering past wars. For example, during the fighting in Afghanistan I had moved up to a Northern Alliance tank position during a mortar exchange. A few moments later, my colleague, a *National Geographic* producer who was standing right next to me, was wounded by an exploding shell that landed just thirty feet from us.

I also remember crawling into an abandoned Taliban bunker and stupidly poking among the belongings they had left behind; fortunately, nothing was booby-trapped. In combat coverage, I knew you had to take prudent risks to get the story, you had to push beyond fear at times, but you also needed to rein in recklessness. It remains a line that's hard for me to see at times; the consequences, though, are not.

OBSCURE BATTLE

During the hostile environment course, I thought about four colleagues who were killed in an obscure and now long forgotten battle on an Afghan hillside called Puze Pulekhomri. There were five altogether, riding on the outside of a Northern Alliance armored personnel carrier (APC) when a pocket of Taliban fighters remaining from recently overrun positions popped up and shot them. Only one, a Canadian journalist named Levon Sevunts, survived.

Sevunts, who is Armenian by birth, had military training as a conscript in the Soviet army. When the shooting started, he hung on to the APC turret while the vehicle retreated; the other four jumped to the ground and were cut down by machine-gun fire.

Sevunts's knowledge and reactions saved his life. Knowledge was essential in these places, which is why I paid even closer attention during the course.

HOSTAGE VIDEO

During a session on hostage situations, the trainers showed us a video of a Russian schoolteacher who had been kidnapped by Chechen rebels.

The tape was used as a hostage note to his family. I watched as his captors grabbed his hand, held it down and cut off his index finger. It was the look on his face that affected me the most. He never screamed or cried out in pain, but he dropped his chin into his chest while they wrapped up his bloody stump. At that moment his captors had killed his spirit. He had lost hope in his ability to influence the events surrounding him. He had lost hope in his future. I only saw the video once, but I'll never forget it.

I remember thinking to myself from then on: I hope I never go to Chechnya. But of course, when you want to avoid something that bad, it's almost certain you will end up there. And so I did—four years later. I knew that if my Hot Zone mission was to cover the armed conflicts of the world, I could not ignore Chechnya. I had to go, but every colleague I spoke with who had worked there warned me about it.

FSB

When I first arrive in the Caucasus region, I am supposed to register with the FSB or Federal Security Service (Federalnaya Sluzhba Bezopasnosti), the successor of the KGB, but I never do.

I am advised by colleagues that because of the short time I have in Chechnya, it would be better for me to work below the radar, to do interviews, shoot footage, even transmit while avoiding the FSB.

It's a risk because if they catch me, they could put me on a plane back to Moscow and likely revoke my visa completely. Chechnya is a sensitive issue and they don't have a reputation for a soft touch with critical journalists.

For me, it means working carefully with contacts on the ground, humanitarian relief organizations that want people to know more about what's going on here. They'll help me meet sources and secretly shoot video from cars of the massive destruction of the Chechen capital of Grozny.

But it is a tempestuous time for them as well. Russian President Vladmir Putin has just signed a new law allowing the FSB to closely monitor foreign humanitarian groups, who they say are being used by Western agents to foment trouble in the region with their human rights and prodemocracy campaigns. I have to be careful not to implicate them with my activities.

CARPET BOMBING

When I reach Grozny, I am shocked by the extent of the lingering devastation of two separate Russian carpet-bombing campaigns; one in 1994 and the other in 1999. Russian authorities said the intent of the bombings was to kill or flush out Islamic separatists who were using Grozny as a base for terrorist operations.

But here and elsewhere around the world, the Russian response was criticized as heavy-handed and punitive.

Everywhere I look, there are the skeletal remains of structures that seem reminiscent of the photographs of devastated European cities after World War II. Six years after the last Russian bombing campaign, half of Grozny's population still hasn't returned.

The other half, it seems, is left to live among the rubble.

ART IN THE RUBBLE

Ramzan Izhaev, his wife, Zareta, and their five-year-old daughter, Maria, live in a building heavily damaged by the bombing in the Leninski District of Grozny.

In a city populated by structures riddled with holes, bomb gaps, missing walls and collapsing roofs, their building is one of the better ones, although only two apartments are habitable. They invite me up to see where they live.

On the fourth floor of the building, they have carved out a cozy space. The walls are covered by the couple's paintings and a gas stove keeps the apartment toasty on this frigid February day. Ramzan sits in front of a wooden easel and paints the ruins of medieval war towers that dot the rocky landscapes of the Caucasus. Soft sunlight, diffused by white lace curtains covering a large window, fills the space.

But outside the window, the ruins are not so picturesque. For as far as I can see, in nearly every direction, there are bombed-out and crumbling homes, apartment buildings and businesses.

"Most people would say that it's difficult to live in such a place," he tells me, "that it at times can be very empty, but you must have something to fill it with." For him and his wife, he says, this something is their daughter and their art.

Friends had owned the apartment prior to the fighting but left and initially decided not to return. Because Ramzan and Zareta's apartment was destroyed during the bombing while they sought refuge outside the city, the friends offered them this place.

"It was November when we saw it," Zareta says. "It was dusty and cold with the wind blowing through all the cracks in the walls—and one of the rooms was completely destroyed by a bomb."

A NEW VOCABULARY

"I want to say I had my doubts about it," says Zareta, waxing philosophical for a moment. "But doubts are the reality of a peaceful place; they can't exist here. Before, in our apartment, I was surrounded by beautiful things, furniture and art. I had to forget about all those things when we moved here. I even had to learn a new vocabulary for a life comprised of doing things to survive."

Like thousands of others living in Grozny today, they pirate gas and electric lines to provide heat and power for their apartment—but the major drawback, they both say, is the lack of running water.

"We need sixty to seventy liters of water every day for cooking, washing and so on," says Zareta. That means five or six trips up and down four flights of stairs to a well in the courtyard. "It's good fitness." She laughs, patting both of her thighs.

They say there are other positive unintended consequences of their circumstance. They used to own a busy shish kebab restaurant in central Grozny, which left them little time to spend on their art, but the bombing also destroyed the restaurant. Now they say they can paint full-time and spend more time together raising Maria.

WE HAVE TO LEAVE

But while they are happy to have a place to live, they worry about Maria growing up surrounded by destruction.

"When I fall asleep every night," says Zareta, "I wonder what I can do to make her life better. Each day I get a little closer to the realization that we have to leave this place."

Zareta says that when they take walks, Maria already asks her questions, like why her school was bombed.

"It's difficult," Ramzan agrees. "But it's good that she has had part of her childhood here. I want her to know who she is—to have a connection to her past. I've seen Chechen children who have grown up in Moscow and they've been completely assimilated. They don't have any connection to their roots."

But already, both parents say they have seen the impact of Grozny's destruction on their child; she is more introspective, different, they say, from other children in other places.

DREAMS OF WAR

And the stress of Grozny's battles has scarred them, too. While taking refuge from the fighting in his home village, Ramzan was wounded and nearly killed by bomb shrapnel that penetrated his legs and chest, collapsing one of his lungs. Zareta, staying with her brother in Moscow at the time, saw the pictures of her wounded husband on television.

"I was worried that he may have lost his legs," she says, "and when I called him on the telephone at the hospital, I asked fearfully, 'Do you need your shoes?' "

Ramzan tells me he also sometimes dreams about the carnage that surrounds him, specifically the image of an aquarium that was destroyed when his old apartment was bombed. He says the heat of the explosion melted the glass and fused it with the blood of the fish in a surreal display of color amid the gray rubble scattered on the floor.

Regardless of what he sees at night, as well as what surrounds him during the day, he says his family will have a good future and that Grozny is and always will be a part of that—wherever they may live.

When I leave, they both give me small abstract paintings from their collected works, presents to remember the afternoon we spent together in this warm, colorful and unsettling place.

INTERMISSION

Bomb U

CHECHNYA

If it weren't for their formidable knowledge of the world and the acute absence of that glazed look that says "You're boring me," I might mistake them for university students anywhere in America. They are, after all, young, fashionably hip and all clutching cell phones.

But this is Chechen State University, well, at least in name. The real university was bombed to rubble by the Russians back in 1994. Now CSU is using a former school for the deaf as its campus—because, well, the buildings are still usable even though everything around them seems to have been blown to smithereens.

I asked my fixer, Bella, to set up a chat with the local students, if for no other reason than that I need a break from the depressing surroundings, and on my journey so far, students everywhere, no matter what they've experienced, always seem to be a bit more optimistic than the rest us.

This group is no different, even though the violence they've lived through would make most of us feel like chronic whiners. These eight young adults crowd into the tiny office of one of their professors to tell me about their lives and aspirations.

A twenty-one-year-old psychology student named Madina opens up the conversation with a story about having to crawl to school in the morning to avoid the shooting during the fighting with Russia. Most of them say they spent many of the war years in the cellars of their homes, waiting out the air strikes.

Hasmajomed, the youngest of the group at eighteen, says that after seeing the bodies of almost twenty people who had been killed in his neighborhood by an artillery strike, he got used to living with death.

"We stopped going into the cellars—we just stopped being afraid."

Many of the students say their sanity depends on not dwelling on the war, but it follows them anyway.

Madina says most Chechen adults suffer from post-traumatic stress disorder; hers actually led her to study psychology. But she says it's even worse in the children, who still only play war games and who hurt each other without empathy.

"I don't want anyone to have the kind of experiences we've had—ever again," she tells me. "My hope is that the next generation will read about this war only in the history books because there will be no evidence left of it in real life."

I smile. It is exactly the kind of talk I came here for.

CHAPTER 14

AFGHANISTAN
Smiling Through the Pain

LWARA, AFGHANISTAN | MARCH 10, 2006

FOB TILLMAN

On a map, the village of Lwara lies within a finger-poke of territory surrounded by Pakistan—making Forward Operating Base Tillman the last official America military outpost on the easternmost border of Afghanistan.

I have just arrived by helicopter, the first reporter to embed with this unit of 10th Mountain Division soldiers who only two months ago replaced a company from the 82nd Airborne. The base is a small piece of real estate on a plateau above the village; it is surrounded by concertina wire and canvas HESCO barriers filled with sand and rock. The feeling of physical and psychological isolation is immediate and unrelenting.

Now that the snows have melted on the mountain passes between Afghanistan and Pakistan, American commanders say Taliban and Al Qaeda fighters have become more active. Attacks on American bases like this one have become almost a weekly occurrence.

FOB Tillman is named after former pro football player turned Army Ranger Pat Tillman, who was killed in a controversial friendly fire incident in Afghanistan in April 2004. At first, his family was told he was killed during an enemy engagement. He was awarded a Silver Star for the courage he showed during that fictional battle. It took two years before the army revealed the full truth about how Tillman was shot by his own men. They say they will not withdraw the Silver Star but will change the story behind it in the paperwork.

THE HURRICANE

Inside the base, I meet with Alpha Company commander Captain Chris Nunn, who at the wise old age of twenty-nine is in charge of hundreds of men, millions of dollars of equipment and a small piece of American's foreign policy objective in Central Asia: stabilizing the volatile eastern border by wooing local tribal leaders and keeping fighters from infiltrating from Pakistan into Afghanistan.

Nunn is a fast-tracking officer who was adopted as a child and grew up on a cattle ranch in Panhandle, Texas. He seems relaxed but has a reputation as a high achiever. His men even nicknamed him "the Hurricane" for his flashes of anger when people are not meeting his performance standards. I learn later just how high those standards are when a fellow officer tells me that Nunn was bitten by a rattlesnake while undergoing one of the army's toughest training programs, the elite Ranger School. Instead of washing out, he was back within forty-eight hours of being bitten and limped through the perilous "mountains" phase of the program, passing the course and earning the coveted Ranger tab.

"TREAT US FAIRLY"

In a room off the TOC, or Tactical Operations Center, Nunn tells me that he has heard about my reputation as the reporter who videotaped the shooting in the mosque.

"My normal reaction," he tells me, "is to support the Marine. But I don't know the full circumstances. All I ask is that you treat us fairly while doing your job here."

I appreciate his candor and will find both him and the rest of his company willing to honestly share their thoughts and experiences in this difficult outpost.

I drop my gear in one of the buildings being shared by military contractors and soldiers on temporary duty here. There are rows of green cots with body armor and care packages from home underneath. While the troops from Alpha Company live in proximity to the Afghan villagers of Lwara, they don't necessarily live like them, though the conditions are nothing like home.

Instead of huts made of sun-dried brick, the men sleep in buildings made of poured concrete. There is a small shack with two sinks and a few showers—as well as some washing machines tended by Afghan workers.

NASTY SMELLS

There aren't toilets here, of course, only pit latrines, poorly positioned near the entrance to the TOC, which exposes the area to nasty smells every time the doors open. Nunn shrugs his shoulders. "Unfortunately, we inherited it this way and haven't had time to set it up in a better location."

The base has a recreation room with a large-screen TV and Internet access, with two computers and drop lines for laptops. The men get two hot meals a day, breakfast and dinner, but the ingredients can depend on when the last supply chopper made it this far east.

Perhaps most surprising in this remote place is the fully stocked, constantly packed fitness center, with benches, free weights, exercise machines and even a treadmill.

"It's where our guys spend most of their free time," says First Lieutenant Rich Holguin, Alpha Company's artillery officer, from Woodlake, California. "There's really not much else to do when they're not on duty."

But today the soldiers seem busy, occupied with tasks to ensure their survival, filling sandbags and building up bunkers along the base's perimeter walls.

OGA

Although the military tends to play this down, bases like Tillman also support the counterinsurgency operations focused on hunting down Osama bin Laden, Mullah Omar and other Al Qaeda and Taliban leaders believed to be taking refuge in the tribal areas along the border.

These activities are mostly the domain of teams of Special Forces and individuals from what has cryptically become known as OGA or Other Government Agencies—such as the CIA and DIA (Defense Intelligence Agency). I have seen these operators and their look-alike Afghan trainees. They all dress paramilitary style—the usual camo pants paired with high-end civilian hiking boots, khaki Ex Officio shirts, Oakley sunglasses and baseball caps or Afghan woolen hats called pakuls, popularized by assassinated Afghan Northern Alliance leader Ahmad Shah Massood. Everything about them screams spook, from their mixed array of small arms to their deadpan looks when asking me not to photograph them.

CARROT AND STICK

It's 6:30 A.M. and I am with First Platoon, sitting in the back of a Humvee on the way to a village called Guyan, which like many on the border appears friendly and cooperative to American forces and the Afghan army during the day yet moonlights with the Taliban at night. First Platoon's mission is to provide security for a two-tiered operation in the village that American commanders hope will provide both a show of military force and effective humanitarian aid.

The carrot and the stick here are just different ends of the same pole: lots of troops on the ground combined with the "wow" factor of a C-130 cargo plane dropping two large containers of relief supplies.

MARIANI

First Platoon commander Lieutenant William Mariani is a former star high school lacrosse player who leads his men like someone working a yo-yo, rather than as an officer who spent four and a half years at West Point. He's constantly rolling it down, then reeling it back up; joking, keeping it relaxed, then pulling the cord taut again when he needs them focused.

"O'Brien," he tells his driver, "don't get stuck today or you'll never see your wife again."

"Don't threaten me with a good time, sir," O'Brien shoots back.

They banter like this for much of the two-hour drive through perilous, nonexistent roads, threading multiton Humvees with nine-foot wheelbases through the needle of sharp-rock canyons, sheep trails and nearly dry riverbeds.

BIBLICAL TIMES

There are fifteen vehicles, forty-nine soldiers, four translators and twenty Afghan National Army soldiers when we leave the compound. In the early morning light, the mountainous countryside exudes a crisp, hard-edged beauty that in many ways is largely untouched by the modern world.

But for those who live here, it is a life of attrition where years of outdoor manual labor turn faces deeply creviced and as dusty as the landscape. The process begins early. We pass children leading a donkey down the road, laden with water jugs just filled from an icy stream.

I have been to Afghanistan twice before, but I'm still mesmerized by the feeling of being transported back to biblical times. As the convoy moves forward, we pass a boy herding sheep with nothing more than a staff and a slingshot. There are women scrubbing clothes against rocks in a streambed and village elders squatting in a circle deciding a legal or business matter for their community.

TEA

When we reach Guyan, Mariani deploys his platoon to secure the field where the airdrop will take place, while more senior officers meet with the village elders, grizzled men in large turbans sitting cross-legged in an expanding circle on the ground. Pitchers of hot tea are served in small, clear glasses with a handful of sugar.

The officers, I am told, will offer the elders funds to build a police station and cobblestone roads and to erect solar lights—if they support American and Afghan National Army efforts against the Taliban and Al Qaeda.

WHITE PUMPS

The villagers look up when they hear the whine of the C-130 engines overhead. The plane's back ramps open and two large containers are pushed out. They float to the ground on round, green parachutes. But the C-130 is off its mark. One container hits the landing zone, but another ends up in a rocky gulch about three hundred yards away.

Afghan workers, under Mariani's supervision, head into the gulch to retrieve the other container, breaking it down and hauling the items out of the gulch on their backs like pack mules. When the container that landed on target is opened up, I get a peek inside. It is filled with such typical necessities as blankets, bags of rice and flour, toiletries, but also, inexplicably, dozens of pairs of women's pumps—white pumps.

In the capital of Kabul, high heels are not such a far-fetched gift. In fact, for those covered head to ankle in the blue shroud of the burka, exposing a smart pair of shoes is often the best fashion statement a middle-class Afghan woman can manage. But here, in the ultraconservative and remote village of Guyan, white pumps could not seem more out of place than if the Pentagon had air-dropped a crate of spandex tights, Rollerblades and a disco ball.

The off-target crate has delayed the goods giveaway by about an hour, and now an open area near the marketplace has filled with eager villagers hoping for some of the bounty that has just fallen from the sky. I ask some of the men waiting in line if they would take this kind of help if it came from the Taliban. They all laugh in a knowing way.

"We like the Americans," says Pir Gul with a sly smile. Tonight, however, they will like the Taliban, others privately tell me.

The Afghan men are lined up by the 10th Mountain Division soldiers, and as they step forward to receive their aid, a civil affairs officer makes a mark on their right hands with a black Sharpie pen to keep them from returning to the line and double-dipping. They are given only one thing: a bag of flour, a carton of tea, a plastic tarp, a blanket, a bag of coal—or perhaps a nice pair of white pumps. Regardless of what they get, I notice, they all leave the line smiling.

CAMERA THIEF

While the distribution continues, I start snapping photos of a boy who has arrived with a pet monkey. The big crowd seems to agitate the monkey, who jumps on the boy's head, clawing into his scalp for a firmer grip. When I reach around for my video camera, usually slung over my right shoulder, I discover it's gone. Someone has cut the cord that attaches it to the shoulder strap.

The boys behind me are giggling when they see the look on my face. They stop giggling when I grab the one nearest me, demanding to know who took it. I move down the line, but they all claim ignorance. The perpetrator is probably already home, recording his first-ever video diary, which will end abruptly and forever once the battery dies. The camera itself is not so costly; it is a temporary replacement I bought in Moscow when my main camera had to be sent home for repairs.

But I am angry about losing the videotape with all the footage I just shot of the off-target airdrop. I make an offer of a cash reward, thinking I might be able to buy it back. No one comes forward.

I know that within a few hours the power will drain, the viewfinder will go black and the camera will lose its magic, becoming nothing more than a trophy and conversation piece among fast-fingered Afghan boys.

ROADSIDE BOMB

An hour into the distribution, Mariani gets a call on the radio that a Humvee hit a roadside bomb while leaving the village. No one was killed, but the driver was injured when his head hit the roof of the vehicle.

Mariani's team babysits the Humvee for two hours until they can make arrangements to have it airlifted out by a Chinook helicopter the next day. It is dark by the time Mariani's First Platoon heads back to FOB Tillman. The mood is somber now, no banter. There's a feeling that the roadside bomb was probably laid by some of the same people from the village that they had just tried to help. Taming Guyan, it is clear, will require more than an afternoon of household handouts.

Later, I ask the Second Battalion, 87th Infantry Regiment commander, Lieutenant Colonel Chris Toner, if the carrot has failed and if Guyan will now get the stick.

"Not yet," he tells me. "We have to give them something first, we have to move ahead with the program, then we can demand accountability after we've followed through on our promises."

The next day when I talk to Mariani, he seems unfazed by what happened in Guyan.

"I'm not here to change their way of life," he tells me. "They have their own culture and you have to respect that. Some people back home might think they are ass-backwards. I don't agree with that. This country has been at war for thirty years. We're here to do what we can to help."

KILL ZONE

A few weeks after I leave Afghanistan, Mariani's platoon and an Afghan army unit are attacked by Taliban fighters while on patrol. According to after-action reports, Mariani went back into the "kill zone" and rescued two Afghan soldiers from their burning pickup.

But two of Mariani's men were also wounded in the attack, which resulted in a likely unprecedented injury in American military combat. A Humvee Mark 19 gunner, Private Channing Moss, was standing in the turret of his vehicle when a rocket-propelled grenade flew through the window, caught the webbing of his ammo belt and finally lodged in his right thigh—unexploded. He was evacuated to a combat hospital, where Army surgeons removed the RPG round without it detonating.

Mariani wrote me this email telling his reaction when he first saw Moss and his feelings afterward:

The RPG wasn't in his leg, but penetrated his abdomen and was be-ginning to exit his thigh. You could see the bulge because it hadn't bro-ken skin. As for my reaction to it, well here we go. At first I had no clue that Moss had a RPG embedded in him. The report I received over the radio was that he had an abdominal wound. It was like an old war movie cliché.

As I was receiving the transmission I could hear Moss screaming and raising hell in the background. It wasn't until everything was said and done in regards to the fight that I actually saw Moss. I made it up to the vehicle he was in just as Doc was pulling him out. That's when I saw the tail end of the RPG sticking out of him. I was aware of the fact that he most likely had live ordnance stuck in him, but it really didn't phase me. I just knew we had to get him out of there as quick as possible.

By this time, Moss was pretty dosed and almost serene. I grabbed his hand and said something to the effect of, "Hang in there buddy, we're going to get you out of here." I then ran off to make sure our security was straight and coordinate for the MEDEVAC. Once I got the word that the bird was on the way, I headed over to check on him again.

SGT Jarrell was there with Moss, holding him and talking to him about basketball and football or something. As soon as I walked up, Moss stopped SGT Jarrell and asked him to just hold him. That hit me pretty hard. I pulled Doc aside and asked him what he thought Moss' prospects were and Doc just shook his head.

At that point I was faced with the possibility that I was going to lose one of my soldiers. I had doubts that he was going to make it, and Doc just confirmed it. All I could do was just make him as comfortable as possible until the MEDEVAC came in.

You wouldn't believe the relief I felt once I heard Moss made it through his first surgery and was stable. It was a pretty difficult situa-

tion for me. I remember once CPT Nunn arrived on the scene, I almost broke down. I can't even remember the last time I cried, but I was pretty damn close at that moment.

I mean, it's one thing to see bad guys blown to pieces. A dead body is a dead body and once you see one, you've kind of seen them all. That, and the fact that the guy was just trying to kill you, kind of makes you numb to the whole thing.

It's a totally different story when it's one of your own. Seeing a grown man ask another to "just hold me" blows away any toughness you think you might have. Thank God Moss is recovering, but I honestly thought he wasn't going to make it.

It's a pretty hard prospect to deal with and I wrestled with it for months after the fact. I always say that you can have all the medals and what not. They eventually fade. My biggest concern is getting all my boys and myself home alive and with all our parts.

NO HOMECOMING

Still, the attack doesn't rob Mariani of his sense of humor. While I'm reporting in Asia, he emails me a photograph of an Afghan boy holding up a dirty piece of cardboard with these words written in English: "Hey Kevin, thanks for the camera."

His easygoing demeanor will be greatly tested ten months later, however, when the company was supposed to have completed its tour of duty in America's "last outpost." But after making a stop in Kuwait on their return trip home in February 2007, they are told they will be extended for another four months because of troops being redirected to Iraq for President Bush's last-ditch "surge" strategy there. The soldiers of Alpha Company are put on a plane and sent back to FOB Tillman in Afghanistan without ever reaching home.

"It was a kick in the nuts," Mariani emailed me afterward. "Everyone is trying to deal with it in their own way."

GULSOMA

When I end my embed at FOB Tillman after a week with Alpha Company, I return to Kabul, where my friend and fixer, Haroon, arranges a story that will become the most widely read and discussed of my entire journey. It concerns a twelve-year-old girl named Gulsoma who possessed the strength to survive an unspeakable ordeal, as well as the grace to keep it from embittering her heart.

Since my video camera was stolen in Guyan, I will have only my notebook and still camera to capture the narrative, but regardless, eight million people will view it on the Hot Zone site and thousands of others from around the world will respond with emails of support for Gulsoma and requests to adopt her. This is her story as it appeared on March 21, 2006:

CHILD BRIDE

Eleven-year-old Gulsoma lay in a heap on the ground in front of her father-in-law. He told her that if she didn't find a missing watch by the next morning he would kill her. He almost had already. Enraged about the missing watch, Gulsoma's father-in-law had beaten her repeatedly with a stick. She was bleeding from wounds all over her body and her right arm and right foot had been broken.

She knew at that moment that if she didn't get away he would make good on his promise.

When I meet her at the Ministry of Women's Affairs I'm surprised that little girl is the same one that had endured such horrible suffering. She is wearing a red baseball cap and an orange scarf—she has beautiful brown eyes and a full and animated smile. She takes one of my hands in both of hers and greets me warmly without any hint of shyness.

"She looks healthy," says Haroon, my friend and translator. I nod. But she looks older than her now 12 years, we both agree. In an orphanage first in Kandahar, then in Kabul, she has had a year to recover from two lifetimes' worth of unimaginable imprisonment, deprivation and torture.

In one of the ministry's offices, she sits in a straight-back wooden chair and tells us the story of her life so far, stoic for the most part, pausing only a few times to wipe her eyes and nose with her scarf. It begins in the village of Mullah Allam Akhound, near Kandahar.

"When I was three years old my father died and after a year my mother married again, but her second husband didn't want me," says Gulsoma, "so my mother gave me away in a promise of marriage to a neighbor's son. They had a ceremony in which I was placed on a horse and given to the family."

Because she was still a child, the marriage was not expected to be sexually consummated, but within a year Gulsoma learned that so much else would be required of her that she would become a virtual slave in the household.

At the age of five, she was forced to take care of not only her "husband" but also his parents and all 12 of their other children as well.

Though nearly the entire family participated in the abuse, her father-in-law, she says, was the cruelest.

"My father-in-law asked me to do everything, laundry, the household chores—and the only time I was able to sleep in the house was when they had guests over," she says. "Other than that I would have to sleep outside on a piece of carpet without even any blankets. In the summer it was OK—but in the winter a neighbor would come over and give me a blanket—and sometimes some food."

Gulsoma says when she couldn't keep up with the workload she was beaten constantly.

"They beat me with electric wires," she says, "mostly on the legs. My father-in-law told his other children to do it that way so the injuries would be hidden. He said to them, break her bones, but don't hit her on the face."

There were even times when the family's abuse of Gulsoma transcended the bounds of the most wanton, sadistic cruelty—as on the occasions when they used her as a human tabletop, forcing her to lie on her stomach and then cutting their food on her bare back.

Gulsoma says the family had one boy her age named Atiqullah who refused to take part in her torture.

"He would sneak me food sometimes and when my mother-in-law told him to find a stick to beat me," she says, he would come back and say he couldn't find one. He would try to stop the others sometimes. "He would say 'she is my sister and this is sinful.' Sometimes I think about him and wish he could be here and I wish I could have him as my brother."

One evening, when her father-in-law saw the neighbor giving her food and a blanket, he took them away and beat her mercilessly. Then, she say, he locked her in a shed for two months.

"I would be kept there all day," she says, "then at night they would let me go to the bathroom and I would be fed one time each day. Most of the time it was only bread and sometimes some beans."

She says every day she was locked in the shed she wished and prayed that her parents would come and take her away—but then she would remember that her father was dead and her mother was gone. But Gulsoma had an inner strength even her father-in-law couldn't comprehend.

"When he came to the shed he kept asking me, 'Why don't you die—I imprisoned you, I give you less food, but still you don't die?' "

But it wasn't for lack of trying. Gulsoma said when her father-in-law finally let her out of the shed, he bound her hands behind her back and beat her unconscious. She says he revived her by pouring a tea thermos filled with scalding water over her head and her back.

"It was so painful," she says, dabbing her eyes with her scarf and sniffling for a moment. "I was crying and screaming the entire time."

Five days later, she says, her father-in-law gave her a vicious beating when his daughter's wristwatch went missing.

"He thought I stole it," she says, "and he beat me all over my body with his stick. He broke my arm and my foot. He said if I didn't find it by the next day, he would kill me."

• • •

That night, left outside where the family made her sleep each night on a thin, ratty strip of carpet, Gulsoma crawled away and hid underneath a bicycle rickshaw.

When the driver found Gulsoma under his rickshaw, broken and bleeding, he listened to her story and took her to the police, who hospitalized her immediately.

"The doctor at the hospital who treated me said 'I wish I could take you to the village square and show all the people what happened to you—so no one would ever do something like this again,'" Gulsoma says.

It took a full month to recover from her last beating—but the fear and psychological trauma may never go away.

"I was happy to have a bed and food at the hospital," she says, "but I was thinking that if and when I get better they will give me back to the family."

However, Gulsoma says when the police questioned the family the father-in-law lied and tried to tell them she had epilepsy and had fallen down and hurt herself, but the neighbor who had helped her confirmed the story of beatings and torture.

The police arrested her father-in-law and told her, she says, "'We will keep him in jail until you tell us to let them out.' Everyone was crying when they heard my story."

Gulsoma says she stayed at an orphanage in Kandahar, but was the only girl in the facility. Eventually, a worker from the Ministry of Women's Affairs in that region told the Minister, Dr. Masouda Jalal, about her story.

Gulsoma was then brought to a Kabul orphanage with both boys and girls where she lives today. She takes off her baseball cap and shows us a bald spot, almost like a medieval monk's tincture, on the crown of her head from where she was scalded.

She then turns her back and raises her shirt to reveal a sad map of scar tissue and keloids from cuts, bruises and the boiling water.

Haroon and I look at each other with disbelief—her life's tragic story etched upon her back. Yet she continues to smile—doesn't ask for pity, seems more concerned about us as she reads the shock on our faces.

"I feel better now," she says. "I have friends at the orphanage. But every night I'm still afraid the family will come here and pick me up."

Gulsoma says also when the sun goes down, she sometimes begins to shiver involuntarily, a reaction to seven years of sleeping outdoors, sometimes in the bitter cold of the desert night. She says she believes there are other girls like her in Kandahar, maybe elsewhere in Afghanistan, and that she wants to study human rights and one day go back to help them.

As we walk outside to take some pictures, I ask her if after all she's been through she thinks it will be harder to trust, to believe that there are actually good people in the world.

No, she says, quickly.

"I didn't expect anyone would help me but God. I was really surprised that there were also nice people; the neighbor, the rickshaw driver, the police," she says. "I pray for those who helped release me."

Looking directly into the camera she smiles as if nothing bad had ever happened to her in her entire life.

"I think that all people are good people," she says, "except for those that hurt me."

A year after I left, Haroon went back to the orphanage to see Gulsoma. He shot videotape of her to show me how much her life had changed.

Now she can study, play and talk with her friends at the orphanage. She is no longer a servant but still waits to eat after serving the other children. Despite her past suffering, I can see on the video that she is full of laughter and life. In only a year, she has turned from a child into a beautiful young woman.

But the suffering she endured can never be completely left behind. There are brief moments on the videotape when I think I can still see on her face, the only part of her body not beaten, the lingering pain of her past—softly pushed back with a smile.

But that resilience, I know, puts her in a dangerous place both for me and for the millions that read her story. She has been so graceful in her survival that there's a danger that her heroism will eclipse her humanity. We'll bookmark her under "inspiring tales" to be referenced when we need an anecdote about child abuse in Central Asia. Though the knowledge of her has changed me, I fear that as the years pass, I will lose her true memory as her smile and scars disappear under the burka she may be forced to wear in the future.

CHAPTER 15

COLOMBIA
The Right to Bear Arms

BOGOTÁ, COLOMBIA | APRIL 10, 2006

CHIN-DEEP

The longer I am on this journey, the more I realize how isolated I am becoming. It is nearly impossible for me to speak on the satellite phone with anyone except my team—and then only to discuss the details of the next day's work. In seven months on the road I have called my parents no more than three times (for their birthdays and Christmas) and prefer to email my girlfriend rather than hear her voice—or perhaps it's to avoid the sound of hearing my own trying to explain what I'm doing. Wading chin-deep into the misfortune of others for so long has shriveled my capacity to interact in a normal way. My commitment hasn't changed, but my energy has. Each profile I do hollows me out with its consistent thread of suffering. Some readers applaud me for making them aware of these people and places—others tell me I have paralyzed them with woe. I am trying to report truthfully about what I see, making efforts not to dehumanize my subjects through their suffering, but there are times, like now, when that's all I can see.

PRAYING MANTIS

It is unkind to even think, but when forty-five-year-old Heliberto Prada Ardila rubs the stumps of his arms together, it reminds me of the forelegs of a praying mantis. The war here has stolen more than his hands and his eyesight; it has, in this brief moment in my mind, taken away the very image of his humanity.

"I was walking out of a gate and there was wire stretched across the bottom connected to a mine. When I tripped the wire the mine exploded," he says. "I lost both hands, my right eye, a testicle and all my teeth. These scars you see on my face—they're all from the mine."

Ardila says the trip mine was set by the ELN, or National Liberation Army, Colombia's second-largest guerrilla group.

Ardila's tragedy is also compounded by the loss of his brother, shot dead by the Colombian army when he did not obey orders to stop. His brother, he says, was deaf. Ardila says his father was killed later by another armed group, but he's not sure which one.

With more than four decades of civil war and unending violence over the cultivation and production of drugs, Colombia has become one of the most heavily mined nations on earth, with leftist guerrillas, right-wing paramilitaries and the Colombian armed forces all sharing responsibility.

"It's us campesinos [peasant farmers] who are the ones that suffer," Ardila tells me at the San Bernabé shelter, a small refuge in west Bogotá. "Both from the paramilitaries, the guerrillas and the government. Campesinos are never allowed to live in peace."

Ardila says that after his accident in 1993 he had to beg on the streets for five years to make enough money to pay for an operation on his remaining eye. Until that time he was completely blind.

The trauma of his experiences continues to haunt him. Unlike many of the other residents at San Bernabé, he mostly keeps to himself, standing away from the others who watch TV in the living room or sit on the porch and talk.

MAMA LISSI

San Bernabé's has cared for the shattered bodies and broken spirits of land mine victims for more than twenty years. German-born Lissi Hansen Victoria has run the shelter the entire time, providing food, shelter and a sense of community for the mostly rural victims while they endure the multiple operations that usually follow a mine accident or while they wait for prosthetic limbs to be constructed and fitted.

"I've had to struggle in life and people helped me," says Hansen, called Mama Lissi by the residents. "I want to help other people."

Ardila's abbreviated arms stick out from the rolled-up sleeves on his white shirt, both tapering into stumps at almost exactly the same distance from his elbows. In the thirteen years since his accident, he has become adept at manipulating objects without fingers, opening doors, pushing his glasses up on the bridge of his nose.

In one of the bedrooms at San Bernabé, he picks up his prosthetic arms, connected by a complex harness of web straps, and slips them over his forearms, pushing the straps over his head and across the back.

"The fingers don't move," he says, "but the thumbs do. They are only good for things like picking up glasses. If you get them wet, you can really damage them."

Once he has them on, Ardila is able to move them around and manipulate the thumbs using wire cables that react when he contracts the muscles of his upper arms.

"My dream is to have my own place," says Ardila, "to open up a little store and to live off of that. But life for mine victims is extremely difficult. The government doesn't help at all. When I leave here I'll probably have to go back to begging."

THREE VICTIMS EVERY DAY

Colombia's government signed the international Mine Ban Treaty that went into effect in 2002, but guerrilla groups and narco-traffickers continue to use land mines to protect rebel encampments and drug labs. According to government statistics, Colombia's land mines kill or wound three victims every day; many of those are children.

In an upstairs bedroom at San Bernabé, Gustina Roma watches her son, Jesus, and grandson, Jonathan, both eight, play on the carpeted floor. Jonathan picks up a yellow Lego brick with his left hand and snaps it into place with the stump where his right hand used to be. Jesus rolls a toy truck across the carpeted floor and cocks his head to the side, almost like a bird, to compensate for his blind right eye. It has been almost a year since the day in June 2005 when both boys came running home bloody and burned.

THE "MICROPHONE"

"We were walking home from school when I saw the bomb. It was close to my house," says Jonathan. "I thought it was a plastic microphone, it was all white." With his left hand, he draws the shape on my notepad, a stick with ball-shaped fins at one end.

"I picked it up and we both were looking at it. Then I squeezed it and it exploded. We both ran home—we felt like we were burning up."

"I washed off the blood from them," Gustina says, "after they arrived at the house. Then I went out looking for Jonathan's hand, but I couldn't find it."

"Both the guerrillas and the paramilitaries operated in the area," Gustina tells me. "Anyone could've planted it. When I asked them, they both blamed the other. No one takes responsibility."

HUMAN TOUCH

But while no one will take responsibility for causing their injuries, San Bernabé—where the boys have spent the last year—is trying to assist in their healing.

Mama Lissi tells me there are usually about fifty residents in the small, three-story house year-round, but the annual operating budget is only twenty-five thousand dollars.

"It's very basic," she says. "Everything you see is donated—all the tables, furniture, much of the food. The house is owned by the [Presbyterian] church, so there's no rent. What we provide our residents is shelter and a human touch."

That human touch can be important—especially when the pain of repeated operations and the frustration of long waits for prosthetics take their toll. Some residents, fed up with the process, look to themselves for solutions.

A REAL WOODEN LEG

Alvaro Armando Toro, thirty-one, lost a leg six months ago to a mine set by guerrillas. He says he got tired of waiting for a prosthetic, so he made a temporary one himself—out of a log.

He demonstrates it for me by walking down the block. While it may seem crude to others, the wood rough-hewn and knotty, Toro is proud. "I haven't fallen once since I made it."

Some of the others sitting on the outside stoop at San Bernabé clap and cheer him on. Heliberto Prada Ardila stands by himself, looking into the distance.

As Toro finishes his demo for me, an ambulance pulls up to the house. A middle-aged woman is pulled out of the back, lying on a gurney and covered by a gray blanket. Despite her circumstances she smiles at me while I videotape her—another land mine victim and the next resident of San Bernabé's Refuge.

GUNS TO GUITARS

César López's comfortable Bogotá apartment is filled with the tools of his trade, a baby grand piano, guitars, amps, as well as the evidence that his subversively creative mind has few boundaries. A classically trained composer, he has chosen a radically different trajectory for his life.

Here is one example: near the piano, on a black stand that resembles a bipod, sits a Winchester lever action rifle. On its polished barrel are four hash marks, representing, López tells me, the four people who were killed by it.

But the Winchester can only be called a gun because of its form, since it no longer functions as a weapon. López has transformed it. Now six metal guitar strings stretch from the midpoint of its wooden stock across the loading chamber, past the fretboard threaded over its barrel, and end at the guitar neck flaring past the muzzle.

KILLER SOUND

López is turning guns from Colombia's long civil war into electric guitars, and this is an early prototype. López then uses these instruments of killer sound in a kind of political performance art on the streets of Bogotá.

"The main idea," he says, "is that weapons can change from an object of destructiveness to an object of constructiveness."

López says he came up with the idea after organizing a group of musicians and political activists tired of Colombia's seemingly endless conflict. They called themselves the Battalion of Immediate Artistic Reaction and were committed to making music as well as antiwar statements.

MEET-UPS

The group uses the concept of Internet meet-up groups, mobilizing participants by emails and instant messaging every time there is a terror bombing in Bogotá. At the site of the violence, López tells me the members serenade the victims and onlookers with soothing music.

López says it was a soldier who gave him the guns-to-guitars idea during the 2003 bombing of the El Nogal nightclub, which killed thirty-six people in the capital's trendy Zona Rosa district.

"We were playing our music on the streets near the club," he tells me, "when I noticed that a soldier was holding his rifle the same way I was holding my guitar." So he thought, why not turn the guns into guitars?

Only a few dozen of the guitar guns have been created so far—most used by members of the Battalion when they respond to acts of violence around the city. López designs the guitars but doesn't build them himself, subcontracting them out to fabricators and metal artists.

TROJAN HORSE

While he lies in a hammock hung between the walls of his apartment, López strums the Winchester, looking like a rock 'n' roll Che Guevara. I ask him if those who have just suffered from violence would really want to be serenaded by musicians playing guns.

"The attitude of most people is very good, except at airports." López laughs. But there are definitely critics.

"It's been very difficult to explain to the military the reason for a campaign like this," he says. "They don't really understand how a gun can be turned into a guitar."

"And is there the potential that one of Colombia's many armed groups could use the gun guitar concept as a kind of Trojan horse?" I ask him. "Pretend they are a member of your artistic battalion but arrive in public wielding real guns instead of decommissioned ones?"

López nods his head—it is a question he says he has considered many times.

"This is my nightmare," he tells me. "That's why we've been very careful to make sure the weapons are decommissioned and who we actually give them to—but yes, people could be killed."

Regardless, he believes real change requires risk and this cause, he says, ending Colombia's cycle of gun-related violence, is worth it.

Besides, he tells me, the transformation is not just for show; the gun guitars truly have a killer sound. He demonstrates by cocking the hammer on the Winchester and then pulling the trigger, creating an electronic twang instead of a bang. López then plays a beautiful, ethereal work on the former weapon that belies the vestiges of its deadly past.

DALAI LAMA

López gets his guns from the Colombian Peace Commissioner's Office and says he has just received a dozen of the world's ubiquitous automatic assault rifle, the AK-47.

When they are completed, he plans to give them to high-profile musicians such as Shakira, Carlos Santana, Paul McCartney and Carlos Vivas. He has also tried to give some of the earlier models to political and religious leaders—without much success.

After offering one to the Dalai Lama, López says he got a letter back asking why anyone would want to give "His Holiness" a gun—with or without strings.

INTERMISSION

Email

SEPTEMBER 17, 2005

C: I couldn't bring myself to wash your clothes yet, I know, I know—but that smell on them is you. But I don't want to be that girl who sits in an apartment smelling her boyfriend's clothes. That's just weird.

K: The airline lost my expedition duffle on the connecting flight. They say it will be in tonight on a later flight. Hope so, since I leave for Somalia 5:30 A.M. tomorrow. The good news is I have all my technical gear with me— the bad news is my usual daisy fresh scent is gone.

OCTOBER 30, 2005

K: Spending my last days in south Sudan, have about 700 thousand mosquito and fly bites and some kind of jungle or heat rash on my arm. Can't believe that I prefer to be in Iraq—at least as far as climate is concerned.

C: I'm so happy to hear from you. I'm glad you will be getting out of Africa— I'm sure you will miss the sun and the bugs. I'm nervous for you to be back in Iraq. I know you will be fine, but you saying you have mixed feelings about it scares me a bit.

NOVEMBER 8, 2005

K: It's 3 A.M. and had to take an armored bus and convoy to get to my staging point for my embed. Sat modem isn't working again so using army computer temporarily.

NOVEMBER 20, 2005

C: *I kind of forgot you had a plant in the kitchen and haven't watered it in about two weeks. I think it will be okay.*

JANUARY 12, 2006

K: Had a few minor epiphanies about my life on the plane on the way back from Iran—some of them kind of disturbing things that aren't quite finished from the past—mostly Iraq stuff. All of the decisions you make in life are such a big part of who you are and what you become.

C: *We're a lot alike—every Christmas I think about dancing again because of the Nutcracker. I miss it so badly and every year I realize I'm slipping farther and farther away. I don't have the closure I want from dance and I know it.*

K: What I was thinking about on the plane was that guy that was still alive in the mosque. He was only slightly wounded. I should've ensured he got somewhere safe—rather than leaving him on the front line. That guy saw everything that happened there and when they decided not to charge the Marine with the shooting, I know investigators probably didn't interview him. Makes me wonder if someone didn't pop him or if they shuffled him off to Abu Ghraib, never to be heard from. He was the primary witness. I think I need to try and find out where this guy is and if he's OK.

JANUARY 29, 2006

C: *I don't know what's going on with you. I know you're burned out, but I don't know what I can do. I have tried to get you to talk to me about it. I don't want to push you, but it hurts my feelings when I feel I'm not giving you what you need from me. Please tell me what you need.*

FEBRUARY 9, 2006

K: So didn't sleep for a couple of days in Gaza because of the shelling—then I was up until 2:30 A.M. filing my story for the next day, so last night I thought I'd sleep well but then had this weird dream: I'm walking down a road completely littered with land mines—I mean everywhere. And there's a kid in front of me, running through them but not stepping on any. I'm stepping very carefully when some other guys come out from a house and throw rocks on the road around me trying to make the mines explode.

C: *The child running in front of you, says to me, you're chasing after something, but there are lots of obstacles.*

CHAPTER 16

HAITI

Life Without a Net

CITÉ SOLEIL, HAITI | APRIL 22, 2006

CITÉ SOLEIL

You smell the inaptly named Cité Soleil before you see it. Haiti's largest slum is crisscrossed with open sewers, fertilized by garbage, infested with gangs, teeming with people—many of them rag-clad children.

This is not another late-night Sally Struthers save-the-kids poverty-porn television appeal. This, unfortunately, is life for the three hundred thousand residents here. As we drive through the area, I see a little girl of about three years old wearing a pair of white underpants and blue yarn ribbons in her hair, nothing else. She is a black speck in the midst of a sea of sun-bleached refuse; plastic bottles, bags, rotting produce, cans. It is, I realize after snapping a photo, her bathroom.

The world's eyes have begun to glaze over with the intensity of stories about Haiti's misery index. According to the World Bank, 80 percent of rural Haitians live in poverty, trying to survive on the equivalent of two U.S. dollars per day. But this should be impossible to ignore.

SLAVE REBELLION

It is difficult for me to stomach that Haiti, a nation born of a slave rebellion and the hope for something better, is still struggling in that effort two hundred years later.

It has been hampered by political instability. From the moment it declared its independence in 1804, Haiti was blockaded by slaveholding nations fearing revolts in their own territories.

After a decade of violence and corruption, much of it influenced by foreign dominance over the Haitian economy, the United States invaded in 1915 and stayed until 1934, even imposing a constitution written by future U.S. president Franklin D. Roosevelt.

ARISTIDE'S OVERTHROW

Many human rights critics complain that foreign interference has never really stopped here, including the purported U.S., French and Canadian involvement in a 2004 coup that overthrew the democratically elected President Jean-Bertrand Aristide (a former Catholic priest). The coup was made up of paramilitary groups, led by a former police chief. Aristide claims the groups were funded and armed by the United States and that he was forced to resign and was flown out of the country by American military forces.

In the aftermath of the coup, Aristide supporters, mostly residing in poor slums like Cité Soleil, fought it out with the forces of the new interim government, supported by the United States, France and Canada. A British publication reported eight thousand murders and thirty five thousand rapes during this period. A year later, nine thousand United Nations peacekeepers, primarily from Jordan and Brazil, occupied Cité Soleil.

PEACEKEEPERS

I see them now in strategic points throughout the slums. They take cover from the blazing sun in the shadows of their armored vehicles. Some eat mangos, cutting out pieces of the yellow fruit, spearing and eating it from the tips of their combat knives. Others talk to the young women who have come to sell them sodas or fruit. Their presence has been a frequent source of friction with residents, who claim they have been heavy-handed in efforts to rein in criminal gangs, often causing civilian casualties in the cross fire.

ONE MEAL?

Near a shack of corrugated tin, I see a woman talking with her neighbors. She seems to be pregnant. I ask my driver to stop so we can talk with her. Inside her tin shack, framed with tree branches, twenty-two-year-old Marijo Joseph tells me her story.

"My husband is a fisherman," says Marijo, "but he's not working today, because he is trying to borrow a net. His was torn and now he doesn't have one."

It is not just a problem but a crisis for Marijo, who already has three children, ages three, four and five, and is pregnant with her fourth.

On days like today, she says, her family may be lucky to eat one meal, usually when her husband can catch some of the small fish swimming in the incredibly polluted shoreline of this seacoast settlement. In a drainage ditch nearby, a large black pig roots among the trash.

Normally the family can get clean water from a source installed by an international aid group, but Marijo says there are days when the taps are dry.

"Then we have to buy water from a local cistern," she says. "It usually tastes salty and my kids get sick a lot."

RELENTLESS VIOLENCE

The poor sanitary conditions around the community mean children regularly get skin conditions such as scabies and impetigo. Marijo's daughter Estella has the sunken and drawn appearance of multiple gastrointestinal illnesses and malnutrition.

But as if the poverty wasn't enough, the family also has to endure the violence that often plagues Cité Soleil. In a clash between Cité Soleil's many gangs and U.N. peacekeeping troops, a stray bullet struck the family's shack and set the dry structure ablaze. Marijo's three-year-old son, Peterson, was inside.

"I ran into the flames to get him," she says, "but by that time the entire right side of his body was burned."

Today he bears a mask of burn scars around his eyes as well as others across his body. Despite the misery in which she has spent her entire life, Marijo refuses to despair.

"I think God will make things better," she tells me. "I think they will change. There will come a day when there is enough for everyone."

But there doesn't seem to be much evidence of that today.

She says after this next child is born, she will ask for birth control from the French aid group Doctors Without Borders.

"I heard they will give it to you for free," she says.

It's very important, she knows, since it will take more than a good net to feed the mouths she already has.

INTERMISSION

The Art of Survival

HAITI

I watch as forty-eight-year-old François Andre, using nothing but a ball-peen hammer, pounds a discarded fifty-gallon metal drum into a nearly perfectly flat sheet. He does this on the side of a hilly street, busy with cars and buses belching black smoke.

He then takes a stencil and draws different-shaped patterns onto the sheet. Then comes his least favorite part: punching out those patterns with hammer and a sharpened chisel. François learned this from his father and his grandfather. He's been at it almost thirty years. His hands, thick with callouses, back up his claim.

But what François is doing here, besides making a modest living, is making art. The fifty-gallon metal drums he flattens and punches will become elaborate sculptures of palm trees and bright Caribbean suns, they will become metal menageries of horses, alligators, salamanders and monkeys. The dull gray metal will be painted in a bright spectrum of tropical colors.

Some of the pieces take as long as a week to make—but will still fetch only a few hundred dollars for François, who sells them in the same roadside shack where he creates them.

He will never get rich this way, but François, like Haiti's other "survival artists," has found hope with a hammer and art in the poverty that surrounds him.

I envy his strength and wonder if I could find it within myself, faced with the same circumstances.

PART V

MY *ASIAN* ODYSSEY

Tamil Tigers, Nepal Maoists,
Karen Rebels and a
Missed Moment with
the Dalai Lama

CHAPTER 17

NEPAL
Where to Mao?

KATMANDU, NEPAL | MAY 12, 2006

RAIN

It is pouring. The rain is coming down hard enough to dent the car—although this 1971 Datsun is already so dimpled it looks like a golf ball on wheels. We have wiper blades, but like faulty brain synapses the electrical circuit from the control knob to the blades isn't making the jump.

Despite the fact that the windshield glass is nearly opaque from the downpour, I'm still able to make out the forms of buildings, colors and people as we whiz past them on this tightrope of streets, swerving and beeping and pushing forward to who knows where.

When I was traveling in regions of Africa and the Middle East, the changes in geography from country to country seemed subtle. There were recurring themes that linked them as kin in continent or terrain.

But this last six weeks, I've hopped continents and hemispheres.

I should feel a bit of traveler's whiplash, but instead there is a strange sense of continuity, like a slow dissolve connecting the disparate sequences of a continuous story spanning too much territory. I see the roads before me blend from one to the other; the dry riverbeds of eastern Afghanistan in a Humvee become the lowlands of northern Colombia in a local taxi, the hillsides of Haiti in my fixer's car become this moment in Nepal in the rain.

I AM A DOG

There is a duality at work here that is hard for me to comprehend. I am enticed by the geographic disjuncture of my journey, the shock of sensory overload, the new smells, structures and lives that wash over me on these drives. Simultaneously, I am lulled by the comfort of it all; the fact that there is too much to understand. Instead of a reporter, for this moment, I am a dog with my head out the window, the rush of air creating a comforting buzz that silences the need to know more—at least for now.

THIS DRIVE

In every new place, this drive is where the journey begins. During this drive, my inability to speak the local language doesn't matter; it is about smiles and pleasantries done in charades. On this drive, there is no negotiation over prices, no cold sweat over the time I have to shoot, write, edit and transmit a half-dozen new stories. There are no technical concerns, no hunger or sleep deprivation—for a moment, even the alternating sense of alienation and loneliness disappear.

Here in Nepal, birthplace of Buddha, I am indeed having that rare moment of Zen that seems to elude me most of my conscious life. But very shortly, the ride will be over and the new reality of where I am will fall full force on my head like a cartoon anvil.

HOPE AND FEAR

The fears, insecurities and discomforts that come with every new place then give way to telling the stories of Nepal, whose history is being rewritten at this moment.

It is a story of the potential end of a conflict, which makes it perhaps the most hopeful of my journey. Only a month ago, prodemocracy demonstrators were in these streets clashing with the police of autocratic King Gyanendra, who dissolved parliament and seized full executive powers in 2005.

Their movement gained momentum and support, but it also had a cost: twenty-one people killed and hundreds wounded in the demonstrations. Their courage pressured Gyanendra to cede his powers, bringing a practical end to the monarchy and allowing for the potential emergence of a new democracy.

On this day, along with my fixer, a local newspaper journalist and pioneering blogger named Dinesh Wagle, I'll fly on an eighteen-passenger plane to the city of Dhangadhi, near India on the western border, to meet with what could be the last obstacle to that democracy—Nepal's Maoist rebels.

CULTURAL REVOLUTION

Sharad Singh-Bhandari is wearing a clean white shirt and square frameless glasses that seem more Berlin than rural Nepal. Despite the wilting heat of the western plains, he looks crisp and seems perfectly nice, but the secretary of the Western Region of the Communist Party of Nepal Maoists is making me slightly crazy at the moment with an important knowledge gap in the history of his own ideology. He insists that Mao's Chinese Cultural Revolution was bloodless.

We are having this conversation in the courtyard of the Bidya Hotel in Dhangadhi, when I ask him why the Nepal Maoists chose to name themselves after a man who created the so-called Cultural Revolution in which millions were terrorized and possibly as many as half a million killed (although the Chinese government still refuses to provide statistics).

"That's a fraud," he tells me without hesitation. "That's a kind of defaming of communism—the massacres of Tiananmen Square were done in the name of communism, but it was not communism. And as far as the Cultural Revolution, it was good since it was only the rich that were dealt with."

"In the Cultural Revolution people were murdered without reason," I tell him, "for their status, being educated, not for crimes."

"People were wrongly killed during Tiananmen," he argues. "But no, people weren't killed during the Cultural Revolution."

I am becoming incredulous but beginning to think that he actually believes this. It has either been whitewashed in his ideological education or he just stubbornly refuses to accept the truth. I know I need to make this real for him—and so I do.

"People were killed during Mao's Cultural Revolution," I insist. "In fact, a member of my own staff, my researcher's father, was killed as a result of the Cultural Revolution."

He continues to shake his head, not believing it. I press on to my point, which is more relevant to our current talk.

"Once in power, will you use violence to achieve your social and economic goals?"

LESSONS

He tells me the Maoists in Nepal have learned lessons from the past and that no one should fear, although it is clear to me from our conversation that some of those lessons should have been a more prominent part of the curriculum.

It's easy for me to see, though, how Sharad Singh-Bhandari became a Maoist. He tells me the story of his younger brother.

BROTHERS

"In 2001 a squad of Royal Nepalese Army soldiers came to the boarding school where he was teaching and asked for him," he tells me. "When he appeared, they tied one end of a rope around his hands and the other to the back of their truck. After dragging him for a distance, they stopped, untied him and shot him dead in front of the crowd that had gathered."

Then they simply drove away. Singh-Bhandari says someone had told the soldiers that his brother was a communist.

"I've had many brothers killed by the army," says Singh-Bhandari. "But this was the only one connected by blood."

THE WAR

I tell him that I want to see his military wing, the members of the Maoists' rebel army or PLA, People's Liberation Army—estimated to be twenty thousand strong. They have waged a ten-year war against the royal government of Nepal in which thirteen thousand people have died and innumerable human rights abuses have been committed by both sides against civilians. But now there is a cease-fire in the aftermath of the prodemocracy "People's Movement," and the Maoists are being brought into the political process.

The Maoists have joined a seven-party alliance, they say, in hopes of permanently curtailing the powers of the king and creating a multiparty democracy.

That has made it difficult to arrange a meeting with the rebel fighters. As active partners in the alliance, the Maoists want to flex their political muscle now, not showcase their military might. I press the point with Singh-Bhandari that showing the rebel army now would likely serve as a reminder of their strength and provide leverage at the bargaining table.

Dinesh negotiates with them for two days before we finally reach an agreement.

THE MEETING

It's 6:30 A.M., and Dinesh and I are riding with Singh-Bhandari, his assistant and a couple of cadres in the back of a rented gold-colored Land Cruiser on our way to meet the rebels.

On the drive, just as we are leaving the city, we see columns of Royal Nepalese Army soldiers in their jungle camouflage, out for their morning run. They are just flashes of green as we whiz by.

"Those are the ones we are fighting," says one of the cadres, while the others laugh a bit nervously.

We drive for an hour and a half and stop in a small village where Singh-Bhandari meets his military counterpart, the Seventh Division commander, a man in a long-sleeved white t-shirt who goes by the party name of "Prajjwal." Both Singh-Bhandari and Prajjwal are just thirty years old.

WAITING GAME

Dinesh and I sit in a tiny shack by the side of the road, eating spicy noodles and sipping tea while the two go off to make contact with their commanders in the field. The noodle shop plays an upbeat and catchy revolutionary song on a boombox. There are lots of other young men milling around carrying backpacks.

"They're Maoists," one shopkeeper tells us. "They've come in from the field and are heading home for a while during the cease-fire."

After an hour of waiting, the two return and we get into the Land Cruiser again and drive another half hour. We stop at another village, where we are swarmed by schoolchildren wearing light blue shirts, their school uniforms.

They're fascinated by the sight of a tall Westerner decked out with camera gear, so I snap their pictures and show them the digital display on the back. They giggle uncontrollably.

Dinesh and I are ushered into yet another roadside restaurant, where we sip more tea and wait. A half hour later we get into the vehicle again, this time backtracking until we meet a motorcycle rider. We follow him off the main road and onto a dirt path leading to the base of the nearby foothills. We park in a large grassy opening that is the grounds of a rural elementary school in the village of Chainpur.

Within minutes of our arrival young men and women, many of them no more than teenagers, begin pouring out of the woods from different directions; members of the People's Liberation Army.

Some are in green camouflage and strung with dark blue webbing with attached ammo pouches; others are in t-shirts and jeans with bandanas tied around their heads. They carry a mix of aging, British-designed Lee-Enfield bolt-action rifles and World War II–era, top-loading Bren light machine guns. But many don't have any weapons at all.

To me, they seem young and not very intimidating, yet the rebels have a reputation for ruthlessness. Much of the force is made up of women. The Maoist commanders say the women are among the fiercest fighters and make up a third of the entire army.

The women in these ranks tell me they fight because they have very few rights in Nepal. They believe the Maoists will bring equality.

Within the group I see a girl who looks to be in her early teens. She is tiny and delicate-looking but carries a compact machine gun over her shoulder. She calls herself Janaki and says that she is sixteen. She has been with the rebels for one year. When I ask her why she joined, she gives a robotic response repeated by many of the other rebels.

"Because I couldn't tolerate the oppression of my people any longer," she says.

"Are you ever afraid?" I ask her.

"No, I'm not afraid," she replies in a soft, tiny voice.

But when I press her on the issue, she just stares ahead, so unsure and uncomfortable with the attention that she can no longer find words.

COMMANDER SAGAT

Their commander, who calls himself Sagat, is thirty-three years old with thick black glasses and a cap emblazoned with the communist red star. He says the soldiers are members of the Lokesh Memorial Brigade, which is normally made up of about 4,000 to 5,000 soldiers but is currently only a fourth of that size since many went home for a few weeks during the current cease-fire.

"We haven't been engaged in any military activities," he says. "But we've been busy publicizing the policy of the party."

Another rebel, Rajeev Thapa, says he is nineteen but looks younger. He wears a blue t-shirt that shows his thin arms while he cradles his AK-47.

"I heard too many stories about people being beaten, raped and killed by the army," he says. "So I had to do something."

COMBAT

Many of the rebels I talk with say they have been in combat several times, including a twenty-five-year-old woman who goes by the party name "Sapana," which means Dream.

"I was in the first line in an attack to capture an FM radio station in Tansen," she says. "It was guarded by an army barracks and one of the soldiers threw a grenade at me. I could see it coming and I moved back, but pieces of shrapnel still hit my leg."

Sapana says four or five other rebels were also injured, but they made it back to their lines and were able to get treatment. She pulls up her fatigues and shows me the scar on her shin.

TERRORISTS

Another rebel, twenty-nine-year-old Bishan Dhami, says he has been with the Maoists four years and has seen combat nearly a dozen times.

I ask him if he is tired of the war, but he says, "No."

"Not until we defeat the monarchists, which we also call terrorists," he says. It is the same label the U.S. State Department has given the PLA, because of its practice of attacking civilians, confiscating land and extortion.

U.S. ADVISORS

Prajjwal, the Seventh Division commander, says his forces have consistently defeated the Royal Nepalese Army and the Armed Police Force. But his biggest concern has been the American-trained Nepalese Ranger battalions, which are better equipped and more motivated than the others.

"Four years ago during a battle in the Rolpa region, we captured three U.S. Army advisors during fighting there," he tells me, "but we released them because our fight isn't with America."

I wasn't able to verify his capture claim, but the U.S. government has sent advisors and more than eight million dollars in military aid and services to the Nepalese government since the rebellion began.

DOG AND PONY

After videotaping, shooting stills and talking with the rebels, I feel that what I have captured of them so far is very superficial. The responses have been rote and predictable, the visuals feel staged and, because of time constraints, I won't be able to pry much deeper.

I had pressed Singh-Bhandari for a chance to see the rebels, but I envisioned visiting their encampment rather than watching a military parade. It's manufactured, but it's my own fault. I have tried to have it both ways, forcing the meeting and then not liking the results.

There certainly is a need to put a face on the PLA; to show them as something other than just an acronym to which both bad and good acts are attributed. The group is also a key factor in Nepal's political future.

I thought, naively perhaps, that I might see them in their natural environment, in the bush rather than this grassy schoolyard. I wanted to see them doing whatever rebels do during a cease-fire: cleaning their weapons, reading *Das Kapital,* playing football, flirting with the female comrades.

DRILLS

They gather under a larger tree and begin a series of awkward drills, so that Dinesh and I may see them in action. Commander Sagat looks at a cheat sheet written on his hand, then barks orders to the rebels. With each command they hop to attention, then either stand, kneel or sit pointing their weapons, or their hands, in the direction of an imaginary enemy. As a precise drilling unit, they are the equivalent of the Grateful Dead—not exactly tight. Their movements are hesitant, awkward, but determined.

BACK TO THE WOODS

At the end of the "drilling," these PLA fighters make their exit as quickly as they did their entrance, proceeding, weapons in hand, in single file back to the woods. There they will wait, say their commanders, until they are needed again, either as a show of force or, if peace talks fail, to actually fight again.

Months later, the Maoists will be guaranteed seventy-three seats in a new interim parliament when they agree to begin disarming and to become integrated into a new Nepal army in January 2007.

CHAPTER 18

KASHMIR
Trouble in Paradise

SRINAGAR, KASHMIR | MAY 24, 2006

PACING

It is late afternoon in Srinagar, Kashmir, and I am pacing the already thread-bare carpet of my hotel room. The small window faces north, letting in very little light and making the space feel even more dreary.

Dar Yasin, my fixer, a talented freelance still photographer, dropped me off here after we finished our reporting earlier today. While there is always the potential of racing out to cover the next act of violence, I should be in for the night. I need to write my dispatch and transmit my video and pictures for the day.

I can't get myself to sit down; can't turn on the computer and do the work I have done nearly every single night since I started this journey almost nine months ago.

I know what's bothering me, but I won't admit it to myself. Not yet.

I am here because Indian-occupied Kashmir has been a flash point for conflict between India and Pakistan for the last fifty years and the location of two of the three wars fought between the two nations.

FIFTY THOUSAND DEAD

Around 1989, Muslim separatists began a violent campaign against India's control of the region. Human rights groups estimate as many as fifty thousand people have died from an average of 2,500 incidents of terror every year and the Indian security forces' response to them.

Now, Kashmir is one of the most heavily armed places on the planet, with an estimated half-million Indian security forces deployed here.

Driving through the summer capital, Srinagar, you see them on every block. Unfortunately, they are no guarantee of order, especially this week, while Indian prime minister Manmohan Singh is visiting for peace talks. Yesterday, Dar Yasin and I scrambled to the hospital to cover the aftermath of a grenade attack on a tourist bus.

Kashmir is considered as beautiful as it is dangerous, and despite the violence, civilian tourists, mostly from India, flock here by the thousands every day to enjoy the lush public gardens, walk in the mountains or relax on a Dal Lake houseboat.

YOUTH AND DEATH

Police do not know who tossed the grenade onto the bus, but the explosion killed two young boys and two teenage girls. I know because I saw their bodies; I photographed them and talked to their grieving parents, who were wearing clothes still covered in their children's blood.

Inside the hospital's morgue, a police officer pulls out a stainless steel gurney holding the broken body of Fanal Hamant Zariwala. He was eight. He is wrapped in a white sheet with purple stripes. The officer pulls it down so we can see him more clearly. His hands are tied loosely together over his chest with a white gauze bandage. He is wearing gray jeans with a bright red patch on one of the legs. Outside the room the heartbreak has a voice; the sobbing, screaming, mumbling disbelief of their parents.

"I told him not to sit in the front of the bus," says Hemant Zariwala, Fanal's father, his shirt and jeans still covered in his son's blood. "I told him to sit in the back with me, but he didn't want to."

BLOOD AND TEARS

Vipin Bai was another tourist on the bus and is describing the scene to reporters, his white undershirt crimson with the blood of the victims, when the mother of one of the victims embraces him and begins sobbing uncontrollably, her tears mixing with the dried blood on his shirt as he consoles her. It is hard to keep my camera on them during their spectacle of grief, but it is equally hard not to.

I know this is a way for others to see what I see, the real face of war; not soldiers in helmets and body armor but the unprotected flesh of civilians.

"It's painful when a child dies," says Dr. Ahmad Shah from the hospital's trauma staff as we talk in the hallway. "But we are used to it. This has been going on sixteen years. We've seen this a thousand times over."

UNCOMFORTABLY NUMB

I share his numbness. I know what a body looks like after it has been hit with mortar fragments, improvised bombs, 7.62 rounds from an AK-47 and 5.56 rounds from an M-16 or an M-4. I know what a human head looks like after it has exploded from a sniper shot. I have seen them burned, blown apart, submerged in cars and wrapped around tall trees from the force of a tsunami.

Here's the problem: as any soldier, police homicide detective, doctor or coroner will tell you, the pit in your stomach that you first feel when you confront the aftermath of violent death eventually goes away. The flood of emotions, the pondering about what if it were my child, parent, friend, me— stops, and soon you feel nothing at all.

During a discussion about this occupational hazard, a close friend told me that the numbness was the survival instinct needed to do the job at the moment that counts; the strength necessary to hold it together to complete the task. And while that may be true, there are times, like when my flash was going off within the grimy, white-tile room of that Kashmir morgue, that I wish I felt something; something for those children still dressed like children in t-shirts, jeans and sneakers despite their shredded bodies and burned faces.

NEED TO GET OUT

Back in my hotel room, I know why I'm pacing. It's because of the anger, the only emotion I can work up at the moment. In this state, I know I'll get no work done, but I also have no idea what to do with myself. It's not like I'm surrounded by friends who can chat this out with me. I'm reluctant to walk it off outside, because I'm not in the mood to be the standout gringo right now. I just don't feel like answering the question, "Where from?" one more time.

But then I get an idea. On the drive back to the hotel, I saw a park with cricket and soccer fields just a few blocks away. I'll put on my iPod and run this anger off on that larger grassy field. It is the perfect antidote for this restlessness. I put on my sneakers, gym shorts and a t-shirt and run from the hotel to the recreation area.

At the field, I see there are soccer games and cricket matches already in progress; young men burning off steam like me after work or school. As I begin my laps around the mesh fence encircling one of the fields, I quickly feel winded and tight since I haven't had an outdoor workout in months. Almost immediately, however, my head begins to clear.

As I run, I begin to draw stares from the players on the field, particularly three high school boys who are kicking around a soccer ball on the sidelines. Seeing someone running when they are not chasing a ball is not a common sight in Srinagar.

THE SOCCER WAR

Every time I pass them, they get a little bolder, kicking the ball a little closer to me. On my fourth lap, pretending to pass from one to another, they kick the ball directly into my running path. I jump over it without breaking my stride or even giving them a look. I am in my own head now and not to be trifled with.

On the next lap, one of the boys, a stocky one, wearing blue soccer shorts and a matching shirt, does an overhead inbounds pass that whizzes past the back of my head. I can hear some laughter through the sound of Depeche Mode playing in my earphones. I'm beginning to be aware of their game. As I blow by them on my sixth lap, I hear the ball being kicked hard from a distance and with good precision as it slaps me on the back of my left arm as I round the corner.

Again, I don't acknowledge the effort to get my attention, but I quietly make a plan. As I approach again, I see the skinny one in a red t-shirt getting ready to toss the ball to the third one in a gray shirt, strategically positioned on the other side of me.

I know where he will throw it—at my head. He does. But I also know it is coming. With my right hand, I block its trajectory and pull it into my chest. Out of my peripheral vision, I can see the one in red is surprised.

He is even more surprised when I take a few steps and then punt the ball hard, sending it on a high arc. When it is finally done rolling it is about seventy yards in the opposite direction of the three boys. I give them a quick wave behind me as I round the corner as if nothing happened.

ATTENTION

I learn that nothing endears you to Kashmir teenagers more than messing with them. They seem to believe that kind of attention can't be bought, especially when it is a gringo dishing it out. They all quickly run after me with smiles on their faces. "Hey, where from, where from?" they ask in English. "How you like Kashmir?"

"It's nice," I say, "except the grenade attacks." They laugh like it's an inside joke that I understand.

As I stretch after my run, they want to know what I am wearing on my arm. I take off my earphones and let them listen to the iPod. The one in red speaks English fairly well. He points at the stocky one in blue and says, "He's what we call a Kashmir cow." They all laugh.

UNIVERSAL LANGUAGE

They ask me if I know how to play soccer. I tell them, a little, and we begin to kick the ball around, keeping it airborne between us using our feet, knees and heads. Without even realizing the transition, I'm not working anymore, I'm playing. I haven't played on the road since a brief game of three-on-three basketball in Tehran.

I become aware, not acutely, just casually, that I am actually having fun on a sunny afternoon in Kashmir, even though I am thousands of miles away from where I would normally be having fun on another sunny afternoon, biking or surfing at home in California.

These high school boys don't want to talk about my work, they just want to know a little bit about how I live and how Kashmir is different from America. After a while, we don't have to talk at all. We just kick the ball back and forth.

ENOUGH

Because of their curiosity, these boys caught the gringo, got him to engage, and for that they earned the attention and respect of others who come to join us. Some of those who gather around to kick the soccer ball with us are other kids, but there is also a handful of middle-aged men, still in possession of some tricky footwork they had when they were younger. We are, despite the language and cultural difference, joined in play, and at this moment that is enough for me.

INTERMISSION

Learning to See

KASHMIR

I'm grateful rather than embarrassed when Dar Yasin helps me with my 35 mm digital still camera. I feel like my photographs are often washed out and overexposed. It's the ball I seem to drop most often as I juggle the three mediums of writing, video and stills on this project.

Here in Kashmir, Dar Yasin is my fixer, but he's also considered one of the best photojournalists in the region. His work captures Kashmir's violence and beauty both, with enviable technical precision.

Perhaps because I feel so exhausted, I'm also more open to help as he doles it out in easy spoonfuls while we work together.

I have a bad habit of keeping my Canon 20D set on green, auto everything, afraid of missing a shot because of operator error. Dar has convinced me to manually bracket and underexpose by at least two stops every time I swing the camera to my face. It is a basic technique, but it immediately adds richness and depth to my photographs through color saturation. More importantly, since I've tried to concentrate on using the still camera primarily for the human face, it gives my story subjects the accurate visual depiction they deserve.

I first notice it one evening at dusk when we stop along the shore of Dal Lake to photograph a family of boat people, local fishermen who live on longboats called shikaras. As we approach them, three young girls—Rosie, nine, Daisy, eight, and Fancy, four—run up to us with their hands out, asking for money.

Their mother, Mahooda, is still on the boat holding a toddler. She tells us of the hardships of their lives aboard the boats, exposure to the elements, hunger, danger. While we listen, we are also photographing the faces of the children and Mahooda, the smoke of their cooking fire and the chiaroscuro reflections on the still surface of the water.

To distract the girls from asking for money, I put down my camera, rip a page from my notebook and show them how to make a paper airplane. When we preview our images after, I feel I've done justice to the lives of Mahooda and her family.

When Dar Yasin shows me his images, I see they include my paper airplane making. As I advance them on his camera's viewfinder, I stop at one that seems to have captured something unusual for me at this point in my journey—a real smile. With this picture, he has done me justice and reminded me of something I don't want to forget, that people are more than just the sum of their misery.

CHAPTER 19

SRI LANKA
Tiger Don't Surf

ARUGAM BAY, SRI LANKA | JUNE 10, 2006

CHECKPOINTS

We arrive in Arugam Bay in the late afternoon after a ten-hour drive from Kilinochchi. It is not the distance but the checkpoints that suck your time. Since we were in Eelam, rebel Tamil Tiger–controlled territory, we had to pass through both Tiger and Sri Lankan government border control. My translator, Sarath, and driver, Rodney, both agree with me that the Tigers seemed more efficient.

It is overcast and drizzly when we check into the Siam View Inn, a little surfer hotel still in the rebuilding phase after the 2004 tsunami. It is owned by a German named Manfred.

There is a bit of daylight left, and it looks to me like the afternoon downpour has ended. I pull on my shorts, walk to a nearby shop, and rent a six-foot, seven-inch tri-fin board, which for my size and modest surfing ability is like a potato chip, too short and not buoyant enough. Growing up in Ohio, I know by nature I am not supposed to surf, but I fell in love with the sport when I worked in Florida during my first job in television news.

PADDLING OUT

Since that time, I have surfed infrequently enough to never be mistaken for good, but I am, in the vernacular of the sport, not quite a "barney," either.

But whether I catch ten waves or none, just paddling out always takes my mind off my worries and puts me firmly in the moment. Now, after nine months of conflict coverage, I need this day-and-a-half break to play in the waves.

Arugam Bay is the place where local fishermen ply the same waters as intrepid surfers from Australia, Japan and Europe. It is a wonderful secret spot for surfers; a right point break can carry you into next week, if you are lucky enough to outpaddle the other fifty hard chargers gunning for the same peak.

DOUBLE WHAMMY

Arugam Bay has been hit, however, with a double whammy of bad luck; the continuing violence between Sri Lankan government forces and the Tamil Tiger rebels—and the 2004 tsunami. According to official statistics, more than thirty-five thousand Sri Lankans were killed by the tsunami, most of them on this eastern coast of the island, where almost no one was untouched by the tragedy. More than a year later, thousands are still living rudimentary existences in thatched houses without water or electricity.

Businesses like the Siam View struggled to rebuild in the tsunami's aftermath, but ongoing violence continues to set them back. Last April, the Tigers tried to kill the Sri Lanka army chief in Colombo, Lieutenant General Sarath Fonseka, by sending a female suicide bomber or "Black Tigress." The attempt only injured Fonseka—but likely killed any hopes for rekindling the tourist trade in Arugam Bay.

"Sixty people canceled on me after that," says K. M. Rifei, one of the managers at the Siam View Inn. "They were from all over the world, too: Germany, England, Australia."

Rifei is troubled by the developments, but he has seen enough tragedy in his life that his emotional range seems wisely shifted to neutral. Rifei says he lost seventeen members of his family in the tsunami, including his one-and-a-half-year-old son.

"When the tsunami hit," he tells me as we sit on the deck of a restaurant overlooking the beach, "my family was all in the water, including my son."

I feel somewhat circumspect that I am about to frolic along the same shoreline where so many lost their lives, but I also know it will take tourists like me staying in local hotels, eating at local restaurants and spending money at local surf shops to revitalize the area.

RIPTIDE

When I reach the spot, a sand-and-rock break at the south end of the bay, there are still about twenty surfers in the water, even though it is beginning to get dark.

I am eager to paddle out and don't take a lot of time to read the waves. This will be my first mistake. When I do get out into the water, I realize there is a very strong riptide that begins to carry me farther out to sea.

I also discover that, because of the way the peninsula juts out into the bay, the waves are breaking parallel to the shore rather than against it. They begin to build near the beach, pushing out into open water and breaking over the shallows about fifty feet from shore. To catch one, surfers need to enter the lineup close to the sandy tip of the shoreline. Quickly, I see that I'm in exactly the wrong place. I struggle to paddle back in, but the rip makes it almost impossible; instead I have to paddle, and the current takes me down shore about a hundred yards.

I emerge on the sand fifteen minutes later, sucking air, my arms rubbery from paddling. Since I haven't been surfing for at least a year, my body is hardly used to this kind of exertion.

IMPACT ZONE

Determined, I walk up the sand and enter the water closer to the break. It is now past dusk and heading fast into twilight. Since the lineup of surfers has thinned out, I know I'll get my chance. The waves seem to be getting bigger, and I notice they are steep-shouldered and closing out hard into frothy white foam. I see one building on the outside, paddle toward it, then turn tail and stroke hard to stay in front of its building face.

But I am too heavy on my potato chip and haven't picked up enough speed. The wave is beginning to crest and I feel the back of my board being pulled up with it. It is not a good position. I know in a moment that rather than smoothly sliding down the face of the wave, it will toss me ass over end into the froth—which it promptly does. I am getting worked, tumbling over and over, my leg leash tugging furiously as the board gets sucked into and out of the wash. The embarrassment would be enough by itself, but I also find some rocks at the bottom as well.

When I try to get out of the impact zone, I'm smacked head-on with another wave that drags me across the jagged rocks in the shallows. I feel like I've just been thrown from a motorcycle and I'm sliding down a swatch of pebbly sandpaper. I finally get to my feet and wade to shore. Both my legs are cut and bleeding, as well as my palms from pushing up against the rocky bottom. I put the board under my arm and limp back to the hotel. The only upside of this session is that it is too dark for anyone to see my cuts or my humiliation.

SINHALESE VERSUS TAMIL

Ethnic tensions between Sri Lanka's Buddhist Sinhalese majority and Hindu Tamil minority have alternately simmered and boiled since the time of Sri Lanka's independence from Britain in 1948.

Sarath and Rodney are both Sinhalese, but Rodney grew up with Tamils in his neighborhood and speaks both Sinhalese and Tamil.

They tell me that Sinhalese and Tamil people live in the same neighborhoods all over Sri Lanka without conflict.

"It is only in the north that things are bad," Sarath says.

They tell me they believe the Tigers' leader, a shadowy figure named Velupillai Pirapaharan, who is rarely seen except in photographs and posters throughout Tiger-controlled territory, is the instigator of the violence. The Tamil Tigers or LTTE (Liberation Tigers of Tamil Eelam) were formed in 1976 and began fighting for a separate homeland for the Tamils. From the very beginning, they have been a determined, and at times ruthless, rebel force.

BLACK TIGERS

The Tigers have an estimated ten thousand fighters and are legendary for the practice of wearing cyanide capsules around their necks and vowing never to be taken alive. They also have their own navy, which sometimes uses suicide swift boats to ram Sri Lankan ships.

That controversial tactic, the use of suicide bombers or "Black Tigers," has put them on the European Union's list of terrorist groups. But the Tigers claim that it is the Tamil civilians who have been terrorized, routinely murdered by government security forces and paramilitaries in their rural villages.

THE COST

Nearly sixty thousand people have died in the conflict, but in 2002 it seemed to reach a turning point when the Tigers and the government signed a cease-fire agreement. The agreement gave the Tigers at least a partial taste of independence, as government forces withdrew from northern Tamil population centers, allowing the Tigers to create their own semiautonomous state, Tamil Eelam, which simply means homeland.

Within their area of control, they have their own uniformed border patrol, customs agents, police department, courts and even uniformed motorcycle traffic cops with Tamil Tiger shoulder patches. The region also has its own newspapers, culture magazines, radio and television studios.

The city of Kilinochchi, the de facto capital of Tamil Eelam, has also been noted in foreign travel guides for its preponderance of memorials to dead Tigers, including a statue to its first female suicide bomber.

Just outside the city there is also a cemetery with row after row of identical black marble headstones, nearly two thousand graves, ground reserved for Tamils who have died for the cause.

INSIDE TAMIL EELAM

Sarath and Rodney have never stayed inside Tamil Eelam overnight but agree to go with me. Getting inside is like entering a foreign country. Our bags are unloaded and thoroughly checked by Sri Lankan Border Patrol agents. We fill out paperwork, show our passports to officials, then our van is reloaded with our bags and we drive a quarter mile through a neutral zone administered by the International Red Cross. At the end of the neutral zone, we're in Tiger-controlled territory, where we go through the entire process again.

Once through the checkpoints, we locate the Tigers' media relations office and meet their official spokesman, a former science teacher from the Jaffna peninsula who identifies himself only as Thaya Master.

He tells me the cease-fire is still in place for now, but is shaky at best.

"The government says they want peace, they're ready to talk peace but their actions are different," he says. "They want to solve the problem but there's no normalcy. Stopping the killing would help with bringing back normalcy."

TIGER CADRES

The next day Master arranges for me to interview four Tiger cadres, two men and two women all dressed in the distinctive tiger-stripe camouflage. Since Rodney speaks Tamil, I want him to translate, but they know he is Sinhalese and refuse.

They want to use their own translator and ask Sarath and Rodney to wait outside during the interview. It is not an ideal situation for me, but there will be no interview otherwise. The Tigers can be very media-shy, preferring to use Tamil.net, their Internet news service, and their own television and radio stations to get their message out.

THE INTERVIEW

The four cadres sit on a couch together with me on the opposite side, videotaping our discussion. I ask what prompted them to join the Tigers. They all tell similar stories of home villages being bombed by the Sri Lankan government; friends and family being killed.

Vikneswaran Malathi, a twenty-eight-year-old female officer, has served the longest of the four, eleven years, joining the Tigers when she was just seventeen. She has also paid the highest personal price, by losing her leg in battle with Sri Lankan forces.

The Tigers have a history of recruiting and using women in combat, but the men and women are separated by gender, with male officers leading male soldiers and female officers leading female soldiers.

LOSING A LEG

"In 1995, I was a section leader of fifteen soldiers during an offensive by the Sri Lankan army to retake the Jaffna peninsula," Malathi tells me. "After landing onshore in an amphibious mission, we fought and advanced for three days up to Palai. On the third day we had stiff resistance and there was artillery fire. An artillery shell landed behind me. It wounded two of my soldiers and knocked me down. I tried to get up but I couldn't stand. I called for support and medics came and carried me back to a field hospital. My right leg, which had been wounded three times before, was hit again with shell fragments. This time—it had to be amputated."

She shrugs it off, as if it were just a couple of stitches.

BLACK TIGER MISSION

"You are also known for your use of suicide bombers, 'Black Tigers,' " I say to all of them. "Would all of you accept a Black Tiger mission if asked?"

"It's not a tradition to be asked to be a Black Tiger," says Aganalagan Veluppilla, a thirty-four-year-old male cadre. "You have to volunteer."

"Well, would you volunteer for a Black Tiger mission?"

"The future will tell us if this is necessary," says Malathi, referring to whether the cease-fire will hold or not.

I want to examine the issue more deeply. "Let me pose a very important question on that point," I say. "While the use of suicide bombers may bring about some kind of tactical advantage for you—aren't you concerned that it's actually backfiring in the court of world opinion? The European Union recently labeled the LTTE [Tamil Tigers] a terrorist organization, in part because of your use of suicide bombers. Now, instead of a rebel army with legitimate concerns, you've been lumped in with the likes of Al Qaeda. Doesn't that hurt your cause?"

"Yes, it hurts, but branding us terrorists is not justified," says twenty-eight-year-old Kumaran Sipathasundaram, who tells me he joined the Tigers eight years ago, after his village was bombed. "It is the responsibility of the people to determine whether someone is a terrorist or a freedom fighter. Every Black Tiger attack was aimed at military targets to help maintain a balance of power. It's part of a military action. It's not against civilians—so it's not terrorism."

After my interview, we walk outside and I continue talking with them, trying to get them to speak with me more casually, but it is not likely with their commanders watching and listening to everything they say.

The Tiger cadres do laugh and joke around with one another as they drift away from my camera and me. Less guarded, they seem almost like goofy teenagers, as if suicide and cyanide were the furthest things from their minds, as if they weren't part of this deadly conflict at all.

The very next day there is a bus attack in a predominantly Sinhalese community. Sixty-four people are killed, many of them children. It is the deadliest attack on civilians since the cease-fire began. The Tigers are blamed for the incident but deny any involvement.

A few days later, there is a land and sea battle between the Tigers and government forces. Thirty people are killed, but both sides say they will hold to the cease-fire, wobbly as it may be.

RECKLESS CHOICES

Back at the Siam View Inn, I have tended to my cuts and am eating a bowl of noodles on the veranda, looking at the ocean. As I swat away flies and mosquitoes, I consider the apt lesson Sri Lanka has just taught me: reckless choices can squander the beauty and potential of a place.

Sri Lanka, I have seen, is a nation embarrassingly rich in man-made and natural resources, including historic religious monuments, pristine rain forests, white-sand beaches, prized tea plantations, rubber trees, sugar cane, rice and a climate where fruits and vegetables seem to grow with little coaxing or effort.

And here, though it is not completely trouble-free, humans seem to cohabitate more peacefully with the wide array of animals such as egrets, storks, leopards and elephants than they do with one another.

The potential value of all these resources, which could help turn a peaceful Sri Lanka into a powerful regional economy as well as an irresistible tourist destination, dramatically improving the lives of the population, has been undercut by the stuttering conflict between the Tigers and the government. It is a conflict that lives in that no-man's-land of "cease-fire," not really war but not really peace, either. Without a resolute effort by both sides to get the peace process back on track, and without greater involvement by the international community, the only potential that Sri Lanka will fulfill is the promise of renewed and bloody civil war.

The next day, wiser from my cuts and bruises, I paddle out into the lineup. I wait my turn patiently, see my opportunity, turn stroke and lift myself onto my board. I make the drop down the face of the wave and ride it as it unfurls its way out to the sea.

When it's over, I drop into the water and smile to myself while I paddle back into the lineup. I want it to signify something more, but I know it was just a nice ride; a small peaceful moment in a beautiful place.

CHAPTER 20

MYANMAR

Oldest Rebels Battle Ugliest Regime

KAREN STATE, MYANMAR (BURMA) | JUNE 22, 2006

ACROSS THE BORDER

Off a well-paved highway running north from Mae Sot, Thailand, my driver, Nibo, makes a sudden left, wheeling the silver Toyota pickup onto a winding dirt pathway leading through a seemingly endless expanse of cornfields.

As usual during monsoon season, it is dreary gray and on the cusp of another afternoon downpour. The rows of green stalks rustle in the wind, lulling me into an almost hypnotic calm, but then, after only a few minutes, the ride is over.

Nibo is out of the vehicle and leading me through the fields. We are mice in a green maze. Emerging on the other side, we are on the southeastern bank of the Moei River, which separates Thailand from what was once called Burma, renamed Myanmar in 1989 by the military junta that rules the country. A long wooden dugout powered by a small outboard motor is waiting for us. We climb aboard and ride it a hundred yards upriver before we tie up on the other side. Myanmar.

On the ledge above us, I spot the silhouettes of two men in uniform. After we climb the bank and I get a closer look, I can see that one is in his early twenties and the other in his late fifties. The older man extends his hand and introduces himself as Sanplo.

BETEL NUT

He is wearing green fatigues and a maroon beret. He smiles broadly, revealing the few teeth he has left, badly stained brown from chewing betel nut.

Betel nut is the bitter seed of the betel palm and is chewed like tobacco, and also like tobacco it is an addictive stimulant known for causing mouth and gum cancer. It is chewed by both men and women over much of Asia and the South Pacific.

"Please excuse me," Sanplo says, "my English is not so good."

I WILL KISS YOU

He leads us over the ridge to an encampment of thatched buildings, including a large meeting place guarded by two young fighters, one armed with a Russian-designed AK-47, the other with an American-made M-16. The one holding the M-16 is named Kapaw.

He smiles when he sees me looking closely at the homemade tattoos on his forearms, both in English: "I will kiss you" and "I love you."

I doubt that in close combat with a Myanmar army soldier able to read English, Kapaw's forearms would inspire much fear.

KAREN NATIONAL LIBERATION ARMY

Inside, a handful of older men dressed mostly like Sanplo await my arrival. I am told they are the leadership of Battalion 101 of the Seventh Brigade of the Karen National Liberation Army, or KNLA.

The KNLA and its coordinating political arm, the KNU or Karen National Union, have waged a fifty-seven-year war for independence of the Karen state in eastern Myanmar. The regime they are fighting has a reputation for being one of the most democratically contemptuous on the planet: the notorious, acronym-loving, Big Brotheresque military junta formerly known as the State Law and Order Restoration Council (SLORC) but now renamed the less ominous State Peace and Development Council (SPDC).

AUNG SAN SUU KYI

The junta changed the name of the country from Burma to Myanmar in 1989 and mysteriously moved the capital from Yangon to an undeveloped inland jungle enclave called Pyinmana in the last year.

This same junta has held the Nobel Peace Prize winner Aung San Suu Kyi under house arrest for ten of the last seventeen years after her opposition party, the National League for Democracy (NLD), won an election landslide in 1990. The regime invalidated the results. She remains under house arrest today despite calls for her release from much of the international community.

The Karen conflict is just one of several different ethnic struggles in Myanmar, but it is considered the oldest civil war in the world. When I meet some of the men who are fighting the war, a few appear to have been around for most of it.

LONG STRUGGLE

The first commander is introduced to me as Colonel Pawdoh, fifty-one, the youngest of the bunch, wearing a beret, striped polo shirt, black cargo pants and zip-up combat boots. He has a mouth full of betel nut. He says he has been with the KNLA since he was twenty years old.

When he sees me photographing Kapaw's tattoos, he holds out his forearms so I can photograph his as well. On his right is a dagger with wings, crowned with a large star; on his left is a crudely inked cross with the words "God is Love," in English. The blue ink has begun to diffuse and the lines are starting to blur.

The second commander is a sixty-three-year-old named Major Thasu, who claims he has fought with the KNLA for forty-four years. The battalion's adjutant is a bespectacled and kindly-looking sixty-five-year-old named Captain Raylo, a veteran of forty-two years.

On the wall behind a lectern is a painting of Saw Ba Oo Gyi, the founder and first chairman of the Karen National Union. Flanking the painting on either side are the KNU's four principles, in English on the left and in the curvy script of Karen on the right. While we make small talk, I write them down in my notebook. They read: (1) For us, surrender is out of the question, (2) We shall retain our arms, (3) The recognition of the Karen State must be complete, (4) We shall decide our own political destiny.

They seem, as I look at them, ready-made demands, both reaffirmation of the struggle's purpose (necessary in one this protracted) as well as clear signposts of deal-breaking points in any negotiations with the SPDC junta.

At this point in its existence, both the KNU and its military arm, the KNLA, need all the reaffirmation they can muster. They are plagued by divisions, aging leadership and shortages of manpower and materials.

"At the present," says Colonel Pawdoh, "we have no operations going on. We are working on peaceful negotiations."

There's a kind of "gentlemen's agreement," as Colonel Pawdoh calls it, between the KNLA and the Burmese military that followed a meeting with the SPDC in Yangon two years ago. It is not so much a cease-fire as a decision to avoid fighting when possible. Still, it seems to be a loose agreement with regular bouts of violence between the KNLA and SPDC, which results in a constant flow of Karen and other Myanmar refugees across the border into Thailand.

"The Burmese [Myanmar] military constantly violates the cease-fire," says Karen National Union general secretary Mahn Sha, from a location in Mae Sot on the Thai side of the border. "If they don't stop their military offensive against the Karen people, we will be forced to defend ourselves."

But it is a toothless threat, since there is little force to back it up. Quietly, many in the Karen leadership concede that the lengthy struggle has sapped the will of many of the Karen people to continue the fight.

BREAKAWAY FACTION

One of the biggest setbacks of the KNU/KNLA's struggle came in 1995, when a breakaway faction called the Democratic Karen Buddhist Army split with the KNLA over what it said was a Christian bias in the KNLA.

Then the DKBA switched sides and began working with the Myanmar army. The breakaway faction's insider knowledge, many Karen people believe, provided the Myanmar military with the information it needed to overrun the Karen National Union headquarters at Manerplaw inside Myanmar in 1995, forcing the leadership and thousands of refugees to flee to the borderlands and even across the Thai border. It was a strategic disaster from which the KNU and KNLA have not recovered.

Another major obstacle for the KNLA in providing a military backbone to the KNU's political pressure is the lack of supplies to equip their army.

WEAPONS

Major Thasu tells me that the KNLA gets lots of verbal support from the international community but few weapons, while the Myanmar government is supplied with arms from both China and India and is possibly also getting new weapons from Russia.

The KNLA, says Thasu, must rely on small arms captured from the SPDC or weapons bought with money funneled to them by the Karen people for work operations such as logging and farming. But the weapons available to purchase, including Vietnam-era M-16s, are often aging as fast as the KNLA leadership.

DRUGS AND CHILD SOLDIERS

Both the Myanmar military and the KNLA have been accused of profiting from the drug trade (Myanmar is the second-largest opium producer in the world behind Afghanistan) and using those funds to purchase weapons.

Major Thasu denies the charges that either the KNLA leadership or soldiers are involved with drugs.

"It's illegal," he says. "We take action against anyone who deals with drugs."

But the KNLA does admit to experimenting with the use of child soldiers in the mid-'80s, when it developed what it called "The Boys' Company," an entire unit of fourteen-, fifteen- and sixteen-year-old boys orphaned or made homeless through fighting with Myanmar troops.

KNU general secretary Mahn Sha says that international law and pressure made them quickly disband the Boys' Company only two years after it started.

However, when I make an impromptu visit to another KNLA battalion, the 22nd, inside Myanmar, I come across a skinny preadolescent boy, easily just eleven or twelve, shouldering an M-16.

I have clearly surprised him and the other adult soldier he is with. The boy nearly runs into the bush while I capture just a few seconds of videotape. He is a fleeting but stark contrast to the wizened KNLA vets I have spent most of the day with.

REFUGEE CAMPS

After going back across the river in the dugout, Nibo drives me to Mae La, one of the many overcrowded Karen refugee camps inside Thailand.

An estimated 125,000 refugees are now living in Thailand, and though they lack legal status they have become inextricably tied to the local economy, providing a constant source of labor cheaper than Thai workers.

Karen leaders say it is a desperate situation in which an entire group of people are stuck in limbo with marginal work and little actual hope of either returning home or becoming fully integrated Thai citizens.

THOSE WHO LIVE BY THE SWORD

Inside Mae La, I meet a thirty-year-old man named Pa No Htoo. He lives in a cinder-block building in the camp that houses land mine victims. Two attendants help him bathe in a dark back room, pouring buckets of water over his soapy head. He is in the shadows, but I can still see the stumps of his arms.

When he emerges, his head is covered with a towel. When he pulls it back, I see for the first time his deeply scarred face. There is just an empty socket where his right eye used to be, and his left eye has been glazed milky white.

I can see that Htoo's right arm was badly amputated above the elbow near his shoulder, creating a jagged, uneven look of a poorly sewn seam. His left arm was more cleanly cut just above the wrist.

Both arms are tattooed with letters and words that once had meaning but now trail off into incomplete thoughts toward the end of his missing limbs. The way he became a blind double amputee seems too obvious an example of the Christian axiom "Those who live by the sword, die by the sword."

Htoo says he was a KNLA soldier, just twenty-one years old, when the incident happened.

"I was laying land mines," he says, "but I forgot where I put the last one—until I put my hand on it."

The cook, preparing food nearby, chuckles at hearing the story, which he has undoubtedly heard many times before. That was nine years ago, says Htoo. He has been here at the Mae La camp ever since.

Most days he says he feels very sad that his life has turned out this way, but he still believes in the Karen struggle, even though it has left him like this. A fleeting happiness comes when he sings, something he never did before the mine incident.

I prod him a little and he agrees to sing, accompanied by another blind land mine victim, who also plays the guitar. Inside the cinder-block building, Htoo sings a Christian religious song. His voice is soft, pleasant and tinged with the sad acceptance that this is likely the best his life will be.

INTERMISSION

Missed Chance: Oh, Hello Dalai

KASHMIR AND JAMMU

What do you do when one of the world's preeminent religious leaders sits behind you on the plane: Dish on China? Share your iPod? Show off your downward dog pose? Or maybe nothing at all?

Location: The aisle of a Jet Air 737 making a stop in Jammu.

You: Bald-headed and bespectacled, wearing an off-the-shoulder scarlet-and-orange robe, smelling of sandalwood incense and lotus flowers, toting a briefcase with a "Free Tibet" sticker.

Me: Long-haired, bleary-eyed foreign correspondent, wearing a dirty black t-shirt and khaki pants, smelling of last night's curry and toting a look of unrivaled disbelief.

The Moment: I was sitting in my aisle seat already, having boarded in Kashmir when we made the quick stop to Jammu on our way to Delhi. That's where I saw you.

Your bodyguards got on first, not the juiced-up, pistol-packing muscle that usually accompanies heads of state, annoying celebrities and corporate robber barons—just clean-cut, average-sized dudes who probably did their time in a Shaolin temple or two and could likely snap spines with a properly pitched shout.

One eyeballed me for a second, shooting a fully disapproving look at my unlaced combat boots and slumpy seated posture.

But all that negativity quickly disappeared when your silhouette pierced the white haze coming from the open cabin doorway.

You looked inside, I can't say whether right at me or not, but it certainly seemed that way, a barely perceptible Mona Lisa smile on your face. Or perhaps you were only adjusting to the light inside the plane.

As you walked by, I wanted to reach out and touch you, thinking that even just a brush against your robes might make me a wiser, kinder, more peaceful man—or at the very least I would know if they were all cotton or some kind of synthetic blend.

I was too awestruck. I just let you pass by without even a word. Then opportunity came knocking again when you climbed into the window seat behind me, but there was another problem. You were with someone else: another Tibetan monk. Now, I'm not saying he was some kind of God digger, but I doubt he would hang around with less karmic figures.

I tried to listen while you gave your lunch choice to the flight attendant; were you a mutter paneer or vegetable korma kind of Dalai? I thought maybe if your friend got up to use the bathroom I could slip in for a second while the seat belt sign was off and buy you a sweet mango lassi.

But he never left your side. Smart. Probably knew some enlightenment-seeking player like me would try to move in on you. I mean, look what happened when you went to Hollywood; that whole Richard Gere affair.

I kept watching you out of the corner of my eye, pretending to listen more closely than I was to Matisyahu on my Nano. I would bet my backup hundred-gig hard drive that you'd get a kick out of hearing a Hasidic Jew singing reggae. I considered offering you my headset, but you just sat there, staring out the window with that blissfully serene look on your face.

I kept trying to think of something witty to say, but nothing came to mind, which with you, I guess, is probably a good thing, seeing that you are always talking about staying in the moment. I thought about asking if you had read *The Da Vinci Code*, but you probably get that all the time. With that mischievous smile of yours, I wondered if the whole thing might have been one of your legendary monkish pranks, spreading rumors to author Dan Brown to get Pope B's vestments all in a bunch.

I can even imagine you double-dog daring the Danish cartoonists just to get the other guys riled up, too.

I guess that is why I was initially attracted to you: forced into exile, you had to grow up fast, decades of cross-legged meditation and a vegetarian diet—yet you are still able to keep your impish sense of humor.

And I have to admit, your professional success is pretty impressive. A lot of people say they want world peace, but how many can actually make a living at it? Also, this was just a bonus, but I don't think I ever felt so safe and secure flying with anyone else, ever.

When the plane finally landed in Delhi, we had that moment during the deplaning where I paused to let you go first, but you waved me ahead. I knew that if I went, we would probably never speak, but just like that, I did. The next thing I know, I'm in the airport shuttle and you're being packed into the back of a white Mercedes and whisked off to who knows where. I pressed my face against the bus window to get one more glimpse, but it was too late.

Anyway, I know there is a very slim chance that you will read this, but if you get my vibe, I'm putting out good thoughts into the universe. Also, I wanted to tell you, that while in the short time we spent together I didn't achieve nirvana, I did come very close (for me, anyway) to having a moment of Zen.

Note: Of all the reader responses I received over the year during my journey, this one, about my Dalai Lama story, was by far my favorite slapdown. Name calling is easy, but this reader turned me into the banjo-playing inbred kid from the film *Deliverance*.

READER RESPONSE

You wrote that you wanted to speak to the Dalai, but couldn't think of anything witty to say. Is that what happened when you sat down to write this report? Writer's block is not pretty, sir. Try writing the same report over, but from the standpoint of the Dalai looking at you, and being jealous of your anonymity and your blog-simple ways, wanting to speak to you about things that he would presume you would be interested in, like trailer parks in the moonlight, or the peculiar timbre of a mantra from a toothless grin, or how many Supercuts you have to endure to get a free one. Oh, the things he could have said to you, sir!!!!

Posted by blouseketeer on Sat, Jun 17, 2006 12:42 P.M. ET

CHAPTER 21

CAMBODIA

Does Justice Lie Among Those Bones?

PHNOM PENH, CAMBODIA | JULY 2, 2006

MONSOON

The summer monsoon shows no signs of letting up. People are squeezing under the awnings of storefronts, half a dozen men pull a plastic tarp over themselves in the bed of a pickup truck and two toddlers lie on their stomachs underneath the wooden platform of their father's pastry cart—all to avoid the downpour.

My driver/fixer, Bon Thim, and I duck into Phnom Penh's art deco–style Central Market with its giant wooden dome. I pull off my plastic poncho and wipe my cameras dry with a black bandana.

Inside the Central Market, there is the comfort of shared purpose. We are all refugees now, fleeing the rain. I snap some photos of a baby, sitting on his uncle's lap, trying to catch raindrops dripping from the roof with claps of his tiny hands.

The market is filled with electronics, gold and jewelry, as well as cheap goods from China and Thailand, clothes and plastic buckets, posters of Thai soap opera stars, pirated music CDs and DVDs, books and food.

I'm getting hungry. While looking around for a snack, I see an opportunity for some adventurous eating—big piles of insects. I circle around the vendors twice, looking over the buckets of black beetles, segmented pupae, brown locusts and hairy black spiders.

I watch what people are buying, and think I'll take my cue from the locals, but most are buying the hairy spiders, the very last thing I want to eat. A no-nonsense, middle-aged woman quickly tongs dozens of them into a small plastic bag, twisting, knotting it and handing it over, taking the cash, making change—all at a blurring speed.

I give Bon Thim my camera and tell him to videotape while I try the different options. I want the clip to be informative, a cultural bridge, but not an episode of *Fear Factor*.

People's different appetites and interests are newsworthy to our home audiences, but I hate it when I see traveling journalists setting up lame punch lines: "Hey, everybody, they eat bugs here! How crazy!"

FIVE-SECOND RULE

The insect vendor is not pleased with me, since our videotaping might keep customers away. I do the on-camera piece fairly quickly and hopefully with some respect, aside from dropping one of the beetles on the ground. I quickly brush it off and pop it in my mouth anyway, figuring the five-second rule applies, and since all the bugs came from the ground to begin with.

While they are all lightly stir-fried, the crunchy beetles are my favorite; all exoskeleton, no squishy insides. The pupae are nutty with the consistency of a lima bean, while the locusts are light, toasty like a rice cake, but dry like them, too. I am disappointed in myself for wussing out on the spiders.

Overall, it seems like a great solution for two problems: hunger and bugs. The ultimate fast food is not only a good source of protein but also plentiful. But with Western addictions to processed snacks, I doubt these would make much of an inroad in American or even European markets.

Bon Thim gives me back the camera and buys a bagful of spiders.

"My wife is pregnant now," he tells me. "She likes to eat these."

While walking around the market waiting for the rain to stop, we are approached at every corner by men trying to sell us books or videos from large plastic baskets tied around their necks with rope.

All these men have one thing in common—missing legs. They are land mine victims. It amazes me that they do not tumble forward, considering the weight of what they carry around their necks. One man in particular seems to have the balance of a circus performer; a double, above-the-knee amputee, he somehow remains upright on two crudely made wooden legs that might have seemed at home in a pirate movie.

HISTORY OF VIOLENCE

These men are just a handful of examples of Cambodia's history of violence, one that culminated in the brief but genocidal rule of the communist Khmer Rouge regime. When the Khmer Rouge seized power in 1975, its leader, Pol Pot, proclaimed it "Year Zero" and renamed Cambodia the Democratic Republic of Kampuchea.

The goal was to transform the country into a workers' agricultural paradise by destroying banking and the monetary system, industry, urban infrastructure—anything and anyone linked to civilized modernity. When the experiment was over, as many as two million people were dead, murdered or starved in a vast wave of violence and chaos that turned the entire nation into a giant killing field.

The genocide finally ended in 1979 after forces from neighboring Vietnam overthrew the regime. Pol Pot and other Khmer Rouge leaders and troops fled into the jungle. But even while their brutal killing frenzy was being revealed to the world, the Khmer Rouge continued to receive support from China, Thailand, and indirectly from the United States, which was funding a coalition of anti-Vietnamese insurgents.

TUOL SLENG

Even though 70 percent of the population was born after the genocide, museums and memorials keep the tragedy's narrative alive. For me, the most powerful and disturbing museum is the former Khmer Rouge prison known as S-21 in suburban Phnom Penh.

A visit there makes it indisputably clear that the Khmer Rouge were very good at two things: killing people and documenting the lives of those victims. The museum, now called Tuol Sleng, translates in English to "Poisonous Hill." Here the faces of the Cambodian genocide are much more than memories.

WALLS OF SHAME

Visitors walking through the hallways of this former high school turned prison must confront the pain, uncertainty and fear of thousands of victims looking back at them from the black-and-white photographs taken by prison guards, mounted on panels throughout the half-dozen buildings that make up the site.

The documentation was a methodical process. The victims were positioned on a specially constructed chair with a boom arm that steadied their head before the photograph was taken. Detailed histories were written for all prisoners, covering the days of their childhood up until their arrest. They were stripped of all their possessions and clothes, leaving them only their underwear.

Some were chained to the floor in tiny individual cells, forced to defecate in ammunition cans. Others were held in groups in open classrooms with one or both legs shackled to larger iron bars on the floor, similar to the method used to immobilize captives on African slave ships sailing to the Americas.

TORTURE

As I walk through the different rooms, it is easy to imagine the agony of the prisoners here. In one section, there are bare iron beds with shackles. These were used as torture rooms, according to the guides. The rust-colored stains on the floor, they say, is the dried blood of victims.

The insides of the buildings seem at sharp contrast to the quiet, peaceful-looking grounds filled with palm trees and benches and neatly lined brick pathways cutting through swaths of manicured green lawn.

But S-21 was not a killing factory. It was a holding area and a place to extract confessions. True to the Khmer Rouge's communist utopian vision of beating the nation back into a purely peasant agrarian society, the killings took place in the countryside, in extermination camps or "killing fields" like Choeung Ek, just outside the capital of Phnom Penh.

The majority held at S-21 were Cambodian citizens from all walks of life—and all ages. The Khmer Rouge had a practice of arresting entire families together, including children and babies. Foreigners were also imprisoned at Tuol Sleng, including Vietnamese, Laotians, Indians, Pakistanis, British, Americans, New Zealanders and Australians.

QUESTIONS

It is a sobering experience for the fifty or so visitors who come to the museum each day. Many whom I spoke to say they didn't know much about the genocide but felt it would be wrong to visit Cambodia without paying respect to its tragic history and the victims. For some, it also raises questions about the past and the present.

"When this was going on," says twenty-three-year-old Canadian Aaron Johnson, "it makes you wonder why the world wasn't more motivated for some kind of humanitarian intervention."

"And the question of genocide seems to keep coming up," says Gabrielle Donnelly, twenty-three, also of Canada. "What about places like Darfur? After World War II, we said we wouldn't let genocide happen again, but it seems like it's still with us."

And like other past genocides, the question of how this could happen still hangs over Cambodia. Although there are few clear answers, there are some clues provided by S-21.

CHILDREN AS PERPETRATORS AND VICTIMS

Many of the prison guards here were just children themselves, usually be-tween the ages of ten and fifteen, sometimes picked out from other camps. Literature from Tuol Sleng says the children usually started out quite nor-mal but increased in their remorseless cruelty toward those they were charged with minding. Eventually, these children were often killed them-selves by the children who replaced them.

Prisoners had to ask permission to do anything, from going to the bath-room to even moving their bodies. Failure to obey immediately would re-sult in savage beatings with electrical wire or electric shock. The regulations were posted in each cell—some of them even prescribing how prisoners should behave during torture, for example,

> Rule #6—While getting lashes or electrification you must not cry at all.

And torture at S-21 took all forms.

"Sometimes victims would be shackled to the floor," says guide K. Eo-lundi, pointing to a painting depicting the torture made by Vann Nath, a former Australian prisoner at S-21 and one of the few survivors, "and the guards would cut off their nipples with these clamps."

In the same room is a large wooden box in which prisoners would be shackled facedown. The box would then be filled with water until they could no longer raise their heads high enough to breathe.

Outside on the grounds, there is what looks like a large wooden goalpost with pulleys on the crossbeam. Here, the guides say, prisoners were hoisted up by the back of their arms, which caused excruciating pain, often dislocat-ing the shoulders. According to the placard beside it, if they still refused to talk, the guards would force their heads into a large clay urn filled with ani-mal excrement.

HUMAN FACE

With the thorough documentation of their victims, the Khmer Rouge ironically helped to put a human face on the atrocities it perpetrated. But now time itself has become an enemy. Without proper chemicals and temperature-controlled storage, many of the documents and photographs of those who passed through S-21 are beginning to yellow and fade. Museum directors say they fear that without adequate funding to preserve them, they could be lost—and the history with them.

But while their photographs may fade, the bones of the victims will not disappear so easily.

KILLING FIELD

The staggering crime of seventeen thousand murders could not be buried in the orchards of Choeung Ek for long—although the Khmer Rouge did try.

In a quiet field nine miles from Phnom Penh, the ground is pitted with 129 mass graves where men, women and children were tossed after most had been killed by bludgeoning with rifle butts, bamboo stakes or logs, to save bullets. Some survivors even describe babies being tossed in the air and caught on the end of rifle bayonets by sadistic Khmer Rouge executioners.

But nature, though a witness to these deeds, was not an accomplice. The shallow graves easily exposed the horrors beneath. One year after the fall of the Khmer Rouge, eighty-six of the graves were dug up and the bodies of nearly nine thousand people exhumed. Most were bound and blindfolded.

Forty-three other graves have been left untouched to this day.

The people who were executed here had primarily been transported from the S-21 prison, Tuol Sleng.

Mao Thel lost his mother, father and uncle in the Khmer Rouge killing frenzies. He says it is possible that his own family is among those that were killed and buried here. He has worked for years at Choeung Ek, giving tours to the dozens of people who visit every day; they are foreign tourists mostly, who, as at Auschwitz or Buchenwald, are usually overwhelmed by the magnitude of inhumanity that took place here.

BONES

A large white pagoda covered by glass on all four sides stands amid the shallow pits now covered with thin layers of grass. Inside the pagoda are ten separate wooden platforms, and arranged on these platforms, according to sex and age, are the skulls of eight thousand of the seventeen thousand victims murdered at Choeung Ek.

"This one was killed by electric wire," says Mao, pointing out skulls on the first platform of the pagoda to six young men and women from the United Kingdom. "This one was killed with a bamboo stake through the head and this one by a hoe."

He raises the last skull to show how it was split completely in half.

The tourists look at the skulls in stunned silence. It is, however, almost impossible to stop looking at them; to first take them in as a whole, a mass of textures and shades, brown, white and gray, an army not of soldiers but of victims—an army of death.

I watch the tourists as they look up and down the platforms, trying to comprehend that there are nine more levels above the one in front of them; the skulls of both children and adults, girls and boys, women and men.

On the floor beneath the first platform are some of the clothes the victims were wearing when they were killed. It reminds me of a memorial at the school in Rwanda that I had visited early in this project, in which victims' clothes were hung across a wire near where their bodies were exhumed. The smell of the clothes somehow forces you to see people when looking at the remains, not just bodies, not just victims.

The pagoda walls are covered in glass only on the outside. Inside the structure, the clothes and skulls are open and exposed on their platforms. You can touch them, pick them up and stare closely if you feel the need. There is little separation between the living and dead.

Inside the pagoda I begin to understand that, whether intended or not, this memorial is not a museum piece. Detaching yourself from this tragedy is hardly an option.

NOT JUST THEIR DEATHS

Eight thousand skulls look back at you from empty eye sockets, asking you to see not just their deaths but also their lives.

Once they laughed, dressed in clothes, ate breakfast, took shelter from the rain, made tea. It was these things they were robbed of and these things they seem to ask you to remember so that they are more than statistics of a heinous crime, more than skulls on a platform.

It is hard for me to walk away from Choeung Ek unmoved; to know what has happened here, to see the evidence, to honor the loss, but also to wonder if, after more than twenty-five years, justice also lies among those bones.

JUSTICE?

After all this time not a single Khmer Rouge leader has seen the inside of a courtroom for his crimes against humanity.

Only now is the government of Cambodia working with the United Nations to establish an international tribunal to prosecute major Khmer Rouge figures—if they can find any to stand trial who are not too sick or already dead.

Pol Pot died of a heart attack in a remote Cambodian village near the Thai border in 1998. He had proclaimed shortly before his death, "My conscience is clear."

On my flight into Cambodia, I met a man named Martin Karopkin, who is a trial commissioner for the New York Police Department. He applied for a place on the United Nations tribunal and was accepted as a reserve judge. He was traveling to Phnom Penh for a preliminary meeting of the panel.

I talked with him later in the week and asked him why he believed it was important to hold the tribunal when so few members of the Khmer Rouge's senior leadership is left.

"Fundamentally it's wrong to ignore an event like this," he tells me in the lobby of his hotel. "An event of this magnitude needs to be pursued as long as it can. On a personal level, I hope it will bring a sense of closure to all involved. The key issue here is that this is being addressed in some fashion. To do nothing, to ignore it, is not adequate."

I ask if there are other pressing reasons to conduct this tribunal, something beneath the surface.

"Unfortunately we live in a time when there have been some shocking genocides and the world needs a way to respond to it," he tells me. "Jurisprudence is one response to meet this unfortunate need. And by addressing it, it may also act as a check against future genocides, that those who perpetrate these kind of things will have a day of reckoning."

MORAL RESPONSIBILITY

As he tells me these things, I feel less optimistic about the outcome but admire Karopkin's willingness and effort to try to see justice served. Without any personal connection to Cambodia or its history, he has come here out of a sense of moral responsibility to help right this wrong.

Strangely, he has received no support from the United States in his role, not even a courtesy briefing at the U.S. embassy in Phnom Penh. The United States could be embarrassed by its history with the Khmer Rouge, having possibly helped bring it to power by destabilizing the country with a secret Cambodian bombing campaign during the Vietnam War—and supporting it after it was driven from power by Vietnamese troops in 1979.

Regardless, Karopkin and I both agree how much more effective it would be to see collective action by the international community at the first evidence of genocide, rather than a tribunal long after its completion.

CHAPTER 22

VIETNAM
Clockwork Orange

HO CHI MINH CITY, VIETNAM | JULY 8, 2006

PEACE VILLAGE

Here in the Peace Village section of Tu Du Hospital, Dr. Nguyen Thi Phuong Tan holds up one of the residents, a four-year-old boy named Quang. At first glance he appears to be a normally formed child with his fingers and toes in all the right places. But something is conspicuously absent. Quang has a mouth and a nose—but no eyes. Not even eye sockets. His jet-black hair frames a forehead of pale skin, nothing more.

Also in the same room is a two-and-a-half-year-old Down syndrome boy named Thanh, who stands in his crib as the nurses say he does every day without making a sound. His eyes follow me around the room as I videotape but seem to register nothing.

In the room next door, Dr. Phuong Tan introduces me to a thirteen year-old girl named Linh, born without arms, and a twenty-year-old woman named Hoan, born without lower legs and without a left hand.

While America's military involvement in Vietnam ended thirty-two years ago, its destructive legacy, Vietnamese health officials say, lives on in places like this—specially designated Peace Villages, eleven in all, created for those they believe to be victims of Agent Orange, the now-infamous chemical defoliant used by American forces.

From 1961 to 1971 in an evolving mission, first code-named Operation

Hades and finally Operation Ranch Hand, the U.S. military sprayed eigh-teen million gallons of herbicides over Vietnam in an effort to destroy the jungle canopy that provided a hiding place for North Vietnamese and Viet Cong fighters. Its secondary purpose was to kill crops or other plants that could be used as food by those forces or their supporters.

The most common and effective defoliant was called Agent Orange, named not for its color but for the orange band that encircled the fifty-five-gallon containers that held it.

Agent Orange was laced with a dioxin known as tetrachlorodibenzo-para-dioxin, or TCDD, a cancer-causing chemical that many global health professionals say turned portions of Vietnam into toxic wastelands and nur-tured an epidemic of birth defects as well as chronic health problems affect-ing three generations of Vietnamese: those directly exposed, their children and now their children's children.

Professor Nguyen Thi Ngoc Phuong, Vietnam's leading researcher on the health effects of Agent Orange, says there is a reason why children are still being affected so many years later.

"In some cases, the toxins within Agent Orange can skip a genera-tion," she tells me. "And someone may be a carrier of genes damaged by the toxins but will only pass it on if they conceive a child with another carrier."

THREE MILLION EXPOSED

The Vietnamese say that three million people were exposed to the dioxins during the war and that as many as eight hundred thousand still suffer from its effects today.

Thousands of American Vietnam War veterans have also complained of illness and birth defects they attribute to exposure to Agent Orange dioxins. The U.S. Department of Veterans Affairs now recognizes a series of condi-tions that may be associated with exposure to TCDD, including skin dis-eases, diabetes, some birth defects and several cancers, such as Hodgkin's disease and prostate and respiratory cancer.

NIGHTMARE SENTRIES

Dr. Phuong Tan unlocks the heavy metal door to a windowless lower floor in Tu Du's Peace Village.

Inside are shelves lined with dozens of jars filled with amber liquid preservative and human fetuses so grotesquely deformed they seem to have been created in the imagination of Hollywood screenwriters rather than in wombs.

They encircle the room like nightmare sentries. As much as I want to, it is impossible to turn away. The curve of the glass only serves to amplify the contents inside. There are conjoined fetuses, fetuses with multiple eyes or a single Cyclops eye, enlarged heads or tiny pinheads, elongated chins, malformed limbs, misshapen and twisted torsos, fleshy or calcified masses. I feel a dizzying sense of peripeteia just having discovered they exist.

These, medical officials here say, are fetuses stillborn between 1974 and 1980 to mothers living in or around areas once heavily sprayed with Agent Orange. The U.S. government says the defects, both then and now, haven't been definitively linked to dioxins in Agent Orange and could have been caused by any number of factors.

HOME

For Hoan and Linh, the debate over the cause of their deformities has little bearing on their lives. With their designation as third-generation victims, the Vietnamese government gives them a place to live since their families can't afford the high economic and psychological costs of caring for them.

Linh combs her hair using a brush she holds with her incredibly dexterous feet and tells me how she first came to the live at Peace Village. "My mother lied to me," she says. "She told me we were going on a picnic, then she brought me here. I hated it at first—but then after a week I felt better."

"I'd like to be a doctor," Hoan tells me, "but without legs and my hand, I doubt I will be accepted."

Hoan has lived in Peace Village for twelve years, Linh for six. In their time here, they tell me, they have become like sisters.

DUC AND VIET

But two actual brothers living in Peace Village are the formerly conjoined twins Duc and Viet, twenty-six. They were born to a family that lived in an area affected by Agent Orange spraying and were separated by surgery eighteen years ago. For Duc, the more fully formed of the two, the surgery was liberating.

Missing only one leg and portions of his abdomen, he has thrived at the center, able to move around on crutches, and even play soccer. He was recently married to a physically normal, healthy woman at a ceremony held at Peace Village.

Viet, unfortunately, has not fared as well. Like a living yang to Duc's yin, Viet has only one leg, but it twists up toward his head like a tree branch. He spends his days lying on a mattress, one wrist loosely tethered to the bed frame in case of seizures. A nurse sits near his bed, turning him to prevent bedsores.

"We are very close to the children. We are like second mothers to them," says Peace Village nurse Truong Thi Ten. "When one of them dies, it's devastating. It is like losing a relative."

LAWSUITS

In 1984, American servicemen who believed they were suffering from exposure to Agent Orange sued the chemical companies that manufactured it, including Monsanto and Dow Chemical. They settled out of court for $180 million. Veterans from Australia, New Zealand, Canada and South Korea were also able to negotiate settlements from the chemical manufacturers.

Ironically, however, the same Brooklyn Federal Court judge, Jack Weinstein, who helped engineer the American veterans' settlement, denied a similar claim by a Vietnamese Agent Orange victims' association.

Many human rights groups see it as an apparent double standard in which American vets are compensated, even though the U.S. military was using chemicals that, theoretically, were banned from combat use by the Geneva Convention. Meanwhile, the victims of those weapons, even first-generation victims (those directly exposed), are not entitled to any compensation whatsoever.

The majority of victims in Vietnam, who do not live in Peace Villages, must try to survive on government subsides equivalent to just five dollars per day. American veterans making successful claims to possible Agent Orange–related illnesses can receive as much as $1,500 a month from the Department of Veterans Affairs.

HARD REALITIES

Life at Peace Village is bittersweet for the two girls, Hoan and Linh. They have each other, but they are also surrounded by children with much more severe mental and physical handicaps. Part of their sense of purpose comes from helping to take care of the other children. It is a comfort level that may, in the future, be difficult if not impossible to leave, concedes Dr. Tan.

Even Hoan seems resigned that this may be her permanent home.

"Becoming a doctor is my dream," she says. "But it is very difficult and may not be realistic."

"It's very hard for them as babies," says nurse Ten, "but as they get older it is even harder on them."

PART VI

THE THIRTY-FOUR-DAY WAR

Putting the Hole in the Holy Land

CHAPTER 23

LEBANON

Dodging Drones and Dead Men's Pockets

TYRE, LEBANON | JULY 23, 2006

THE ROCK, PART I

We're on the grounds of a secondary school that has been converted into a refugee camp for people from frontline villages in the south, such as Maroun al-Ras and Bint Jbeil, which are Hezbollah strongholds.

My current fixer, Ali; driver, Abdullah; and I are in the eye of an angry storm, surrounded by women and children on the inner rings, adolescents on the second and third rings and, finally, by mildly bemused but not totally disinterested adult men on the outside.

I have come to see the conditions here, which I've been told are not good: little food, sporadic water and as many as 1,500 people, mostly families, sleeping shoulder to shoulder in empty classrooms.

But I never get that far. While the men are initially accommodating and willing to show me around, handfuls of angry women swarm us. Ali tells me later they say that we are spies for America and Israel and that as soon as we leave, the bombs will begin raining down on their heads just as they had in their villages.

I tell them that I am only here to document their lives as displaced people. Some of the men nod and give me a quick walk through the ground-level classrooms, but we are pursued by the angry women for the entire three-minute tour. As I raise my camera, the shouting becomes louder. Finally, even the men acquiesce to the women's protests. No pictures, I am told, unless we get a letter from Hezbollah giving us permission.

With the sound of Israeli jets and drones overhead, I assume that anyone from Hezbollah's leadership might be a little hard to find.

While I have accomplished very little here, I do gain one insight, a moment that allows me to gauge the depth of anger here and the cohesiveness of south Lebanon's Shiite Muslims behind Hezbollah. While we stand next to Abdullah's old 200-series lapis blue Mercedes, Ali makes one last, futile plea for access. Out of the corner of my eye, I see a ten-year-old boy and turn to give him my full attention.

He is in a fighting stance, with his left foot forward and his eyes locked on to me. His face shows no emotion, no anger, no fear, nothing but intense focus. A glance down at his right hand, and I quickly realize why I am the object of his resolve. In his hand is a rock the size of a cue ball.

GLOBAL TINDERBOX

This is a conflict I simply hoped would go away, but it doesn't. In fact, with each passing day the Israeli-Hezbollah war seems to grow larger while I am haplessly out of place doing a retrospective on the American war in Vietnam.

As a part of my Hot Zone project, I had already covered Lebanon in December, including an interview with Hezbollah. I had also reported from Israel in February. At the moment, I am not eager to go back.

After covering conflicts in nineteen countries for almost a full year, I am burned out and feeding a growing anger at the senseless violence that plagues the globe. Nearly all the wars I have reported on, with the exception of Nepal, have gotten worse rather than better. I would like to finish my two remaining conflict zones, the Philippines and Korea, and go home. But this current Israeli-Hezbollah fight has all the makings of a global tinderbox with its spectrum of opposing religious and political alliances: Iran and Syria backing Hezbollah Shiites, the United States supporting Israel, the governments of Saudi Arabia, Egypt and Jordan providing at least verbal support to Lebanese prime minister Fouad Siniora, himself a Sunni Muslim who has called for Hezbollah to disarm.

The escalating violence has the potential to grow into an even bigger regional conflict—or worse. I know what I have to do. I make arrangements with my team back in California and board an Emirates flight for Amman, Jordan.

While I'm in the air, my producer, Robert, contacts a fellow journalist and University of Maryland scholar named Jad Melki who was in Beirut doing research prior to the lastest fighting. Melki, who was born in Lebanon, is still well connected. By the time I land, he has arranged for a driver willing to travel against the refugee exodus for an eight-hour ride from Jordan to Beirut. The fare is a war-gouging $1,600. I will stay in Beirut just one day before heading south to Tyre and the most serious fighting.

KABUKI PLAY

The seaport city of Tyre is like a semisafe refuge for the displaced from border villages being bombed around the clock by Israeli warplanes and artillery. It is also a haven for the Lebanese and international journalists covering the war.

Even though there have been earlier strikes against suspected Hezbollah offices and residences in town, this one today in the dead center of the city is both enormous and a bit of a surprise. I am conducting interviews with recent refugees outside a hotel nearby when the concussion and sound wave of the explosion seem to pass right through us.

A plume of gray smoke rises in the distance about a third of a mile away. Ali and I jump into the Mercedes and Abdullah guns it, racing an ambulance to the location by simply following the smoke trail. At an intersection we begin to see people running out of a street covered in blackness. I sprint toward them, my video camera rolling. As the smoke clears a bit, I see two women outside a building next to the one that was destroyed.

They don't seem to be hurt physically, but they are screaming uncontrollably as a bearded man carries out an infant boy. The boy is calm, as if he had just woken from a nap. The only evidence of his trauma is that his entire face has been turned ghost-gray from the soot that filled the air after the explosion. His curious wide eyes are ringed in black while he watches the commotion around him. A few moments later, the boy's mother comes running out of the building as well, screaming, "Where is my baby, where is my baby?"

Her face is also covered in soot, and when she takes the boy in her arms their dust-painted faces make them look like characters from a Japanese Kabuki play. I drop the video camera that is slung over my right shoulder, pull up the digital still camera that is slung over the other and begin squeezing off frames of their faces. There is so much soot in the air that my auto focus has a hard time locking on an image. I will discover later that only one or two of these dramatic images will be sharp enough to post on the Web site. I have better luck shooting video.

When I enter the adjacent building to see if there are any casualties, young men inside begin to yell at me and try to push my camera away. It's an anger and frustration that has been growing with this two-week-old war that has killed hundreds, destroyed billions of dollars of infrastructure and unraveled Lebanon's hard-won economic progress.

LEFT HOOK

As I continue shooting, I see one of the guys coming at me through my viewfinder. He throws a wild left hook that connects with my camera but not my head. As far as punches go, this one is mild but strong enough to snap off my top-mounted microphone and flip on my night-shot switch, which puts the camera into infrared mode, turning video green until I can switch it back.

I know as a journalist to expect this kind of reaction at scenes of violence. It is normal for people to want to lash out in traumatic situations when they are overwhelmed with emotions. If you're first on location, you're going to be their target.

I move to the side, adjust my gear and go back to work. As the wounded are evacuated, my attention turns to the smoking rubble that was the target of the missile strike. It is a seven-story building with forty apartments that seem to have collapsed on themselves, leaving sections of the roof scattered over the top like broken ice floes.

As I look over the wreckage it seems incredible to me—both the precision of this weapon and its destructive power, able to take down one specific building completely.

Soon, young shirtless men are swarming over the rubble, trying to put out flames by swatting them with pillows and blankets. They also begin salvaging things. One bends down to pick up a copy of the Holy Koran. He dusts off the cover and tosses it to another man.

"I WILL FIGHT AMERICA"

One older man walking amid the rubble is a doctor who works for the city. I talked with him at his office earlier.

"This was my house," Dr. Raed Ghassan says to me.

"Where is your family?" I ask.

"Not here," he says angrily, kicking at the rubble.

I ask him why he thought the building was targeted.

"This is an example of American democracy," he says. "This is your human rights. This is why I hate America. I will fight America, every day, every time."

When the firefighters arrive, they pull a hose through the wreckage and quickly put out the remaining fires. As more and more journalists get to the location, a dozen young men begin doing pro-Hezbollah chants for the cameras just as they did after missiles hit a house in the same neighborhood two days before.

I ask one man that I had seen at the earlier missile strike why the Israelis keep targeting the neighborhood. He says something vague about a mosque being nearby and then walks away.

NO HEZBOLLAH?

"There was no Hezbollah in this building, man," another says to me. "None."

It is not until later that I learn the possible reason why the Israelis struck this building. The Israelis claim it contained the offices of Sheik Nabil Kaouk, Hezbollah's south Lebanese commander.

Twelve people were injured in the attack, but no one was killed. All the injured lived in surrounding buildings. People on the street say the one destroyed was empty for weeks before the missile strike, a good indication that both the residents and the Israelis knew it would be a target sooner or later.

MUMMIES

I'm not surprised the day is ending like this. It has been marked by segments of individual and collective grief. It began at the site of Tyre's mass graves, where the city says it places the civilian victims of Israeli air strikes. They are put in plywood coffins and buried quickly in adherence to Islamic tradition. They may be reburied, officials tell me, when the fighting is over.

Later, at Jabal Amel Hospital, I see the victims of a recent Israeli air strike that hit a civilian bus, leaving three dead and thirteen injured, the majority women and children trying to flee the area.

The victims include Rhonda Shaloub and her fifteen-year-old niece, Radije. When I see them, they are mummy-wrapped in gauze bandages with openings only for their noses and mouths. The little I can see of their faces is deeply disturbing: blood seeping at the edges of Rhonda's bandages and lacerations on Radije's lips stitched closed.

Later, when I visit the city morgue, hospital workers will show me the bodies of two men recently recovered from Lebanon's dangerous roads, where anything moving can become an Israeli target—even Red Cross ambulances responding to attacks. I ask how they were killed. The first, I'm told, was driving a car that was hit by an Israeli missile fired from a helicopter. His name is Jihad Ammad Murtada.

They unwrap the blanket from around his body to show me that they weren't able to find his head. His hands are clenched tightly into fists.

DEAD MAN'S POCKETS

One of the men reaches into the dead man's pockets to pull out his personal belongings: a set of keys, a wallet, things that would seem very normal for someone breathing but that take on a near-mythical quality for someone without a head.

Next to Murtada is the body of Hassan Ibrahim Said. According to his brother, Said had come to the city to buy food and milk for his eight-month-old daughter, Fatme, and was struck by a missile while riding home on his motorbike.

They unwrap the blanket to reveal that his body has nearly been split in half, bending from the top into a Y. His face hangs to one side like a rubber mask. Most turn from the gruesome scene, except two young boys who have sneaked into the compound to get a closer look. Hospital workers chase them away.

The bodies are wrapped in black plastic, then bound with white medical tape, their names written on it with marker. For now they will be stored in a refrigerated truck with the five other bodies recovered today.

Inside the morgue's office, a Lebanese police officer sorts through Said's wallet and other belongings while his brother waits for the items to be turned over to him. The officer opens the wallet and removes some Lebanese currency and slips of paper with different phone numbers written on them.

In the middle of the wallet's fold, under a plastic sleeve, is a picture of Said's wife, Sabah, who is at the same time, I notice, beginning to sob at the entrance of the office, perhaps just beginning to realize the reality of her new life without a husband and father for her child.

Finally, the officer pulls out Said's identification card with a small square picture revealing what he looked like in life. He is a dark-haired, handsome

man, probably in his early thirties. It is hard for me at this moment to reconcile the photograph with the image I have just seen outside, wrapped in
black plastic.

DRONES

Each night after my reporting, I have to turn the information I have gathered into stories for three different mediums—a text dispatch, similar to a
newspaper story; video clips, similar to a television package; and a slide
show of still photographs.

It is a difficult task after the day-to-day emotional and physical exhaustion of covering this high-casualty, high-intensity conflict. On this night, I
finish writing my dispatch by 2:30 A.M. and need to feed everything to my
producers in California using a satellite modem connected to my laptop.
But as I prepare to go to the rooftop of my small hotel, the owner, Mohammed, warns me against it.

"You can't go up there, Kevin. You know the Apaches will be out," he
says, referring to Israel's American-made attack helicopters that circle the
Lebanese sky at night, looking for targets.

My only other option is to feed from the deserted street below. I carry
my gear, looking for an opening to the south where I can direct the satellite
signal between buildings. Depending on the amount of material and transmission speed, it can be a painfully slow process. Tonight it is.

While I am waiting I become aware of how bright the display is on my
Apple PowerBook in a nearly blacked-out city.

I also recall that the Apaches, whose rotor sounds seem to be getting
closer, have thermal imaging. Media or not, sitting outside next to a computer and arrayed satellite modem I will likely draw some suspicion. I think
of the two halves of Hassan Ibrahim Said's body in the morgue. I don't want
to end up the same way.

The chopper passes, but then there is another noise. This one is the high-
pitched whine of an Israeli spy drone. It seems to be working the coastline
behind me and getting closer. I slap down the lid of my PowerBook to kill
the light, but that also kills the transmission. When the sound passes, I have

to reboot the computer and the modem and start all over again. Halfway through the second transmission attempt, I hear the sound again, but this time it is growing really loud. I am sure it has located me. The whine seems lower this time, like it is almost right on top of me.

I push the lid down again, put my hand over the glowing Apple logo and hold my breath. It is so close I can almost feel it against my neck, the buzz filling my ears, louder and louder. I close my eyes and wait for the sound of missile release. It never comes. In fact, the sound whizzes right by me.

My body unclenches; I open my eyes. "Goddammit," I say aloud, and then laugh in release of stress. The "drone" is a late-night motorbike rider passing on the street behind me. By the time I finish transmitting, it is 4:30 A.M. My day will begin all over again at 7:00.

TRAGIC, POLARIZING, MUDDLED

Qana. Here the circumstances seem a fitting representation of this conflict so far—tragic, polarizing and muddled.

Here the war's most poignant images surfaced: the bodies of Lebanese children being pulled from the rubble of a house hit in an Israeli air strike. When my colleague, Jad, and I arrive, one of the Red Cross workers opens the doors to reveal the bodies of five boys ranging in age from five to fifteen. He pulls the blankets back to show the bruised and dusty corpses.

He picks up the body of the smallest one and holds it up for a second to show us. The boy is dressed in green shorts and a white sleeveless t-shirt. Aside from the white dust that covers his body, there are no signs of the blast trauma and falling concrete that likely killed him. His eyes are closed, and the only evidence of his violent death seems to be the slight gritting of his teeth.

By early afternoon a contingent of United Nations soldiers from China arrives in Qana with a large backhoe and, together with a bulldozer from the Lebanese army, begins digging through the piles of heavy concrete and twisted rebar.

It is a slow and frustrating process. Two stories of the three-story building have collapsed completely from the explosion, making a twisted mess not easily pulled apart. After two hours of digging there is still no sign of more bodies.

This house was only one of many buildings bombed in Qana overnight. Driving to the location, I see huge swaths of destruction, including everything from residences and a supermarket to a small mosque.

Under a pile of rubble at the mosque, I pick up a small sign of life, a handwritten note on white lined paper. It is a letter from a local woman telling a man that she doesn't love him because he hasn't shown her respect. Jad reads portions of it aloud as we walk: "Joseph, love alone is not enough for me. I want respect and dignity. We cannot build a future on love alone without trust and understanding and I did not find any of those in you except disrespect and humiliation. . . . You used to be my hope and my dreams but you destroyed all that in one instant . . ."

In another time the letter would seem quite important, at least to the two people involved, but here in this destroyed city, it is just another thing scattered on the streets.

I ask a man at the scene, who calls himself Abbas Kassab and works for Amal, a political party aligned with Hezbollah, why the Israelis would strike Qana. He insists that Hezbollah doesn't operate in the village.

"There's no resistance here. Israel is lying. There are no resistance fighters here. Children are playing, there is no resistance at all," he says. "There was a mother with a seven-month-old child who was killed. Was she a resistance fighter?"

I ask him who he blames for what has happened here.

"America. Only America," he says.

"Why?"

"America gave the green light for Israel to do this. Israel can't shoot one bullet without America's permission. America is responsible. There are no resistance fighters here. Only kids playing. Even if there were, why would they kill civilians? Let them fight in Bint Jbeil, where the resistance is. Let Israel go to Bint Jbeil and see what they can do."

The quick worldwide repercussions of Qana were easy to gauge: condemnation on one side, damage control on the other.

The death of children, like rape and pillage, is a powerful mobilizing force in time of war. This case is no different. It becomes a clarion call for Hezbollah and a moment of regret for Israel.

But the truth, as usual in war, is more complex and more difficult to establish.

After the incident, Hezbollah was accused of using the dead children as props in a campaign to generate backlash against Israel and support for Hezbollah when one of its members, wearing a green helmet, appeared in a photograph holding up the body of a dead boy. The same man appeared in other press photographs in similar poses in places with heavy civilian casualties.

Israel apologized for the mistake but blamed Hezbollah for putting rocket launchers in civilian areas and using women and children as human shields. Rescue workers and villagers initially said that at least fifty people were killed. But I stayed the entire day and saw that no other bodies were removed from the wreckage beyond the initial twenty-five killed.

The number in the wire service reports for the next two days stated that between thirty-eight and fifty were killed. No one tried to correct the numbers on the Lebanese side, but Israel's defenders pointed out the discrepancy as soon as it became apparent.

Still, I wondered, did the final numbers lessen the tragedy by half; conversely, did the initial larger numbers amplify the loss?

Regardless, the numbers, like the images, became issues that journalists had to struggle with as we attempted to report accurately on a war where collateral damage became both an issue and a weapon.

OBJECTIVITY, HUMANITY

After the incident at Qana, Israel says it will suspend air strikes in south Lebanon while it investigates what went wrong there.

For Lebanese trapped by the fighting in frontline cities, this is a chance to dash to safety in the north. For journalists kept on the war's perimeter by the air campaign, this is a chance for us to dash south and see the destruction.

Jad and I hire a driver to take us to Bint Jbeil, the frontline city that has been pounded for two weeks by Israeli air strikes and artillery. When we arrive, we see that Hezbollah flags still fly from nearly every lamppost, at least those that are still standing.

The town center has been pulverized, almost everything reduced to rubble with the exception of a few scattered buildings stripped to their steel and rebar skeletons. Store façades are blown away, exposing interiors of chocolate shops, clothing retailers and jewelry stores with portions of their merchandise seemingly intact, still on hangers or in display cases, the rest scattered along with shards of glass on the ground.

As we walk, videotaping and shooting photographs, something strange happens: people begin to emerge from the rubble.

They trickle out, just a few at a time, mostly too old or too poor to escape, like so many others. They sit on slabs of broken concrete in the middle of their broken town, parched with thirst and bone-rattled to the core by an explosive fury many said they thought would never end.

They are exhausted. Most can't take one more step. The sight of their suffering is too much for even war-hardened journalists to stand by and do nothing.

So, in an unusual twist, the journalists begin to help. They begin guiding the elderly through the rubble to reach ambulances at the bottom of the hill. Some carry the old people in their arms like babies, others in stretchers made from blankets.

A journalist for Britain's *Daily Telegraph* picks up an old man named Mohammed Bazzi, blind and seemingly as frail as a paint chip, and carries him over his shoulders, fireman-style, to the rescue teams below. He stops for a moment to take a rest, holds the old man in his lap like a child, pours a little water on his own hand, softly pats the back of Mohammed's neck to cool him down, all the while saying, "It's OK, Haj," a sign of respect for an older Muslim man.

I carry one old woman piggyback style. Her name is Fatina al-Sayeed Mohammed. She is so weak she can barely keep her arms wrapped around my neck, so another journalist holds them there for her. I feel a little uneasy when another journalist takes a photograph of me carrying Fatina. I didn't want to give the impression that we were taking sides, but it seemed the obvious thing to do. These people were not combatants but civilians—and they were dying.

The photo later ran on the Associated Press wire. While I wish it hadn't been published, seeing it served to remind me of the time I hadn't helped: when I let an old man bleed to death in front of me in Iraq—and just walked on.

I was told by Jad that the old woman, Fatina, lived for three months after the war ended, long enough to see her family again.

THE ROCK, PART II

Back at the school turned refugee shelter in Tyre, I see that the boy with the rock, staring at me, is just waiting for the signal from someone else, to hurl it with all his might at my head.

If it connects, I'm certain it will do damage. This moment should probably not be a revelation for me, but it is. The potential violence I see here, both in this boy and in the women, is obviously deep and generational.

And maybe I am projecting a bit, but it appears disciplined as well. He is holding so far, not throwing. To me, that is control that real anarchy wouldn't allow.

When this war is over, that potential for violence will not go away, but if it can stay disciplined, held back like at this moment—then there is at least as much of a chance that a rock in the hand will be dropped as that it will be thrown.

I watch as the boy loosens his fingers and lets it fall to the ground.

CHAPTER 24

ISRAEL

The Equality of Fear

METULA, ISRAEL | AUGUST 5, 2006

THE BORDER

Theoretically, this is what the whole war is about. The border. The so-called blue line between Israel and Lebanon is, of course, not blue at all, but a double-thick chain-link fence topped with concertina wire.

I learn later that the fence is electric but not electrified. It's an important distinction. Electrified means it will shock me if I touch it. Electric means it has electric sensors attached that will let monitors know when someone tries to climb it, cut it or blast through it.

I just stare at it with my colleague, Haggit, a freelance television producer from Tel Aviv. It is, we both seem to think, somewhat remarkable. On the side where we stand in Metula, Israel, there are groves of green apples and reddish nectarines.

On the Lebanese side there are some bullet-ridden buildings and houses, including one that is now just a pile of rubble. A single, cedar-crested Lebanese flag and two yellow and green Hezbollah flags, hanging from lamp-posts, flap in the strong breeze. A poster of Hezbollah leader Sheik Hassan Nasrallah looks out toward Israel from a pockmarked wall.

Haggit has two brothers in the Israel Defense Forces (IDF): one on active duty fighting inside Lebanon and another in a reserve artillery unit that was called up and is now based here in northern Israel.

"I'm really surprised," she says, "to see those flags flying right on the border."

But this spot, aside from the sound of Israeli artillery and Hezbollah rockets arcing overhead, seems almost completely abandoned.

We can't stop staring as we walk along the fence line. I joke with Haggit that I'll climb over and get her one of the Hezbollah flags as a souvenir. But then we discover climbing won't be necessary. Here, in front of us, is a large gaping hole cut through both fences.

TICKET TO TEL AVIV

I have traveled through Amman's Queen Alia International Airport dozens of times on my way to conflict. It is usually my final stop before heading into the maelstrom of Iraq. Most times the procedure is routine. This time it feels very different.

I have just finished my reporting from south Lebanon and now I am heading to cover the other side of the story, Israel. With so many Lebanese taking refuge from the war in Jordan, anti-Israeli emotions here are particularly high.

Jordan and Israel signed a peace deal in 1994. They have diplomatic relations and until recently, Israeli tourists traveled to Jordan to visit Petra or the Sinai in Egypt. But while Royal Jordanian Airlines still flies to and from Tel Aviv, few Israelis are making the trip, realizing they might be less than welcome.

I knew the process to take this forty-five-minute flight was going to be uncomfortable. Passing through the first security point, the guards always ask where you are going.

"Tel Aviv," I say softly, trying not to arouse the attention of fellow passengers behind me. He just looks at my passport and raises his eyebrows before handing it back to me.

And because of all the technical equipment I carry, I am always yellow-carded by airport security screeners who also ask me where I'm going. While one of the officers goes through my bag, I await the question and what I assume will be a lengthy interrogation and dissection of my gear once I say "Tel Aviv."

But after a cursory shuffling of items from one compartment to another he gets distracted and waves me through; a rare, small gift from the travel gods.

But I still have to pick up my prepaid ticket at the Royal Jordanian ticket counter, so instead of saying my destination I simply hand the woman behind the glass partition my passport and confirmation numbers. After inputting the keystrokes on the computer, she prints out the ticket and finally looks at it.

"Tel Aviv?" she asks loudly. "Tel Aviv!" I just nod once as she tosses the ticket dismissively onto the counter near my open hand.

Thankfully, there are not any incidents at immigration. I walk to my gate and sit with the others waiting to board: a group of Korean Christians and young Israelis returning from a trip to Asia. As I board the plane, the flight attendant looks at me scornfully and will not return my greeting.

After the flight, at Tel Aviv's Ben Gurion Airport, I get flagged for additional questioning at immigration. I knew this would happen, as it usually does here. My American passport is filled with entry and exit visas to Iraq, but because of the mix of civilian and military flights I have taken there, the exit and entry stamps don't match. The Israelis are quick to spot them. After a short question-and-answer session with a more senior officer, I am cleared to go.

RAIN OF ROCKETS

It is the kind of day in Kiryat Shmona when the air raid sirens never seem to stop.

A pall of gray smoke, like low-lying clouds, hangs over the tree lines where Hezbollah Katyusha rockets have just exploded on the hillside.

Unlike the high-velocity Israeli 155 mm rounds whistling into south Lebanon, the Katyusha rockets just stroke the air with a whooshing sound but are no less frightening as they fall into northern Israel.

Today they fell like rain, 160 of them, 66 on this northern town alone.

Despite their numbers they aren't deadly today, causing only two minor injuries, but set ablaze acres of dry grass and bamboo. It burns dangerously close to buildings where a few holdout residents, who have not fled to the south, are still hunkered down.

Firefighters Doron Malol and and Hay Yamin wrestle a hose through the thick brush to wet down a trench line to keep the fire from jumping across the vacant field toward the apartment buildings.

The entire area is covered with heavy smoke and dancing black ash. Flames jump from thrushes of dry bamboo stalks and race in different directions. Malol and Yamin have to cut it off before the whole neighborhood goes up in flames.

"Normally, we'd have two teams on this and we work from both sides and meet in the middle," Malol says, "but we've had six or seven calls already today and the other units are out on different fires—so we have to do it all by ourselves."

The firefighters push deep into the brush, spraying on each side until they can go no farther; the hose running from their truck has reached its full length. Within minutes, another firefighter runs to their location with an extension, which they quickly connect and continue with their mission.

Overhead, a single-engine Piper drops loads of orange fire suppressant over the area. Within an hour of responding to the call, the firefighters have put out much of the blaze and contained the rest. But there will be no break today; as soon as they wrap up their hoses, they head out to another call.

This is the reality of northern Israel now as diplomatic initiatives to end the monthlong war continue with few results.

Like the residents of south Lebanon who have fled north toward Beirut to escape the bombing, most of the people in northern Israel have done the converse, fleeing south toward Tel Aviv. But there are some in small towns like this one who still can't bring themselves to leave. For them, days and nights are spent in concrete bomb shelters located in schools around Kiryat Shmona.

Alice and Abraham Buskila have taken refuge in the bomb shelter of a private religious school for the entire month.

"My husband was in a car accident," says Alice, "and it's too hard to move him around."

Other members of her family are also staying in the shelter with them, including her twenty-nine-year-old son, Shlomi, and her new daughter-in-law, Maya.

KATYUSHA WEDDING

Shlomi and Maya famously married in the shelter two weeks ago when the war didn't end in time as they expected. Instead of hundreds of guests, it was attended by about twenty people, including the mayor of Kiryat Shmona and members of the international media.

I ask Shlomi how he feels about getting married under these conditions.

"If you start out in life on the wrong foot," he tells me, cuddling on a shelter bed with Maya, already three months pregnant, "you'll probably end up on the right foot."

RESERVES

Unlike the regular Israeli army, which has uniform and grooming standards, reserve soldiers, by law, cannot be forced to cut their hair or conform too much. In call-ups like this one, some report for duty in dreadlocks, others in ball caps, as well as those who wear Jewish yarmulkes under their helmets.

Captain Amit Sharan's Battery B is based on an open field near the border. It's made up of men like Max Lieberman, an immigrant from Uzbekistan, whose regular job means hanging from rappelling ropes on high-rise buildings as a window washer. Now, clad in a red bandana and a black-and-white camouflage t-shirt, he runs 155 rounds and charges to the loader in one of the mobile artillery units.

Omer Gazit, thirty, manages a tire business and has plans to get married in two weeks. But at the moment he is in charge of one of the Battery B guns firing volleys of high-explosive shells into south Lebanon.

The wedding will go forward as scheduled, he says, since it would take more than a war to stop the 350 guests already invited. He is only concerned that some of his family, also called up because of the fighting, may not be able to make it.

He has heard about the civilian casualties in Lebanon, but since they have no access to television or the Internet they have not seen any of the images. Still, he believes what they are doing is right.

"It think this is a just war. We withdrew from Lebanon, we withdrew from Gaza, we declared we want to withdraw from the occupied territories. To me this is a just war."

The unit's medic, a twenty-eight-year-old doctoral student in Jewish history named Dotan Arad, was in Lebanon ten years ago as a conscripted soldier during one of the earlier occupations.

He believes the current conflict is more complicated for both sides.

He is also aware of the civilian casualties in Lebanon, specifically the incident at Qana, where twenty-five civilians, the majority of them children, were killed by an Israeli air strike.

"It's sad when I heard about the event at Qana—that is not our goal. I have a lot of Muslim friends. I'm a volunteer in organization of interfaith dialogue," he says. "And I met a young lady from Cairo and she says she believes the IDF has a mission to kill Palestinian kids. But I know this army. These are my friends; we do not do things like that. It's not our goal. Sometimes there are mistakes. But that's not our mission."

Arad says he thinks there is a distinct moral difference in the way the IDF is fighting this war as opposed to Hezbollah.

"They don't try to make any difference," he says, "between civilians and military. They just fire their rockets into cities."

When the reservists in the unit find out that I have just come from Lebanon, they ask me what the Lebanese are feeling about the war.

"Are they mad at Nasrallah?" another soldier, Alon Harel, asks me, thinking that the Lebanese might turn against the Hezbollah leader for bringing so much destruction to Lebanon.

"No, they're mad at you," I tell them, "at least the ones that I've spoken to. Some in Christian neighborhoods in the north were angry with Hezbollah at first, but that seemed to change when you attacked infrastructure in the north, like bridges and roads."

They're surprised and saddened to hear this, wanting to believe that the strategy of punitive strikes against Lebanon might actually drive a wedge between Hezbollah and the Lebanese people. That doesn't seem to have happened, I tell them.

PROPORTIONAL, ASYMMETRICAL

These words, common in diplomatic speak, have a new application in this war.

The first use is in the form of a commonly asked question: is Israel's all-out offensive proportional in response to Hezbollah's killing six IDF soldiers and kidnapping two?

The second use is in the form of a statement: this is an asymmetrical conflict in which a state, Israel, is fighting a conventional war against a guerrilla force, Hezbollah, armed and supplied by other states, Syria and Iran, but which is based in the host state, Lebanon.

These words have particular significance for news organizations covering this conflict as well. For example, is our news coverage response proportional to this asymmetrical conflict? Most large media companies have reporters on both sides of the border simultaneously, allowing them to ping-pong back and forth from one front line to the other. Yahoo! News has only me to cover both, so I must report them one at a time since I am unable, effectively anyway, to step back and forth across the border of each country to follow each violent action and reaction.

The question then becomes, How much time or how many stories for each side?

While I was in Lebanon, many readers responded with seething emails about the "one-sided reporting" from Lebanon. Where was the reporting from the Israeli side? they asked. Similarly, as I began reporting from Israel, readers asked me how I could cover a "grass fire" started by a Katyusha rocket in northern Israel when south Beirut was being turned into rubble.

Surely, there is no question that civilian deaths are equally tragic when caused by Israeli air strikes or Hezbollah rockets, but the real dilemma for myself and other journalists is how to factor the numbers in. Should Lebanon get more coverage because that is where the most deaths and injuries are occurring as well as the majority of structural damage, or does equality in war reporting simply mean putting reporters on both sides of the conflict?

To me, the answer has been elusive and its pursuit dizzying.

It was extremely difficult for me to watch the death and destruction in Lebanon caused by Israeli air strikes and artillery. To see civilians suffering under the destructive power of the world's most high-tech weaponry is not something you can see unmoved.

But now, here in Israel, while the death and destruction is not quantitatively the same as in Lebanon, it is just as easy to understand the fear of ball-bearing-laden Hezbollah Katyusha rockets fired haphazardly at civilian population centers, forcing people, just as in Lebanon, to huddle in shelters or flee to safer ground.

Proportional? Asymmetrical? The terms mean little to the majority of Israelis, who according to most polls supported the offensive against Hezbollah, even though they did not expect it to unfold like this.

"We are fighting for the survival of Israel," Sam Seidner, the father of a wounded Israeli soldier, tells me later at a hospital in Haifa. "When have the Jews ever felt secure?"

EMERGENCY CALL-UP ORDER 8

It is a sentiment I hear over and over throughout Israel, whether talking to civilians, soldiers or those who, at this moment of conflict, happen to be both.

"Emergency Call-Up Order 8—this is a rare animal that is both particu-

lar and peculiar to Israeli society," says Lior Taylor, a major in the IDF reserves, talking about the summons that took him from his job and family
and sent him to war in Lebanon—for the second time.

"It's understood," he tells me from his base just across the border from
Lebanon, "they don't use this for superfluous reasons. If you get one, the
gravity of it makes the switch for you."

For thirty-eight-year-old Taylor, that switch had to come fast. He is one of
the operations officers for the IDF's 609th Reserve Infantry, a unit that has
already seen plenty of action in south Lebanon, reportedly killing sixty Hezbollah fighters and capturing ten, so far without losing a single soldier of
its own.

On the roof of the operations center, covered with machine-gun and 40
mm grenade shell casings, we look across the valley into south Lebanon.
Taylor points out a pile of rubble on the hilltop in Lebanon, directly across
from us. It has an Israeli flag flying above it. He says it used to be a Hezbollah
command post that they destroyed when the fighting broke out. They placed
the flag there as a bit of triumphalism. He says he went to Lebanon for the
first time in 1986, just four years after Israel invaded in an attempt to destroy
Yasser Arafat's Palestine Liberation Organization.

Taylor says the terrain is the same but the dangers have changed. He
says Hezbollah has some of the best weaponry in the world, including
American-made antitank TOW missiles.

"It's complicated," Taylor tells me from personal experience. "It's not
army-versus-army warfare. They do have an organized fighting doctrine,
but it's not based on making contact. It's more guerrilla warfare tactics. They
want to draw you into an area where they have booby traps and they can use
their antitank missiles."

Those antitank missiles have been blamed for the bulk of IDF ground
force casualties in south Lebanon, as Hezbollah fighters used them against
tanks, but also against the houses and buildings where IDF soldiers took
shelter.

Taylor says the one tactical area where the IDF has been particularly effective is also the area where it has been the most criticized; attacks on villages where it believes Hezbollah supplies are stockpiled.

"The villages are used as logistic bases," he says, "but they usually fight from bunkers in outlying areas. They have tunnel systems with camouflaged entry points where they can enter in one place and exit somewhere else. We've been fairly successful at cutting off the supplies from the villages. Which forces them to come out eventually."

The way to fight them, he says, is to outlast them in a war of nerves.

"The name of the game is patience," says Taylor. "You have to be methodical, moving forward slowly, and see who makes the first mistake—then capitalize on it."

At this base in western Galilee, reserve soldiers rack out on the floor of the operations center, catching some sleep between missions. Others play cards outside or, like soldiers all over the world, sit around smoking cigarettes and talking about their lives back home.

A month into the offensive, and Taylor himself looks tired and war weary.

He has left a wife and three children back home in Haifa and a job with a multinational company for combat missions in the hills of south Lebanon and "hot-racking," sleeping in shifts on whatever cot is available, when he is back at base.

He believes the sacrifices are essential for the preservation of Israel.

"This is like a test case," Taylor says. "They interpret an open society as a weak society. Our response has to be definitive."

He pauses for a moment, becoming circumspect. "If there's one thing that pains me about all this, it's the fate of the Lebanese people. Medieval-thinking forces have dragged them into this. If they could be masters of their own destiny, I know there would be peace. But instead of progress and enlightenment these forces drag the Lebanese into darkness."

KIBBUTZ FUNERAL

At the Nachsolim Kibbutz, on a small hilltop under an elm tree, Ya'ar Ben-Giat, a nineteen-year-old soldier, is being laid to rest. He was killed in south

Lebanon along with twenty-four other soldiers from the Israel Defense Forces in the worst single day of fatalities for Israel since its monthlong offensive began.

And in an irony befitting this conflict filled with tragic missteps, these deaths occurred while both Israel and Hezbollah intensified their fighting, trying to strengthen their positions prior to a United Nations–brokered cease-fire that will kick in on Monday. Despite the sadness of the occasion, it is a beautiful and serene place to be buried, only a few hundred yards from the gently breaking waves of the Mediterranean.

In the late afternoon, family and friends begin to gather at the kibbutz. Ben-Giat's unit is still fighting in south Lebanon, but many of his friends from basic training have come to pay their respects; they are young men and women, barely out of high school, dressed in the olive green uniforms and light green berets of the Israel Defense Forces Infantry.

There is, I learn from Haggit, an iconic dimension to the death of a young soldier in Israel. Countless films have been made here romanticizing the sense of sacrifice and loss as well as the concept of the young soldier now made ageless for the rest of time. I can't help but think of how similar it is in some ways to the mythology I witnessed in Iran toward its own war martyrs, with their young images frozen in time, carved into the stone slabs covering their graves.

Patricio Weinberg, a soldier in Ben-Giat's basic training unit, was one of his closest friends.

"I was talking to him on the telephone about a week ago," he says. "We were saying how after a few years we would move to a big city and maybe open up a pub." He pauses, his eyes welling up with tears.

One by one, wreaths of flowers are laid over the casket draped with the Israeli flag. There is a wreath from the IDF, from the Northern Command, from Ben-Giat's Nachal Brigade, then from his battalion, as well as the kibbutz and other civilian organizations, family and personal friends. Soon the casket disappears under the pile of flowers.

"God full of mercy sitting high above," says the rabbi presiding over the ceremony, "please give him rest."

As the ceremony continues, the air raid sirens begin to blare and within moments there is a muffled explosion on a distant ridgeline followed by a rising plume of gray smoke. Mourners turn toward the impact, one of 250 Katyusha rockets that Hezbollah will fire into northern Israel this day, killing one man.

They point and murmur among themselves, forgetting the funeral for a moment. Many pull cell phones from their purses or pockets, calling their children, friends or relatives, telling them to go to the bomb shelters. Eventually, they turn back to the ceremony and a popular song for troubled times is played over the loudspeakers. It's a small prayer for peace.

It's not a dream the day shall come. The day for which we've waited 2,000 years has arrived. The last war. We will go back home. We will go back to our friends. We will take off our olive-colored uniforms and wait for other days to come.

When the funeral ends, there is no twenty-one-gun salute, which would be traditional. Some say it would not be wise during a time when there is already so much gunfire.

THE PEOPLE THAT SUFFER

In Haifa, after the cease-fire has gone into effect, I meet an Arab Israeli named Haj Assad in a park. Assad is a plumber and has brought his two daughters out to play after they have been cooped up inside for more than a month out of fear of Hezbollah's Katyusha rockets, which twice landed in their neighborhood.

"When we heard the air raid sirens we tried to take shelter under the stairs," he says, "but we never even made it. We didn't have any damage, but the whole house trembled."

He says Israel has a right to defend itself but should not have started a war over the two soldiers. He says he, like so many others in his neighborhood, has relatives in Lebanon.

I ask him how his neighborhood reacted to the images of the destruction in Lebanon and of civilian casualties, specifically the pictures of the children killed at Qana by the Israeli air strike.

"Anyone would be angry at that," he says, "whether you are Jewish or Arab—these are horrible things. It's a tragedy no matter who you are. People can see that Arabs don't have green blood; we are the same."

While he sits at the table, his six-year-old daughter, Sally, comes to him crying loudly and itching her arms and legs. Assad cradles her in his arms and calms her down.

"She's allergic to grass," he explains, holding her tightly.

"Is Sheik Hassan Nasrallah [the leader of Hezbollah] popular in your neighborhood?" I ask. His answer surprises me with its simple, penetrating insight.

"It's not about Sheik Nasrallah," he says. "He is a leader and like other leaders, like those in the Israeli government, they make decisions away from the people without really thinking about them. The people are only abstractions to them. But when you start a war it's really the people that suffer."

THE HOLE

Back on the border, the opening in the fence is the rabbit hole I cannot resist. It's not some kind of danger dilettante's thrill for me, but just the niggling concept that I had reported the war on that side of the border only a few days earlier, so why did I have to be kept on some arbitrary dividing line now? Perhaps by crossing the border, I rationalize to myself, there might be a clue to finding that elusive sense of balance necessary to cover this conflict fairly and objectively.

But as I crawl through I begin to wonder if this is a wise choice. Hezbollah could have easily left snipers in some of the surrounding buildings, or maybe an IDF patrol could mistake me for a guerrilla fighter carrying a rocket-propelled grenade launcher rather than a digital camera.

I walk along the rubble feeling vulnerable, but also exactly in the middle, no longer bound by the physical constraints of being on one side or the other. In the short period of time I am in this no-man's-land, I don't find much, except for a strangely fitting piece of grafitti on a wall next to a pile of rubble. In English, with a missing vowel, it reads: "T B or not To B."

Regardless of the writer's intent, it is a question with which both Lebanon and Israel grapple. Can Israel survive, surrounded by hostile enemies like Hezbollah just on the other side of the fence? Can Lebanon's fragile democracy survive, beset by internal divisions over Hezbollah and external forces like the Israeli military?

Perhaps in this conflict, that's where the balance might finally be found, in an equality of fear.

PART VII

MY THIRD-WORLD AMERICA

A Wealth of Information,
a Poverty of Knowledge

CHAPTER 25

COMING HOME

Dreams, Death and the Hardest Truth

SOUTHERN CALIFORNIA | MARCH 20, 2007

DREAMS

It is perhaps the most penetrating question I have ever been asked. It's a Tuesday night in March, and I'm talking to journalism students at the University of Southern California about the Hot Zone project.

I have been home for six months now, and my reentry to "normal" life has been less dramatic than I imagined. I have been writing this book, reporting stories for an upcoming Yahoo! project and giving presentations, like this one, to journalism students and professionals around the country.

I am prepared for all the usual questions: what equipment did I use, where did I sleep, what did I eat—even a few deeper questions about the personal toll the journey had on me. But I am not prepared for this one:

"What do you dream about?" a very tall, earnest-looking guy asks me.

He catches me off balance, both for the perceptive nature of the question and because of the vivid dream I just had last night, one so disturbing I had to write it down.

I think for a moment about how much I should reveal in front of a group of strangers on a topic I have never discussed in public. I decide that if he is bold enough to ask, I should be bold enough to answer. So I do.

"This is the dream I had last night," I tell them.

I am in the woods somewhere and there are lots of people around. It reminds me of my brother's farm in Virginia. Is it a hunt? It seems that way. A large buck comes loping up to us in a clearing. It has been shot, but I can only see one side of its head. When I look on the other side, I can see that half of its brain has been blown away. It staggers and falls to the ground.

Someone says it needs to be put out of its misery. Maybe I should do it. We look for a gun but cannot find one. I have two handguns in a black bag near the steps to my brother's house. But the bag is open and someone has kicked dirt into it by accident.

The dirt has gotten into the guns as well. I pull out my Springfield XD 9 mm and the ammo that was in the bag. I load the weapon and walk up to the deer, but now the deer has become a black-haired man with a mustache and wearing a white t-shirt.

The others in my group are pulling up a clear plastic tarp in front of him to keep the blood from splattering all over. I point my pistol at him, but I can see him distorted from behind the plastic. He is stretching out one of his hands, trying to tell me to stop. In the dream, I know he has changed from the deer to a man, but I still think the objective is the same. I need to shoot him.

It is clear, though, he does not want to be shot. I ignore his out-stretched hand and I am trying to pull the trigger, but the trigger pull feels very stiff, very hard to fire.

When I finally do succeed, there is only a click. The gun has jammed. When I slide back the action, I find three large rounds all packed in different directions in the chamber. It's a mess.

Also, they are long and thin, more like 7.62 rounds for an AK-47, rather than stumpy 9 mm rounds. It is the wrong ammunition. They are also maroon-colored and feel like plastic dummy rounds, rather than real shells.

The man/deer that I was pointing the pistol at now slumps back on his arms. The others tell me to shoot again, but now I see that this is a man, not a deer, and he does not want to be killed.

THIRD-WORLD AMERICA

I know I have some issues, but they were somewhat mitigated by a scuba-diving detour I took with my girlfriend to the Micronesian islands of Palau and Yap after the Israel-Hezbollah cease-fire. It was there that I lost myself temporarily in the silence of deep blue waters, the warring world left on the surface that we dove under, among the graceful shadows of giant manta rays.

I believe I could have been happy never to resurface, but eventually your air runs out and you have to come up.

When we finally did, my baggage was waiting for me there; the heaviest was a growing self-righteous contempt for the almost willful ignorance that American citizens have about the rest of the planet.

We have unparalleled access to information, yet on the most important matters of our responsibility as global citizens, we live in information poverty. America is a third-world nation in its per capita knowledge of the people, issues and events outside its borders.

One of the reasons I wanted to do the Hot Zone project was to help educate the American public about places they barely knew existed. My expectations were unrealistic, but when it ended and there was no miraculous wellspring of newly aware Americans, I felt defeated—then angry. It has yet to subside.

That anger sometimes manifests itself in strange, vulnerable ways. I find myself shouting at television commentators about their simplification and misrepresentations of war. I become enraged to see that we have so lost the connecting synapses between reality and fiction that we have to petition the producers and writers of TV dramas like *24* to throttle back the torture scenes a bit—lest we give our troops any more ideas (beyond our own practices of rendition and suspension of habeas corpus through the Military Commissions Act).

I yell at politicians, both Republicans and Democrats, who voted to approve the war in Iraq, then simplemindedly blame the Iraqis for not doing enough to clean up the mess we made.

I find myself dismissive of those who say they have followed my journey but look at me blankly when I speak of any conflict other than Iraq and Afghanistan. I would prefer to speak of the weather or Britney Spears shaving her head rather than endure another monologue by folks on the right or left whose sum total of foreign news knowledge is culled from Fox's Bill O'Reilly or Comedy Central's Jon Stewart (though at least Stewart knows that what he does is pretend news).

Ever since I began covering conflict (the first time in 1986 while the United States was trying to overthrow the Nicaraguan Sandinista government, tasking Marine Lieutenant Colonel Oliver North to covertly arm and fund rebel Contras), some of the supercharged emotions of these experiences seep out at night.

The nightmares are impressionistic and metaphorical, rarely literal representations of the things I have witnessed. For instance, I have never specifically dreamed of the mosque shooting, though the impressions will never leave my memory.

When the nightmares do come, they are usually in the form of supernatural demons, and their purpose is not to harm me but rather someone I care about. My terror is not being able to stop it. I never can. As the demon gets closer and closer to my loved ones, I am frozen in place, I can't move my arms, legs or even my tongue. I am desperately trying to say "stop," but all that emerges from my lungs is a primitive, guttural noise—enough to wake me up and end the dream.

MY COMPLICITY

I hadn't thought about it for the longest time, perhaps because I didn't want to know the truth myself, but early in 2006, I was seized with an unshakable dread on a plane ride from Doha, Qatar, to Amman, Jordan. It concerned my own complicity in the possible death of a man. I pulled out my laptop and wrote this down:

> *1.09.06*
> *Whatever became of the man who talked to me after the [mosque]*
> *shooting? Why didn't I stay and make sure he was transported some-*

where (he was a witness)? These are things I'm even afraid to write down. Did I do any of the right things in that mosque, let alone at all? Intentions are everything; the result is only the result, what was in my heart? Those moments that you wish you had a lifetime to think about, but it's only their consequences that you live with forever. The decision takes but a moment.

The man whom I was writing about on the plane was the young insurgent under the blanket who tried to talk with me after the mosque shooting.

TALEB SALEM NIDAL

His name was Taleb Salem Nidal, and like the four other insurgents, he had been wounded during the initial Friday afternoon battle at the Falluja mosque but was left behind by the Marines only to be attacked again the next day, even though they had already surrendered and were unarmed.

I had seen him and videotaped him that Friday afternoon. He was lying next to a large pillar on a red blanket. He had only a superficial wound to his hand and upper left thigh, which had been bandaged.

The next day, Nidal covered himself with that red blanket while the Marine lance corporal executed another insurgent, Farhan Abd Mekelf, just a few feet away from him, captured on my video.

Nidal pulled the blanket from his face after the Marine who fired the shot walked away. I went over to Nidal after confronting the lance corporal and videotaped him while he tried to speak to me.

He was the only insurgent not fired on again when the lance corporal made his sweep of the mosque on Saturday. Since he spoke in Arabic, I couldn't understand what he was saying without an interpreter. Later, after the video was translated, I found out what Taleb Salem Nidal was trying to tell to me.

Yesterday I was shot ... Please ... Yesterday I was shot over there ... And I talked to all of you on the camera. Yesterday over

here . . . I am one of the guys from this whole group . . . I gave
you information . . . Speak Arabic? Because I want to give you
information.

ANOTHER MURDER

At the time, I felt confused. Maybe I should stay with him, but I also believed I had to get a response from Lieutenant Colonel Willy Buhl, the commanding officer of the 3.1 Marines, concerning the shooting I had just
witnessed.

The field HQ for the 3.1 was several miles away, and there was a Humvee
headed in that direction. I got on it and, in doing so, left Taleb Salem Nidal
to be murdered.

I wouldn't know this for certain until three years and two months after it
happened.

In November, a month after I returned home from the Hot Zone project,
I made a Freedom of Information Act request for the Naval Criminal Investigative Service (NCIS) report concerning the mosque shooting. NCIS is in
charge of investigating suspected cases of criminal wrongdoing concerning
U.S. Navy or Marine personnel and handled the mosque shooting case.

The report arrived in January 2007 at my Yahoo! News office. It was four
hundred pages long, the size of a Los Angeles phone book. I sat down and
began reading immediately. Much was blacked out for privacy or purported
national security reasons, but I could follow the depositions of all the Marines involved, as well as my own.

There was so much that I didn't know, so much that I hadn't been aware
of—even though I had been a central player in the entire event. The lance
corporal who shot Farhan Abd Mekelf had also admitted to shooting two
other insurgents in the mosque prior to that.

The lance corporal, who was from a sniper platoon attached to India
Company of the 3.1 Marines, says he entered the mosque, fired a round
from his M-16, which jammed, then drew his 9 mm Beretta pistol and fired
it into two of the three wounded, unarmed insurgents before clearing his
jammed rifle.

When I arrived in the mosque a few minutes later, the same lance corporal says he saw Mekelf move, like he was reaching for something. I was only twenty feet away and saw no movement aside from Mekelf's breathing. That is when the lance corporal raised his M-16, peered down the scope (although the muzzle was no more than three feet away) and fired.

According to the report, Mekelf and one of the other insurgents had cards identifying them as members of the Iraqi Police; the ID cards had been processed by the First Marine Expeditonary Force.

In the report, the NCIS investigator notes that the lance corporal was bothered by what happened after he pulled the trigger.

> *[Blacked out] reported the results of the gunshot wound to V/Mekelf's head disturbed him. [Blacked out] had never been that close to a person during a firefight and the severity of the wound was unexpected. . . . When asked to review a copy of the videotape [blacked out] indicated that he did not want to observe the shooting again as the wound disturbed him and he was trying to get it out of his mind. [Blacked out] stated he believed any Marine would have acted in the same manner if they had been in the same position.*

And then I came to it on page 195. I got a deep and hollow pit in my stomach. The report read:

> *A fourth AIF [Anti-Iraqi force or insurgent] Taleb Salem Nidal, who spoke and appeared injured in the videotape, was found deceased several hours later.*

I had to make another request to the Armed Forces Institute of Pathology to get the autopsy report on Nidal. When it arrived, I discovered that Nidal had been shot twenty-three times after I left. Almost all of the entry wounds were in his back—execution style. A bullet fragment recovered from his knee was 5.56 caliber, the same type of standard-issue ammo carried by U.S. soldiers and Marines. The bodies of the other insurgents were also sprayed with bullets, one fifteen times, another ten—though the autopsy results show they were probably already dead after being fired on for the third time following their surrender.

What is certain is that Taleb Salem Nidal was very much alive when I left the mosque. There is little doubt that a Marine or Marines killed the only living Iraqi witness to all that had occurred inside that mosque.

The report states, however, *"The involvement of US/Coalition troops in the death of Nidal remains unresolved."*

In another section it states, *"This investigation is pending additional interviews in an attempt to clarify the circumstances of the death of Nidal."* Later, a friend who speaks Arabic will point out another aspect to the story that I had not realized; the irony behind the meaning of Taleb Salem Nidal's name.

Taleb means "asker" or "seeker," *salem* means "safe" or "safety" and *nidal* translates to "struggle." When I was speaking to him in the mosque, Taleb Salem Nidal was seeking safety in the struggle, but because I was preoccupied with the shooting I had just recorded and unmindful of the dangers he still faced, he found only death.

According to the NCIS report, five days after the shootings the entire mosque was destroyed by a Marine air strike. The NCIS says the investigation scene was "degraded" by the attack. The Marines say it was not an attempt to cover up evidence. Five months later, Major General Richard Natonski, commanding general of the First Marine Division, will decide that the lance corporal's actions inside the mosque were "consistent with the established rules of engagement for the armed conflict." He will not be charged.

It raises questions for me about what the actual rules of engagement for Falluja were, or were orders to abide by the laws of land warfare and the rules of the Geneva Convention simply followed up with a wink by commanding officers? Also, did Natonski's decision send a message to other Marines in his division that they could get away with murder?

A year later, in November 2005, members of the Third Battalion, First Regiment, Kilo Company, will be involved in the killing of as many as two dozen Iraqi civilians in the town of Haditha, after a fellow Marine was killed by a roadside bomb. Later, eight will be charged in the biggest U.S. criminal case of civilian deaths to come out of the war.

In July 2007 there will be yet another report, alleging that members of 3.1 Kilo Company executed between five and ten unarmed Iraqi captives during the 2004 battle of Falluja—three days before the killings in the mosque.

Now, almost two and a half years after the shooting, as I read the report, I am sick with my own stupidity for not staying in the mosque with Nidal or taking him with me back to battalion headquarters. The decisions I made directly contributed to his murder and probably the ease with which the entire incident was made to disappear.

But why should anyone care about the death of an Iraqi insurgent, someone who probably fought and may have killed American soldiers or Marines? Perhaps because being true to our ideals means doing the right thing consistently during the most morally difficult moments—like war.

I think back to the interview I did with the 3.1's commanding officer, Willy Buhl, just a day or so before the Battle of Falluja. In it, he made the "we're the good guys" speech:

> *We're the good guys. We are Americans. We are fighting a gentleman's war here—because we don't behead people, we don't come down to the same level of the people we're combating. And that's a very difficult thing for a young eighteen-year-old Marine…*

It is so sadly and perfectly ironic. Whether he believed it or not, none of it, I realize now, is true—except the "difficult" part.

There are few good guys in this war—or in the majority I have seen.

LOSING OUR HUMANITY

In conflict everyone, whether they are invading forces, government troops, rebels or insurgents, even journalists who help perpetuate the myth of war, has chosen violence over diplomacy, guns over statecraft, and when that happens we all lose a little bit of our humanity with every casualty.

In this case, as Americans, we have failed our ideals. Some will say the only way to win in this kind of war is to fight the way "they" do.

If that is the case, if we decide to continue to accept the practices of rendition, torture and summary executions of our enemies, we have already lost.

At the end of this journey, I wish I could say I am more optimistic, more hopeful. But I am not. I have seen the good in people and their resilience, but our violent nature is a formidable opponent.

It feeds on the myths and lies we tell ourselves about war, that it is about the armies and the combatants, when truly, it is about the destruction of civil life; not just innocent people but our ideals and our humanity. The only hope may come from preserving and sharing the truth.

WHAT DID I LEARN?

When my year in the Hot Zone was over, the numbers looked like this:

- 368 days (from departure to final return home)
- 71 airplanes
- 30 countries (traveled)
- 21 conflicts (reported) (Rwanda not included in this book)
- 1,320 still photos posted
- 153 text stories written
- 131 video stories produced

But more important than the numbers—what had I actually learned from my year at war? Was there a cohesive picture that emerged from all the fragments of places, people and stories I had collected?

When I started the journey, I hoped some kind of "truth" would rise to the surface for me at its end, both obvious and indisputable. It was an unrealistic expectation but, surprisingly, it did. And it was this:

War poses as combat but is really collateral damage.

From East Bukavu to West Beirut, societies are encouraged by their leaders to romanticize warriors and their weapons, emphasizing the sacrifice of the soldier, rebel or martyr—while avoiding thoughts of the legacy of civil destruction they also bring.

What I learned from my repeated, consecutive exposure to these conflicts was that the actual fighting between armed groups is a small and infrequent element, while the violence they radiate on civil society and themselves will last for generations.

For example, a study by the International Rescue Committee found that for every one combat-related death in the Democratic Republic of the Congo, there are sixty-two noncombat deaths related to the fighting, such as disease from living in overcrowded refugee camps, starvation from loss of farmable lands or the absence of wage earners conscripted into armed groups.

But the evidence of war as collateral damage goes beyond the civilian death toll and destruction of economic infrastructure—it extends to the mental and physical health care burdens for the members of a conflict-traumatized society: victims of land mines and sexual violence; child soldiers; and alcohol, drug addiction and domestic abuse problems associated with returning veterans. Almost as soon as they leave the battlefield, combatants become victims, too.

To have a remote chance of lessening the perpetual cycle of global conflict, we must first learn how to reject the myths and propaganda, seeing war not in its short pose of epic drama but in its long reality of civil destruction.

It will take commitment, as Rev. Martin Luther King, Jr., said during his Nobel Prize lecture of December 1964 on the threshold of a major U.S. military escalation in Vietnam, "It is not enough to say, 'We must not wage war.' It is necessary to love peace and sacrifice for it."

ACKNOWLEDGMENTS

Special thanks to these local fixers, humanitarian groups and conflict information sources who made our coverage possible:

Afghanistan	Haroon Khadim
	Ahmad Ahmadi
Cambodia	Bon Thim
Chechnya	Bella Tochieva
Colombia	Ignacio Gómez
	Scott Dalton
DR Congo	Amani Matabaro Tom
Gaza	Sami Abu
Haiti	Paul Christian Namphy
Indonesia	Mila Wati
	Mohammed Rinaldi
Iran	Darius Anvari
	Ibrahim Mahmoudi
Northern Iraq	Mohammed Jalizada
	Tofiq Abdol
Israel	Haggit Erez
Kashmir	Dar Yasin
Kenya	Frank Liang Fan
Lebanon	Jad Melki
	Ali Dia
	Henri Ghantou

Myanmar	Thuza Win
	Nyaw Nyaw Simon
Nepal	Dinesh Wagle
Somalia	Duguf Farah
Sri Lanka	Sarath Gamini
	Rodney Perera
Syria	Rhonda Roumani
	Nawara Mahfoud
Vietnam	Quynh Huong
IRC, South Sudan	Richard Haselwood
	Julie Steiger
IRC, Chechnya	Mike Young
IRC, DR Congo	Xavier Bardou
IRC, New York	Melissa Winkler
IRC	*www.theirc.org*
Save the Children	*www.savethechildren.org*
Save the Children, Jordan/Lebanon	Dennis Walto
International Institute for Strategic Studies	*www.iiss.org*
International Crisis Group	*www.crisisgroup.org*
BBC	*http://news.bbc.co.uk*
Information International	*www.information-international.com*

ACKNOWLEDGMENTS

First and foremost, my deep gratitude to Lloyd Braun for having the heart to greenlight the Hot Zone project, to Joel Behr for having the idea, to my sister Shawn for connecting us and all her support, to Scott Moore for having the faith to keep us going, to Neil Budde for backing us every step.

Without my Hot Zone "mission control team" this project had every opportunity to lose its focus, direction and momentum. They kept "it" and me circling the globe: Senior Producer Robert Padavick, Producer Erin Green,

Researcher Lisa Liu, Travel Coordinator Farah Ravon, Documentary and Special Segments Director Jeff Porter and Editor Steve Neilson. Also, thanks to Jessica Young, researcher and writer of this book's Conflict Appendix.

My respect and thanks to Judea and Ruth Pearl for believing that our project in some way mirrored their son Daniel's work, to Christine Egger and Najla Osseira and her students for caring enough to actually help the people they read about on the Hot Zone, Yubaraj and Gulsoma.

Cheers to all the folks at Yahoo! who helped get us started and keep us going, including: News: Neeraj Khemlani, Ezra Palmer, Peter Roybal, Ron Parsons and the full coverage team. Design: Paco Vinoly, Josh Payton, Jimmy Santos and Yun Woo. Legal: Oren Katzeff, Rick Danis, Roshanna Sabaratnam. Public Relations and Marketing: Tanya Singer, Brian Nelson, Charlene Fitzgibbon, Karin Timpone, Christina Bohling, Eric Mai, Alexandra Bresnan. Engineering: Seth Bertalotto, Jeff Boulter, George Diaz, Gary Tauscher. Video Production: Matt Smith, Jon Brick, Ben Heffner, Darlene DeVries, Russell Lee, Paul Neumann, Dorian Robinson.

Thanks to the Lavin Agency for its support: David Lavin, Tom Gagnon, Sally Itterly, Dave Twombly, Johnny Perna, Ruth Weaver, Vera Wong, Katie Thomson, Natalie Van Dine.

Much appreciation to these colleges, universities and learning institutions for asking me to share my journey with them: my alma mater, Northwestern University, Medill School—Dean John Lavine, David Nelson; USC, Annenberg School—Patricia Dean; Columbia University—Asst. Dean Elizabeth Fishman, Sree Sreenivasan; UC Berkeley—Lanita Pace-Hinton, Paul Grabowicz; SUNY New Paltz—Bruno Battistoli; Johnson and Wales University—Deb Ridolfi; Akron-Summitt Public Library—Bob Ethington; West Virginia University, Reed SOJ—Dean Maryanne Reed; Delta College—Nancy Vader-McCormick; California Institute of Technology—Rosalyn Sayaman; Illinois Wesleyan University—Jean Kerr; and the United States Military Academy—Superintendent Lieutenant General William Lennox, Commandant Brigadier General Curtis Scaparrotti.

My thanks to these colleagues, who have supported my work, given me opportunities, shared sources, taught me something, defended my reputation or helped me in the field: Darrin Mortenson, Kimberly Dozier, Fred Francis, Babak Behnam, Karl Bostic, John Zito, Doug Adams, Scott Peterson, Brian Williams, Danny Noa, David Verdi, Levon Sevunts, Bill Skinner and Ricki Goldberg.

My appreciation to those who first helped get me into the blogosphere: Richard Murphy, Xeni Jardin, John Parres and David Ulevitch (whose generosity allows me to keep a permanent online archive).

Much gratitude to my editors, John Williams and Amy Baker, to my copyeditor, Thomas Pitoniak, and the Harper Perennial team for supporting "difficult" journalism: Carrie Kania, David Roth-Ey, Jennifer Hart, Dori Carlson, Rachel Elinsky.

And a very special thanks to all of these special people who had faith in my purpose and pushed me forward: my pop for his emails, my mom for her prayers, my brother, Tim, for his "open" letter, my sister, Kathy, and her family for the distracting laughter. Finally, to Caitlin, for being strong enough to say good-bye more than anyone ever should. You are a rare, beautiful and undeserved gift.

Please remember and continue to support the work of **Marla Ruzicka**, fearless voice of compassion and founder of Campaign for Innocent Victims in Conflict (CIVIC), killed by a suicide bomb in Iraq, April 16, 2005.

CIVIC: *www.civicworldwide.org*

WEB SITES

Kevin Sites in the Hot Zone
http://hotzone.yahoo.com

Kevin Sites Blog (archive)
www.kevinsites.net

People of the Web
http://potw.news.yahoo.com

COMMENTS OR SUGGESTIONS?

ksinhz@hotmail.com

APPENDIX A

OPEN LETTER TO THE DEVIL DOGS OF THE 3.1

The following is one of the early, unabridged versions of my "Open Letter to the Devil Dogs of the 3.1." It is not the final version which appeared on kevinsites.net on November 28, 2004—but I include it here because I believe it is more raw than the original and may provide a fuller context.

Devil Dogs of the 3.1:

I'm getting about 500 hate emails a day. Most expressing admiration and support for the Corps—and outrage that I could "betray" you by shooting and airing a video showing one of your own firing a round into the head of a wounded and unarmed insurgent.

I've been called traitor, scumbag, asshole, dirtbag, leech, money- and fame-grubbing, Al-Qaeda-loving, enemy-abetting, liberal media whore.

Many of the people behind these emails posed reasonable questions along with their anger, accusations and outrage about why this video was aired on television. They deserve answers and explanations, as do you.

To those who proudly expressed racist hatred cloaked in patriotic and religious justifications—I'm satisfied to let them warm themselves next to the burning crosses of their own ignorance.

Some threatened my family. I'm sure they would love the chance to go after my wife or children or torch my home—if any of those things existed.

I gave up all of that in order to do this job. As some of you know, I have spent more time in combat than many of the soldiers and Marines I've spent the last three years covering.

I wish I were still on the frontlines of Falluja with you. Sharing your crappy MREs, listening to your goofy running dialogues about POGs (people other than grunts) and pampered movie stars who pretend to do on the screen what you do in real life, seeing pictures of your wives and girlfriends, learning about the hardships you've endured in your young lives, hearing what you're going to do once you get back home.

What I miss most is that bond under fire. The surreal moments in the Humvee, like when Frey has ducked out of the Mark 19 turret for a moment and is leaning back against Bevins, cracking jokes while sniper rounds whiz by us. Wolf is complaining about how everyone else has it so easy back in the real world and Bejarn is behind the wheel, as always, just soaking it all up—probably still worrying about how Burns is doing back in Germany after he got hit by a sniper round in the midst of heavy fighting on Elizabeth Street the first day in Falluja.

To share a war zone together and then quickly, after the incident in the mosque, to be gone—it's a difficult physical and psychological whiplash.

We didn't get a chance to talk about what happened. But I want you to hear from me, in my own words, what I saw—without imposing on that Marine—guilt or innocence or something in between.

I want you to know about the process I had to go through as a journalist to fulfill my obligations—not to NBC or the media as a whole, but to the truth.

I want you to make up your own minds about whether you think what I did was right or wrong. All the other armchair analysts don't mean a damn to me.

Here it goes.

It's Saturday morning and we're still at our strong point from the night before, a clearing between a set of buildings on the southern edge of the city. The advance has been swift, but pockets of resistance still exist. In fact, we're taking sniper fire from both the front and the rear.

Weapons Company uses its 81s (mortars) where they spot muzzle flashes. The tanks do some blasting of their own. By mid-morning, we're told we're moving north again. We'll be back clearing some of the area we passed yesterday. There are also reports that the mosque, where ten insurgents were killed and five wounded on Friday, may have been reoccupied overnight.

I decide to leave you guys and pick up with one of the infantry squads as they move house-to-house back toward the mosque. (For their own privacy and protection I will not name or identify, in any way, any of those I was traveling with during this incident.)

Many of the structures are empty of people—but full of weapons. Outside one residence, a member of the squad lobs a frag grenade over the wall. Everyone piles in, including me.

But while the Marines go into the house, I follow the flames caused by the grenade into the courtyard. When the smoke clears, I can see through my viewfinder that the fire is burning beside a large pile of antiaircraft rounds.

I yell to the lieutenant that we need to move. Almost immediately after clearing out of the house, small explosions begin as the rounds cook off in the fire.

At that point, we hear the tanks firing their 240-machine guns into the mosque. There's radio chatter that insurgents inside could be shooting back. The tanks cease fire and we file through a breach in the outer wall.

We hear gunshots from what seems to be coming from inside the mosque. A Marine from my squad yells, "Are there Marines in here?"

When we arrive at the front entrance, we see that another squad has already entered before us.

The lieutenant asks them, "Are there people inside?" One of the Marines raises his hand signaling five.

"Did you shoot them," the lieutenant asks.

"Roger that, sir," the same Marine responds.

"Were they armed?" The Marine just shrugs, and we all move inside.

Immediately after going in, I see the same black plastic body bags spread around the mosque. The dead from the day before. But more surprising, I see the same five men that were wounded from Friday as well. It appears that one of them is now dead and three are bleeding to death from new gun-shot wounds.

The fifth is partially covered by a blanket and is in the same place and condition he was in on Friday, near a column. He has not been shot again. I look closely at both the dead and the wounded. There don't appear to be any weapons anywhere.

"These were the same wounded from yesterday," I say to the lieutenant. He takes a look around and goes outside the mosque with his radio operator to call in the situation to Battalion Forward HQ.

I see an old man in a red kaffiyeh lying against the back wall. Another is facedown next to him, his hand on the old man's lap—as if he were trying to take cover. I squat beside them, inches away, and begin to videotape them.

Then I notice that the blood coming from the old man's nose is bubbling. A sign he is still breathing. So is the man next to him.

While I continue to tape, a Marine walks up to the other two bodies about fifteen feet away, but also lying against the same back wall. Then I hear him say this about one of the men:

"He's fucking faking he's dead—he's faking he's fucking dead."

Through my viewfinder I can see him raise the muzzle of his rifle in the direction of the wounded Iraqi. There are no sudden movements, no reaching or lunging.

However, the Marine could legitimately believe the man poses some kind of danger. Maybe he's going to cover him while another Marine searches for weapons.

Instead, he pulls the trigger. There is a small splatter against the back wall and the man's leg slumps down.

"Well he's dead now," says another Marine in the background.

I am still rolling. I feel the deep pit of my stomach. The Marine then abruptly turns away and strides away, right past the fifth wounded insurgent lying next to a column. He is very much alive and peering from his blanket. He is moving, even trying to talk. But for some reason, it seems he did not pose the same apparent "danger" as the other man—though he may have been more capable of hiding a weapon or explosive beneath his blanket.

But then two other Marines in the room raise their weapons as the man tries to talk.

For a moment, I'm paralyzed still taping with the old man in the foreground. I get up after a beat and tell the Marines that this man—all of these wounded men—were the same ones from yesterday. That they had been disarmed, treated and left here.

At that point the Marine who fired the shot became aware that I was in the room. He came up to me and said, "I didn't know, sir—I didn't know." The anger that seemed present just moments before turned to fear and dread.

The wounded man then tries again to talk to me in Arabic.

He says, "Yesterday I was shot . . . please . . . yesterday I was shot over there—and talked to all of you on camera—I am one of the guys from this whole group. I gave you information. Do you speak Arabic? I want to give you information."

In the aftermath, the first question that came to mind was why had these wounded men been left in the mosque?

It was answered by staff judge advocate Lieutenant Colonel Bob Miller—who interviewed the Marines involved following the incident. After being treated for their wounds on Friday by Navy corpsman (I personally saw their bandages) the insurgents were going to be transported to the rear when time and circumstances allowed.

The area, however, was still hot. And there were American casualties to be moved first.

Also, the squad that entered the mosque on Saturday was different than the one that had led the attack on Friday.

It's reasonable to presume they may not have known that these insurgents had already been engaged and subdued a day earlier.

Yet when this new squad engaged the wounded insurgents on Saturday, perhaps really believing they had been fighting or somehow posed a threat, those Marines inside knew from their training to check the insurgents for weapons and explosives after disabling them, instead of leaving them where they were and waiting outside the mosque for the squad I was following to arrive.

During the course of these events, there were plenty of mitigating circumstances like the ones just mentioned and which I reported in my story. The Marine who fired the shot had reportedly been shot in the face himself the day before.

Also, there have been times when dead and wounded insurgents have been booby-trapped. Supposedly including an incident that happened just a block away from the mosque in which one Marine was killed and five others wounded.

War is about killing your enemy before he kills you.

No one, myself included, would ever deny that a soldier or Marine could legitimately err on the side of caution under those circumstances.

But if that had indeed been the case, it bothered me that the Marine didn't seem to consider the other insurgents a threat—the one very obviously moving under the blanket, or even the two next to me that were still breathing.

I can't know what was in the mind of that Marine.

He is the only one who does.

But observing all of this, bearing in mind the dark perils of this conflict—even with the mitigating circumstances—it appeared to me very plainly that something was not right.

According to Lieutenant Colonel Bob Miller, the rules of engagement in Falluja required soldiers or Marines to determine hostile intent before using deadly force.

I was not watching from a hundred feet away. It was the distance of a bedroom. Aside from breathing, I did not observe any movement at all.

Making sure you know the basis for my choices after the incident is as important to me as knowing how the incident went down.

I did not in any way feel like I had captured some kind of "prize" video. In fact, I was heartsick with the potential burden of what this could mean for the vast majority of Marines like you, who have displayed unrelenting professionalism in the face of very difficult and dangerous circumstances.

I knew that perception of who you are and your conduct in Falluja could end up being unfairly tainted by this incident. And I knew you might believe that all along, everything we had experienced together was just some kind of prelude to betrayal. Immediately after the mosque incident, I told the unit's commanding officer what had happened. I shared the video with him, and its impact rippled all the way up the chain of command.

It was a complicated story and, if not handled responsibly, could have the potential to further inflame the volatile region.

At that point I had to leave the battlefront, to begin working to fully understand and accurately report what had happened in the mosque. Marine commanders immediately pledged their cooperation and I offered to hold the tape until they had time to look into the incident and begin an investigation—providing me with information that would fill in some of the blanks.

For those who don't practice journalism as a profession, it may be difficult to understand why we must report stories like this—especially if they seem to be aberrations and not representative of the behavior or character of an organization as a whole.

The answer is not an easy one.

In war—there are plenty of opportunities to see the full spectrum of good and evil that people are capable of. As journalists it is our job is to report both—though neither may be fully representative of those people on whom we're reporting.

For example, acts of selfless heroism are likely to be as unique to a group as the darker deeds. But our coverage of these unique events—combined with the larger perspective—will allow the truth of that situation, in all of its complexities, to begin to emerge.

That doesn't make the decision to report events like this one any easier.

After the video had been shot, none of the choices that remained were good ones.

If we were going to be faithful to this truth, the video had to be released. But we also had to consider the unintended consequences.

Would it become a propaganda tool for insurgents—and lead to more bloodshed? This was not a question that could be dismissed by anyone with a conscience. It has, for me, led to an agonizing struggle—the proverbial long, dark night of the soul.

I knew NBC would not be irresponsible with the footage. But there were complications. We were part of a video "pool" in Falluja, and that obligated us to share all of our footage with other networks.

After discussing the matter with my bosses, we agreed that the gunshot itself was too graphic and possibly traumatizing for some viewers. We could convey the story accurately without it. It was the same justification we used to not show videotape of terrorists beheading hostages in Iraq.

But I had no idea how our other "pool" partners might use the footage. It created a lingering dilemma and I disagreed with my bosses about our obligations to the pool.

I considered not feeding the tape to the pool—or even, for a moment, destroying it. But that thought created the same pit in my stomach that witnessing the shooting had.

It felt wrong. Hiding this wouldn't make it go away. There were other people in that room. What happened in that mosque would eventually come out. I would be faced with the fact that I had betrayed truth as well as a life supposedly spent in pursuit of it.

When we did finally air the story forty-eight hours later, we did so in a way that attempted to highlight every possible mitigating issue for that Marine's actions. We wanted our viewers to have a very clear understanding of the circumstances surrounding the fighting on that frontline.

Many of our colleagues were just as responsible. Other foreign networks have made different decisions. Whatever the results, I have to live with the possible unintended consequences of my choices just as you have to with yours.

But here is how I plan to resolve some of those burdens for myself.

Some have claimed I reported this story to further my own ambition. Nothing could be further from the truth. It is, in many ways a career-ender as far as conflict zone reporting with the U.S. military, the primary way I make my living.

While I may be able to secure an embed in the future, I have also secured a new reputation of having been the shooter of the mosque video. That will likely make soldiers or Marines skittish around me—reluctant to trust. This job cannot be done under those conditions.

Others have suggested this story was released in pursuit of personal glory or recognition. Anyone who has seen the video knows there is no glory in this for anyone.

I was in the wrong place at the right time. That is all.

And because of that, I have become the conflicted conduit who has brought this to the world.

There are people out there who think it's okay to bury the truth if the ends justify the means.

But even the most glittering, polished exterior can't remain so for long when something is rotting inside.

The Marines have built their proud reputation on fighting for freedoms like the one that allows me to do my job, a job that in some cases may appear to discredit them. But both the leaders and the grunts in the field like you understand that if you lower your standards, if you accept less, then less is what you'll become.

You don't have an easy job. You've been trained to kill one second, then to flip the switch and become nation-builders the next. It's not just confusing, sometimes it's impossible.

But regardless of whom you face as an enemy—no matter how barbaric their tactics—the execution of CARE director Margaret Hassan is a perfect example—you know you cannot become them.

Even though there are many in our own country that want you to consider it. People who would weaken your institution and our nation by telling you it's okay to betray our guiding principles by not making the tough decisions, by turning a blind eye to wrongdoings and injustice.

I interviewed your commanding officer, Lieutenant Colonel Willy Buhl, before the battle for Falluja began. He said something very powerful at the time—something that now seems prophetic. It was this.

"We're the good guys. We are Americans. We are fighting a gentleman's war here—because we don't behead people, we don't come down to the same level of the people we're combating. That's a very difficult thing for a young eighteen-year-old Marine who's been trained to locate, close with and destroy the enemy with fire and close combat. That's a very difficult thing for a forty-two-year-old lieutenant colonel with twenty-three years experience in the service who was trained to do the same thing once upon a time, and who now has a thousand-plus men to lead, guide, coach, mentor—and ensure we remain the good guys and keep the moral high ground."

Heed his words. I have.

I'm not some dilettante with a camera who doesn't understand the vagaries of war. And I have never in my career been a "gotcha" reporter—hoping for people to commit wrongdoings so I can catch them at it.

Despite the fact that some in the fringe press are trying to paint me as some kind of anti-war activist—you know that isn't the case. Anyone who has seen my reporting on television or has read the dispatches on this Web site is fully aware of the lengths I've gone to play it straight down the middle—not to become a tool of propaganda for the left or the right.

Before this incident—your fathers, mothers, wives and girlfriends sent me emails every day thanking me for telling it like it is—showing you doing your jobs. You know that because you read those emails yourselves.

You've seen me with you in the thick of combat emerging from the smoke of RPG explosions so I could continue to tell your story, helping to carry wounded Marines because as part of the unit, I felt that was my responsibility too. You know I'm not a coward. Cowards don't go into a fight without Kevlar—only superstitious idiots do that, not cowards.

I wasn't with you long enough for you to know me completely, but I'm hoping that it was long enough for you to realize I'm not some duplicitous bastard.

I am not a Marine but a reporter who saw the different threads of your stories, both before and during the fight in Falluja—and tried to weave them into honest, representative accounts.

Like the identical Turner Twins from Dallas both working as gunners on the same convoy, the four horsemen—Kenny, David, Lloyd and Doc—creating a little piece of home for themselves by taking care of four Iraqi horses (see script following this posting). Grohman—the Marine Corps' own version of Bob Vila—fixing up Camp Abu Ghraib one concrete bunker at a time; Elkins trying to juggle his soap opera love life on my Thuraya sat phone. I'll remember taking rides with "G" behind the wheel and "Snake" in the turret of what at times felt like my own personal Humvee. I marveled at the verbal mastery of Sergeant Moore and respected how Lieutenant Jason Milbrandt and Corporal Richard Ross forced their way back to Iraq after being sent home with serious injuries.

After the fifth day of fighting in Falluja I asked Sergeant Matthew Henderson—a man who wanted to be a Marine since he was four years old—about the black line with hash mark tattoo on the underside of his forearm. He said it was a pre-Celtic language—and this was the word for courage—something I saw him display numerous times on the battlefield. Staff Sergeant Sam "Mortar Magnet" Mortimer—even after this mosque incident came to trust us—"You guys are all right," he said. "I think you get what we do."

A Marine I came to admire greatly was CAAT (Combined Anti Armor Team) platoon leader Lieutenant Ryan Sparks. It was impressive watching this twenty-nine-year-old officer, a former enlisted man and elite-force Recon member, calmly and flawlessly choreographing the movements of a seventy-man fighting force equipped with some of the military's most advanced weapons.

After the mosque incident I talked with him about what I had to do. He was concerned about it's impact on the Marines and it's potential as a propaganda tool—but he didn't condemn me for doing what I believed was right.

"The public doesn't really want to know the truth about war," he told me, "they want it over quick and with no casualties. Then they want to forget about it. But there's so much more to it. So much gray area."

He is right, of course. And that has become the journey of the moment. Delving into that gray area where things are hard to see, harder to grasp. Eventually, it clears, though. And that's when we both have to make the right decisions.

We each have allegiances to important principles. Sometimes mine make it seem more difficult to do your job. But ultimately, those principles make you more credible and deserving of the honor, which is rightly so important to you.

The man I most see as the Marine's Marine—Colonel John Coleman, the chief of staff for the First Expeditionary Force—sat with me for a moment at the chow hall in Camp Falluja after our story had aired.

He was somber, but there was no judgment. He thanked us for being fair in the reporting of the incident. But by the pain in his face, it was clear how difficult it was for him to see his beloved Corps take a hit—just as it would be to see a Marine get wounded. But he knows that when recovered, a wounded Marine is stronger and wiser for the experience.

It's foolish to believe there won't be atrocities in war. The line between right and wrong can be so thin to the point of at times seeming to disappear completely.

But to me, what would be truly remarkable would be to watch an organization consistently correct perceived wrongdoings and pursue justice even in the midst of battle. Perhaps the realization of that ideal provides the moral high ground required for lasting victory.

So here, ultimately, is how it all plays out: when the Iraqi man in the mosque posed a threat, he was your enemy, when he was subdued he was your responsibility, when he was killed while I was recording videotape—he became mine.

The burdens of war are unforgiving for us all.

APPENDIX B

EMAIL TO YAHOO! ABOUT THE CHINA SITUATION

April 23, 2007
Dear Terry, Jerry and David:

I was in the middle of my Hot Zone journey last year when I read an article from the BBC online concerning Yahoo!'s aiding and abetting Chinese authorities in jailing journalist Shi Tao and blogger Li Zhi.

As the first reporter hired by Yahoo!—you can imagine that at that moment, I too felt a sense of betrayal. I asked for a conference call with Yahoo! public relations and legal representatives that would provide more insight into the story.

After the telephone call I was shocked by the unapologetic, cavalier explanation that, "we have to abide by the laws of the countries we operate in."

I can only say, especially in a case where human beings are being jailed through our direct participation, this smacks of a rationalization so transparent and morally hollow that it echoes with callousness.

Yahoo!'s mission statement is, "To connect people to their passions, their communities and the world's knowledge." It says nothing about connecting people to lengthy prison terms for expressing democratic aspirations.

From a business perspective, China is of course a huge potential market and Yahoo!'s competitors are also doing business there. But Yahoo! can't absolve itself simply by being in the "bad" company of other transgressors. It also can't wait for the U.S. government to pressure China on human rights issues—when people have already been jailed because of Yahoo!'s complicity.

As a journalist who was given a once-in-a-lifetime opportunity by Yahoo! to do consistent and meaningful reporting around the globe last year, I implore you to show the same kind of vision and sense of moral responsibility through the following actions:

1) Immediately cease helping Chinese authorities identify and jail political dissidents through Yahoo! email accounts

2) Set up a legal defense and family support fund for Shi Tao, Li Zhi and any other Chinese dissidents jailed because of Yahoo!

3) Work with Yahoo! competitors to create a united front against these kind of undemocratic and anti-free expression demands from Chinese authorities

4) State a deadline to cease and withdraw Yahoo! business investments in China, including strategic partnerships with Alibaba.com—if Chinese authorities do not release the dissidents about whom Yahoo! provided information

As difficult as it may be, Yahoo! has the opportunity to take the moral high ground here—and renew the loyalty and respect of millions of customers worldwide. Thank you.

Kevin Sites

STATISTICS

AFGHANISTAN

(Casualty figures since start of U.S.-led military campaign in October 2001)

AFGHAN DEAD: nearly 9,000 (3,000–5,000 of those estimated to be civilians)

DISPLACED: as many as 134,500

REFUGEES: 2 million–4 million

AMERICAN DEAD: as many as 380

AMERICAN WOUNDED: as many as 1,180

COALITION DEAD: 182

COALITION WOUNDED: 679

TIMELINE

DECEMBER 1979: Soviet forces invade Afghanistan. Mujahedin insurgents (supported by United States, Pakistan, Saudi Arabia and others) battle Soviets. Soviets execute leader Hafizullah Amin and install Babrak Karmal.

1980s: Osama bin Laden recruits Mujahedin to fight in Afghanistan.

1986: Karmal replaced by Mohammad Najibullah.

APRIL 14, 1988: Geneva Accords signed by Afghanistan, Soviet Union, United States and Pakistan promising noninterference, return of refugees and Soviet withdrawal.

Statistics as of May 2007.

MAY 1988: Final troop withdrawal by Soviets begins.

FEBRUARY 15, 1989: Soviets complete withdrawal. But Mujahedin rebels disregard accord after being snubbed during negotiations and form interim government in Pakistan, fueling civil war.

1992: Alliance of Mujahedin forces take Kabul, topple Najibullah and form a new government, which soon disintegrates into power struggles between warlords. Much of Kabul is destroyed and as many as fifty thousand people are killed in fighting.

1994: Taliban, disillusioned Mujahedin rebels supported by Pakistan, pose challenge to fractious Afghan government.

1996: Taliban rebels take Kabul, winning control of more than half the country. Impose hard-line Islamic government and ban women from the workplace. Taliban give sanctuary and base of operations to Osama bin Laden and Al Qaeda in return for financial support from Pakistan and Saudi Arabia.

1997: The Northern Alliance, led by former Afghan defense minister and anti-Soviet Mujahedin Ahmad Shah Massood, forms in opposition to Taliban control.

SUMMER 1998: Taliban takes control of Mazar-i Sharif, massacring at least two thousand. United States suspects Taliban of harboring bin Laden and launches missile attacks.

1999: Taliban leaders refuse to relinquish bin Laden.

2000: Taliban forces occupy 90 percent of country. Allegations of widespread human rights violations, especially against women. Suppressed minorities retaliate by killing 2,500 Taliban soldiers.

2001: Civil strife, poverty, drought, land mines and destroyed infrastructure escalate tensions. Fighting between Taliban and Massood's forces continues in north.

SEPTEMBER 9, 2001: Taliban- and possibly Al Qaeda–backed agents, posing as journalists, assassinate Massood. Many say Massood taken out to ensure Afghanistan's cooperation before September 11 terrorist attacks on United States.

SEPTEMBER 11, 2001: Bin Laden and Al Qaeda launch terrorist suicide attacks in United States.

FALL 2001: United States intensifies demands for Taliban to surrender bin Laden but is refused.

OCTOBER 2001: United States and Britain launch air strikes against Afghanistan and support Northern Alliance fighters with weapons, support and Special Forces advisors.

NOVEMBER AND DECEMBER 2001: Taliban and Al Qaeda forces retreat. Mazar-i Sharif and Kandahar captured by Northern Alliance. Kabul falls; many Taliban flee to border areas near Pakistan.

DECEMBER 22, 2001: Hamid Karzai sworn in as head of new interim government.

2002: Karzai receives four billion dollars in international pledges to rebuild Afghanistan.

SEPTEMBER 5, 2002: Attempted assassination of Karzai.

JANUARY 2004: New constitution adopted by grand council of faction officials and tribal leaders.

OCTOBER 2004: Karzai declared president after country's first democratic presidential elections.

DECEMBER 19, 2005: National Assembly inaugurated, marking first Afghan parliament in more than thirty years.

2006: United States turns over military leadership in Afghanistan to NATO.

2007: Afghan army and NATO forces launch new offensive against resurgent Taliban in southern strongholds.

CONFLICT STATUS: ACTIVE

The porous Pakistan border continues to provide an access route into Afghanistan for Taliban rebels, who have vowed to increase their attacks, including suicide missions against government and NATO forces. However, the Taliban's chief military commander, Mullah Dadullah, was killed in combat with U.S. and Afghan troops. Reconstruction efforts are moving at a snail-like pace and have been complicated by a lack of basic infrastructure, essentially obliterated during decades of civil war. Osama bin Laden still eludes special operations teams on the eastern border, and poppy cultivation has skyrocketed. The number of violent insurgent attacks has risen sharply since September 2006, and there is little security or presence of the national government outside the capital of Kabul. Additionally, President Hamid Karzai's authority has been undermined by local warlords—many of whom refuse to integrate their personal militias into the national army.

CAMBODIA

DEAD: 2 million–3 million (executed or death from starvation/illness during reign of Khmer Rouge, 1975–79)

TIMELINE

1965: Prince Norodom Sihanouk cuts off relations with United States. During escalating Vietnam War and with Sihanouk's green light, Viet Cong rebels set up camps in Cambodia to wage attacks on U.S. and South Vietnamese troops.

1965-70: United States launches bombing campaign in North Vietnam as well as Cambodia and Laos to dismantle Viet Cong infrastructure there, destabilizing Cambodia and increasing support for Khmer Rouge communist guerrillas.

SPRING 1970: Sihanouk deposed while out of country, replaced by pro-American General Lon Nol in coup. Violent riots ensued, ethnic Vietnamese killed. Nol soon sends troops to fight North Vietnamese on Cambodian soil.

1975-79: After years of guerrilla warfare, Khmer Rouge rebels (supported by exiled Sihanouk in China) oust Nol and rise to power under Pol Pot in 1975. They begin catastrophic campaign to create agricultural communal society with no social or economic differentiation. Private property, traditional medical care, education, religion, banking and communication networks are banned. Civilians forcibly relocated to labor camps and ordered to farm. Starvation, exhaustion, illness abound. Torture centers and killing fields target political opponents, educated middle class, others perceived to be disloyal or disobedient.

1977-79: Vietnamese forces invade in 1978 and seize capital, Phnom Penh, early in 1979. Pol Pot and Khmer Rouge insurgents retreat to territory near Thailand border.

1981: Pro-Vietnamese party wins National Assembly elections, but government not recognized by many countries.

1985: Guerrilla warfare intensifies.

1989–90: Faced with international pressure, Vietnamese troops withdraw.

1991–93: Peace accord signed with intent of demobilization, eventual elections. Khmer Rouge violates cease-fire. Monarchy restored, Sihanouk becomes king.

1994–99: Many Khmer Rouge guerrillas surrender in amnesty offer. Efforts to create genocide tribunal. Deputy Prime Minister Hun Sen stages a coup against Prime Minister Prince Ranariddh. Hun Sen eventually becomes prime minister. Pol Pot dies in jungle hideout in 1998.

2002–04: Hun Sen's Cambodian People's Party wins first multiparty local elections. Hun Sen reelected prime minister.

2006: Genocide tribunal judges sworn in, but trials not set to start until 2007.

CONFLICT STATUS: PAST

A tribunal was established to prosecute Khmer Rouge leaders for crimes of genocide, but the process has been painstakingly slow. There are valid concerns that many of the Khmer Rouge leaders are already dead, like Pol Pot, or too old and sick to stand trial, which may leave the country with little hope of bringing justice to those responsible for historical massacres as well as providing a sense of healing for the nation.

COLOMBIA

DEAD: 65,600 (since 1963)
DISPLACED: 2 million–3 million
REFUGEES: 300,000

TIMELINE

1948–57: Civil war erupts after assassination of Bogotá mayor, as many as three hundred thousand killed. Conservative and liberal parties create National Front and ban other parties.

1965–72: In face of widespread unemployment and poverty, many leftist guer-

rilla groups emerge, including Revolutionary Armed Forces of Columbia (FARC), National Liberation Army (ELN), People's Liberation Army
(EPL) and M-19.

1980s: Drug trade explodes. Judges and presidential candidates murdered by
rebels and drug cartels, that become increasingly intertwined. Guerrillas
provide security to drug lords in exchange for arms and money to fund
their operations. Right-wing paramilitary forces form with the help of
wealthy ranchers, military and, some allege, the Colombian government, to counteract kidnapping, violence and extortion by leftist rebels.

1993: Drug kingpin Pablo Escobar killed by security forces.

1990s: United Self-Defense Forces of Colombia (AUC), an alliance of paramilitary outfits, consolidated to offer security and economic protection,
becomes involved in drug production and trafficking. AUC involved in
massacring political opponents, villagers. AUC, FARC, ELN all named
terrorist organizations by United States and European Union, which allows upgraded military and intelligence support to Colombian authorities to fight them.

Colombian president Andrés Pastrana Arango grants FARC a safe
haven, off limits to the military, to spur peace talks. Ultimately unsuccessful.

2000: Pastrana devises "Plan Colombia" and is awarded nearly one billion
dollars from the United States in military and economic assistance to
fight the drug trade and groups protecting it.

2002: Pastrana breaks off peace talks with FARC after three years, safe zone
rescinded. Alvaro Uribe elected president, vows to crack down on rebels. FARC attacks Bogotá as Uribe is sworn in, twenty people killed.
AUC signs cease-fire, engages in peace talks with government, begins to
disarm.

2003: Government, AUC sign Accord of Santa Fé de Ralito, Colombia. AUC
required to demobilize by end of 2005.

2004–2006: Government military offensive against FARC, ELN intensifies.
Uribe reelected in landslide.

CONFLICT STATUS: ACTIVE

More than 2,100 deaths were reported in 2006, and security is still fragile. FARC has refocused its efforts in urban areas, but progress has been made in the government's peace negotiations with the ELN. More than twenty-five thousand paramilitaries in the AUC are estimated to have demobilized, although unresolved issues remain with leaders' amnesty and potential extradition to the United States to face drug charges—as well as past paramilitary connections to the government. And with 3,353 people killed by land mines in just three years, 2002–2005, Colombia is one of the most heavily mined nations in the world.

DEMOCRATIC REPUBLIC OF THE CONGO, DRC (FORMERLY ZAÏRE)

DEAD: nearly 4 million (since 1996)
DISPLACED: as many as 2.3 million
REFUGEES: as many as 430,000

TIMELINE

JUNE 1960–64: Congo granted independence from Belgium. The charismatic Patrice Lumumba becomes prime minister. After army revolt, Lumumba arrested and murdered, allegedly with Belgian and U.S. approval.

1965: Joseph Mobutu (later added Sese Seko) seizes power in coup. Renames Congo as Zaïre. Exploits Congo's mineral wealth and amasses a multi-billion-dollar fortune during his reign.

1990–94: Mobutu harbors Hutu genocide ringleaders fleeing from Rwanda after Tutsis topple the Hutu-led government there.

1996–98: Laurent Kabila, leader of the Alliance of Democratic Forces for the Liberation of Congo-Zaïre (ADFL), with support of troops from new Tutsi-led Rwandan government and Ugandan troops, overthrows Mobutu, who flees to Morocco. Rwanda troops inside Congo seek to root out Hutu Interahamwe militia, who are there after carrying out Rwandan genocide. Once in power, Kabila's primary supporters,

Rwanda, Uganda and Burundi, turn on him and support other rebel efforts to overthrow him. Kabila rallies support from Angola, Chad, Namibia, Sudan, Zimbabwe, Zambia, Tanzania. The cauldron of violence and tangled alliances becomes known as Africa's World War.

1999–2000: Cease-fire agreement signed by six African countries and major rebel groups involved in warfare. U.N. Security Council sends peacekeeping troops whose ongoing presence of seventeen thousand makes it the world's largest, most expensive peacekeeping operation.

JANUARY 2001: Kabila killed by bodyguard. Son Joseph Kabila takes over.

2001–02: U.N. foreign troop withdrawal plan approved. Rwanda, Uganda start pulling out. U.N. panel reports combatants prolonging conflict to compete for Congo's vast natural resources. Reserves of diamonds, gold, coltan (mineral used in cell phones) plundered by all sides.

2003–06: Joseph Kabila signs provisional constitution setting up interim government. Former rebel leaders sworn in as vice presidents, parliament inaugurated. Several coups attempted, more fighting between Congolese army and rebel groups fueled by desire for mineral wealth. U.N. calls Congo "world's worst humanitarian crisis" in March 2005.

JULY–DECEMBER 2006: First free elections in four decades yield no clear winner. Rival groups fight in capital, Kinshasam, over results. Joseph Kabila declared winner in fall runoff election. Sporadic postelection violence in capital of Kinshasa between DRC security forces and supporters of electoral runner-up, Jean-Pierre Bemba.

CONFLICT STATUS: TENTATIVE PEACE

Africa's World War was a tangled web of alliances and counteralliances that involved national troops, rebels and foreign armies. The race for control of Congo's rich resources has always been the underlying factor for combatants entering the fray. Many of the occupying forces terrorized the Congolese population with looting, rape and murder. The newly elected government has taken power, but U.N. peacekeeping forces remain—and the violence, especially in the eastern portion of the country, continues.

HAITI

TIMELINE

1956-86: Haiti under Duvalier dictatorships when François "Papa Doc" Duvalier seizes power in military coup. Son Jean-Claude "Baby Doc" Duvalier named as successor before father dies. Tens of thousands killed, exiled under Duvalier regime. National debt skyrockets, unemployment rates rise and Haiti becomes one of poorest countries in world after having economy rich in sugar, coffee production. "Baby Doc" Duvalier flees to France with U.S. assistance when widespread protests escalate.

1990-93: Jean-Bertrand Aristide, popular priest, elected president by wide margin. U.S.-favored candidate finishes second. New government promises to rid country of past corruption. But Aristide is ousted by Lieutenant General Raoul Cédras (supported by disaffected military personnel) during bloody coup in 1991. More than one thousand killed in first days of conflict, between three thousand and five thousand total dead in next three years of brutal military rule. International sanctions imposed.

1994-96: Cédras relinquishes power in the face of imminent U.S. invasion. First contingent of twenty-one-thousand-strong multinational force arrives to oversee restoration of constitutional government. Aristide reinstalled. First national civil police force created under U.N. peacekeepers. Ally René Préval elected to replace Aristide when term ends.

1997-99: Préval moves to establish pro-market economic reforms: Aristide opposes program. Political gridlock with fractious parliament paralyzes country's progress.

2000-01: Aristide wins election as president for a second, nonconsecutive term, amid allegations of election fraud. Aristide is also accused of corruption and using violence against political opponents with criminal gangs.

2004: Aristide faces a violent uprising, reportedly made of ex-police and security forces. He is forced into exile (with United States arranging for departure) when Front de Resistance rebels take Port-au-Prince. Aristide later claims United States, France backed the rebels and forcibly removed him from the country. Dozens killed in clashes between Aristide supporters and new interim government.

2006–07: Préval wins first elections since overthrow of Aristide, despite ballot irregularities. United Nations forces launch initiative to disarm, demobilize, reintegrate gangs by offering money, food, job training. Longtime U.S. embargo partially lifted.

CONFLICT STATUS: UNSTABLE

Haiti is one of the poorest and least developed countries in the world. International peacekeeping missions have failed to control increasing levels of election fraud, street-gang violence, kidnappings and transshipment of drugs. Armed gangs loyal to the exiled Aristide have been implicated in many killings. Cité Soleil, a slum in Port-au-Prince, was raided and hundreds arrested during multiple operations by U.N. troops and local police in January 2007. Haiti remains unstable and in crisis.

IRAN

TIMELINE

1953: Iranian prime minister Mohammad Mosaddeq is overthrown in coup orchestrated by the United States and Great Britain. Shah Mohammad Reza Pahlavi returns to power.

1963–78: The shah's abuse of power and attempts at Westernization unleash demonstrations, riots. Martial law declared.

1979: Shah forced into exile. Islamic leader Ayatollah Ruhollah Khomeini returns to Iran from exile.

1979–81: Islamic Revolution dismantles monarchy, Iran declared Islamic republic following referendum. Khomeini becomes "Supreme Leader." Islamic militants take fifty-two Americans hostage in U.S. embassy, demand extradition of shah, to be put on trial in Iran. Hostages are held for 444 days.

1980: Iran-Iraq War begins when Iraq invades Iran after border skirmishes, waterway dispute; eight hundred thousand to one million killed by 1988.

1985: United States sells arms to Iran and secretly uses money to fund Contra rebels in Nicaragua in violation of U.S. law; becomes Iran-Contra scandal.

1988: Iran, Iraq agree to U.N.-negotiated cease-fire agreement.

1990: Iran, Iraq resume diplomatic relations. Iranian earthquake kills forty thousand.

1997: Reform-minded Mohammad Khatami elected president, beats out Islamic conservative; but political tension causes deadlock.

2000: Liberal reformists win victory in parliamentary elections but are stymied by powerful Islamic conservatives. Disenchantment grows when promised reforms fail to materialize.

2001–03: U.S. president George W. Bush lists Iran as part of "Axis of Evil" during State of Union address because of support for militant Muslim groups such as Hezbollah. Iran later stays neutral during U.S.-led war in Iraq. Iran voluntarily agrees to suspend uranium enrichment and allows inspections by nuclear watchdog.

2004–05: Conservatives take back power in parliamentary elections in 2004 after Islamic clerics (Council of Guardians) controversially disqualify thousands of reformist candidates. Ultraconservative mayor of Tehran, Mahmoud Ahmadinejad, wins election; becomes first noncleric president in almost twenty-five years. He immediately alienates West with anti-Israeli remarks and breaks off nuclear negotiations with West. Diplomatic showdown intensifies.

2006: Iran resumes nuclear research and development, announces its success in enriching uranium. United Nations debates response.

CONFLICT STATUS: POLITICAL TENSIONS

Some analysts believe Iran has become a dominant regional power in the Middle East, bolstered in part by the U.S.-led war in Iraq, which toppled the regime of Saddam Hussein, Iran's biggest security threat, and by the success of its Lebanese proxy, Hezbollah, in its "July War" with Israel in 2006. Iran has been emboldened to ignore threats of U.N. sanctions by moving ahead with uranium enrichment while tensions with the United States continue to be stoked with claims that Iran is providing military aid and advice to Shia militias in Iraq. But a stagnant economy and Ahmadinejad's volatility have created political problems for him at home, potentially setting up an internal power struggle.

IRAQ

(Casualty figures since U.S.-led invasion of Iraq, March 2003 to May 2007)

IRAQI CIVILIANS DEAD: 63,000–70,000 (est.)

IRAQI CIVILIANS WOUNDED: unknown

IRAQI CIVILIANS DISPLACED: 1.6 million–2 million

IRAQI REFUGEES: 1.8 million–2 million

IRAQI MILITARY: as many as 8,600

AMERICAN MILITARY DEAD: 3,323

AMERICAN MILITARY WOUNDED: 24,000–26,000

COALITION MILITARY DEAD: 268

COALITION MILITARY WOUNDED: 600

FOREIGN CONTRACTORS DEAD: 800*

FOREIGN CONTRACTORS WOUNDED: 3,300

TIMELINE

1990-91: Iraq invades Kuwait. United Nations demands full withdrawal, imposes economic sanctions. U.S.-led coalition of more than five hundred thousand formed to oppose Iraq. Coalition bombing campaign and ground operation liberates Kuwait. Iraq accepts cease-fire terms. U.N. resolution peace terms stipulate that Iraq disclose information on weapons of mass destruction programs, creates team of inspectors; also designates Iraq "no-fly zone" along northern and southern parallels to protect rebellious Kurdish and Shia populations from retaliation by Saddam Hussein's military.

1994: Saddam Hussein becomes prime minister, winning referendum in 1995 for presidential term. Iraqi government recognizes Kuwait's independence, borders.

1996-98: Attempted coup by Iraqi National Accord (sponsored by CIA) dis-

* Source: Associated Press

covered, more than one hundred executed. Coalition aircraft patrol no-fly zone, frequently firing on Iraqi antiaircraft installations. Inspectors from U.N. Special Commission to Oversee the Destruction of Iraq's Weapons of Mass Destruction (UNSCOM) find proof of nerve gas VX. Iraq ends cooperation with program, UNSCOM staff evacuated. United States, Britain launch air attacks to destroy defense installations and nuclear, chemical, biological weapons facilities.

2001–02: After September 11, 2001, terrorist attacks, U.S. president George W. Bush lists Iraq as part of "Axis of Evil" in State of Union address, asserts Hussein has ties to Al Qaeda, paving way for subsequent invasion.

MARCH 20, 2003: Hussein refuses U.S. ultimatum to leave Iraq. Circumventing the United Nations, the United States (with Australian, British, Polish contingents) launches invasion of Iraq, which reaches Baghdad by April 9, toppling the regime.

2003: United Nations lifts economic sanctions. U.S.-led Coalition Provisional Authority (CPA) takes over government responsibilities, rife with mismanagement and corruption. Iraqi insurgents begin campaign of guerrilla warfare. Hussein's sons killed in Mosul battle. Hussein captured near his hometown of Tikrit on December 14.

2004–05: Suicide attacks kill hundreds of civilians as sectarian violence escalates. Extended U.S. siege of Falluja ends in hundreds of casualties. Personal photos of U.S. troops abusing Iraqis in Abu Ghraib Prison are leaked to the media. In June 2004, United States transfers power to interim government headed by Prime Minister Iyad Allawi. Eight million Iraqis vote in first multiparty elections in half century to install Transitional National Assembly in January 2005. Shiite United Iraqi Alliance wins majority, Kurdish parties come in second. Surges in car bombings, gunfire in spring 2005 nearly double monthly civilian death toll. Voters approve constitution that sets up Islamic federal democracy, cast ballots for first full-time parliament since Hussein deposed. Saddam Hussein's trial for crimes against humanity begins.

2006: Waves of sectarian violence continue after bomb attack on Shiite shrine, killing hundreds. Some analysts claim Iraq has descended into civil war. United Nations reports more than one hundred civilians on

average killed in daily violence. Abu Musab al-Zarqawi (leader of Al
Qaeda network in Iraq) killed in air strike. Hussein found guilty, sentenced to death and quickly hung, but critics claim execution was
botched—Hussein appearing composed in the face of jeering witnesses.
Ethnic strife, corruption, unemployment, deep mistrust of local officials
and American troops continue to derail security and reconstruction
efforts.

2007: Bush proposes last-ditch deployment of twenty thousand more
troops—in a so-called surge strategy. Members of the new Democrat-
controlled Congress are critical.

CONFLICT STATUS: ACTIVE

While an elected Iraqi government is in place, it is dominated by Shiites and
Kurds, with marginal Sunni participation. Sectarian violence between Sun-
nis and Shiites has led to ethnic cleansing in some formerly mixed neighborhoods surrounding Baghdad while a multiheaded insurgency, consisting
of Iraqi nationalists, Al Qaeda supporters, foreign fighters and Shiite militias continues to wreak havoc. Attempts to stabilize and reconstruct Iraq
have proved to be dangerous, exasperating and expensive. American public
support for the war has plummeted with each passing year while U.S. troop
deployments are routinely extended. The Bush administration and Congress continue to spar over a timetable for withdrawal of U.S. forces from
Iraq.

ISRAEL (HEZBOLLAH VERSUS ISRAEL)

(Casualty figures for thirty-four-day war, July–August 2006)

LEBANESE CIVILIANS DEAD: as many as 1,000

LEBANESE CIVILIANS WOUNDED: as many as 4,400

LEBANESE CIVILIANS DISPLACED: 700,000–900,000 (est.)

HEZBOLLAH DEAD: 500 (est.)

HEZBOLLAH WOUNDED: not reported

ISRAELI CIVILIANS DEAD: 43

ISRAELI CIVILIANS WOUNDED: 1,489

ISRAELI CIVILIANS DISPLACED: 500,000
ISRAEL DEFENSE FORCES DEAD: 119
ISRAEL DEFENSE FORCES WOUNDED: 400

TIMELINE

1975-77: Lebanese Civil War (which continues in phases until 1990) begins when right-wing Christian gunman opens fire on bus full of Palestinian passengers in Beirut, killing twenty-seven in retaliation for alleged guerrilla attack on nearby church. Syria deploys peacekeeping troops after establishment of Arab Deterrent Force. Lebanon consistently used as pawn by neighboring nations, warring factions that use country as personal battlefield.

1978: Israel launches invasion of Lebanon in effort to end Palestine Liberation Organization (PLO) attacks along northern border, starting occupation that will span more than two decades. U.N. resolution calls for Israel to withdraw, cease military action. U.N. peacekeeping force established to stabilize area, help Lebanese government restore its authority. Israel transfers southern territory to Christian Lebanese militia (linked to Israel Defense Forces).

1982-83: Israel launches full-scale invasion, establishes self-declared safe zone. Hezbollah (Lebanon-based Shiite paramilitary group, later supported by Iran) forms to resist Israel's occupation of southern Lebanon. Israeli siege of Beirut forces PLO retreat from Lebanon. U.S., French, Italian peacekeepers arrive in Lebanon. Right-wing militiamen massacre thousands of civilians in Palestinian refugee camps. Hundreds of U.S., French soldiers killed in suicide bomb attack on base. Fourteen thousand Lebanese killed in Beirut during ongoing civil war.

1985-87: Buffer zone between Israel, Lebanon becomes Hezbollah headquarters.

1988-90: Interim military government splits with Muslim factions in West Beirut and Christian factions in East Beirut. Syrian military intervention helps end civil war, but troops remain, exert de facto control over Lebanese government.

1991-93: National Assembly orders militias to disband, but Hezbollah granted exemption. Israel launches Operation Accountability with heavy bombardment against Hezbollah and Palestinian nationalist organizations in southern Lebanon.

1996: Israel launches Operation Grapes of Wrath, bombing Hezbollah bases in southern Lebanon and Beirut. Israeli attack on U.N. base kills more than one hundred Lebanese refugees. Hezbollah, Palestinian guerrillas agree to U.S.-negotiated truce. Monitoring group formed to ensure parties follow terms.

1998: Israel agrees to withdraw from Lebanon—if Lebanon and Syria guarantee security of Israel's northern border; negotiations collapse.

2000–02: Israel releases thirteen Lebanese prisoners held for more than a decade without trial. Hezbollah advances on Israeli positions. Israel withdraws troops. Hezbollah kidnaps soldiers at northern border.

2003–05: United Nations calls for withdrawal of foreign troops from Lebanon. Spate of political assassinations carried out, most notably of former Lebanese prime minister Rafik Hariri, once a Syrian ally but turned outspoken critic. Cedar Revolution sparks pullout of Syrian troops, ending nearly three decades of occupation.

JULY 12, 2006: Hezbollah kills eight Israeli soldiers, captures two in cross-border raid. Israel launches air strikes, sends ground troops into Lebanon.

JULY 13–15, 2006: Israel bombs Beirut airport, kills more than forty civilians in air strikes. U.S. blames Hezbollah, while Britain, Italy, Russia, France blast Israel for disproportionate use of force. Israel demands release of soldiers, Hezbollah disarmament to end offensive.

JULY 16–20, 2006: More killed in bombings, including forty-three Lebanese in Israeli strike. Hezbollah rejects cease-fire terms. United Nations plagued by disagreement. Foreigners evacuated. At least seventy civilians killed on July 19 in deadliest day of conflict.

JULY 21–25, 2006: Israel warns of potential invasion of Lebanon, mobilizes thousands. Syria warns of retaliation if Israeli troops invade.

JULY 26–31, 2006: U.N. observers killed in allegedly deliberately targeted Israeli air raid. Summit on Middle East conflict held, no cease-fire resolution realized. Fighting intensifies, Israeli air assaults increase. Lebanese infrastructure continually decimated. More than thirty Lebanese civilians killed in air strike on Qana, most of them children.

AUGUST 1–9, 2006: Israeli ground troops, Hezbollah rebels clash. Scores killed. Hezbollah fires hundreds of rockets at Israel. International community still at odds over U.N. resolution draft. Lebanon rejects resolution. Lebanon mobilizes reservists. Humanitarian aid groups unable to distribute relief because of destruction of roads, bridges.

AUGUST 10–13, 2006: Israel scales back offensive for attempts at diplomacy, but Israeli tanks still enter Lebanon, Hezbollah rockets are stepped up. Israel orders expanded ground offensive when talks collapse. Israel, Hezbollah eventually agree to U.N. resolution.

AUGUST 14, 2006: Truce goes into effect after thirty-four days of fighting. Later, U.N. and Lebanese forces deploy as a buffer between the warring parties. Israeli forces withdraw from Lebanon.

CONFLICT STATUS: CEASE-FIRE

In the aftermath of the conflict, human rights groups have criticized both Israel and Hezbollah for not doing more to distinguish between civilians and combatants during the fighting. Hezbollah's indiscriminate firing of Katyusha rockets and Israel's use of cluster bombs have both been singled out as violations of international law. Some analysts claim Hezbollah came out ahead politically in the conflict simply by surviving the Israeli military onslaught—though its initial actions in kidnapping the Israeli soldiers cost more than one thousand Lebanese lives and tens of millions of dollars in damage to Lebanese infrastructure. Israel did not achieve its two stated aims in the conflict: rescuing the two captured soldiers and destroying Hezbollah's military capability. A postconflict report in Israel points out missteps in the handling of the war by Israeli prime minister Ehud Olmert, prompting calls for his resignation. The United States has also been criticized for what some say was a failure to push aggressively for a cease-fire in the midst of the hostilities. Lebanon was undoubtedly the biggest loser in the fight, with large numbers of dead and wounded, billions of dollars of economic setbacks and a further undermining of the relations between Lebanese sects and religious groups.

KASHMIR

DEAD: 50,000 (since 1989, inside Kashmir only)

TIMELINE

1947-49: India and Pakistan granted independence. Kashmir, a buffer parcel between the new nations, sparks contentious territorial dispute. Kashmiri maharaja Hari Singh awards control to India. Indian troops arrive in Kashmir. Tensions escalate into war between India and Pakistan, ending with U.N.-sponsored cease-fire, peacekeeping force deployed. Line of demarcation established.

1965-71: India and Pakistan fight second war over Kashmir. Both nations accept U.N. resolution, agreeing to adhere to Line of Control terms in 1972.

1974: India completes first nuclear test.

1989: Uprising begins in Kashmir with armed resistance (trained and armed by Pakistan). Pakistani rebels breach borderline, Indian army criticized for repressively squelching separatists. After fighting against Soviet Union in Afghanistan, Islamic fighters arriving in Kashmir create more unrest. India accuses Pakistan of supporting cross-border terrorism.

1998-2000: Arms race with India escalates, Pakistan conducting further nuclear tests. United States orders sanctions. Pakistan-backed forces again cross into Indian territory in Kargil; India launches retaliatory air strikes. Hostilities leave seven hundred dead, two thousand wounded. Military coup in Pakistan installs General Pervez Musharraf.

2001-2002: Major clashes erupt after India fires on Pakistan bases. Substantial troop buildup along India-Pakistan border follows escalating tensions. Pakistan-backed Kashmiri rebels blamed for attack on Kashmir's assembly in Srinagar that kills thirty-eight, offensive against Indian parliament in New Delhi that kills fourteen.

2003-04: Cease-fire defuses conflict, but bloody attacks continue.

CONFLICT STATUS: ACTIVE

There is an average of 2,500 violent incidents in Kashmir every year and continued allegations of human rights abuses by both militants and Indian security forces. In March 2007, representatives of the Organization of the Islamic Conference and Kashmiri authorities called for Kashmir's vague status to be resolved. Peace negotiations are ongoing.

LEBANON (CEDAR REVOLUTION)

TIMELINE

1976: Syria begins occupation of Lebanon in effort to end Lebanese Civil War.

2004: U.N. Security Council adopts resolution that calls for foreign troops to pull out of Lebanon, recognize sovereignty. Lebanese prime minister Rafik Hariri, once allied with the Syrians, now resigns to protest Syrian political interference and opposition to constitutional amendment extending term of President Émile Lahoud (pro-Syrian).

FEBRUARY 14, 2005: Hariri assassinated in car bombing, which kills about twenty, wounds one hundred. Syria emerges as culprit in death of Hariri. Cedar Revolution triggered by series of mass demonstrations condemning the assassinations and Syria's possible involvement.

FEBRUARY 21, 2005: Tens of thousands of activists (supported by United States, France) protest in Beirut to demand Syrian withdrawal, formation of commission to investigate assassination and resignation of pro-Syrian Lebanese politicians. Weekly demonstrations follow.

FEBRUARY 25, 2005: United Nations threatens Syria with sanctions unless it withdraws troops from Lebanon.

FEBRUARY 28, 2005: Pro-Syrian government resigns, calls for new elections to be held. But opposition leaders insist on complete Syrian withdrawal.

SPRING 2005: Pro- and anti-Syrian counterdemonstrations in Beirut. More bombings kill high-profile journalists and politicians.

APRIL–JULY 2005: Mounting international pressure, especially from United

Nations, forces Syria to end occupation. Syria withdraws fourteen thousand troops after nearly three decades in Lebanon. During U.N. Hariri probe, two Lebanese security chiefs implicated in assassination. Lebanon's pro-Syrian government collapses, replaced by fragile, multi-party coalition. Fouad Siniora becomes prime minister, but pro-Syrian Hezbollah also gains parliament seats and cabinet representation.

OCTOBER 2005: Ghazi Kanaan, Syria's interior minister, commits suicide after U.N. commission interviews him in connection with Hariri's assassination. U.N. report released about the killing concludes that Syrian and pro-Syrian Lebanese intelligence officials were likely aware of the plan.

CONFLICT STATUS: PAST

There is much disagreement over the formation of an international tribunal to try suspects in Rafik Hariri's assassination. Saudi Arabia has agreed to mediate the dispute.

MIDDLE EAST CONFLICT

TIMELINE

1948: Declaration of Israel as Jewish state. British leave Palestine. Egypt, Syria, Iraq, Lebanon, Jordan, Saudi Arabia declare war on Israel.

1949: Armistice ends the fighting. Israel has gained 50 percent more territory than allotted by original U.N. partition plan.

1967: Israel launches strike on Egypt, Syria, Jordan in Six-Day War; captures Sinai and Gaza from Egypt, West Bank from Jordan and Golan Heights from Syria. U.N. resolution calls for Israeli withdrawal. Yasser Arafat becomes chairman of Palestine Liberation Organization (PLO).

1973: Yom Kippur War, surprise attack by Egypt and Syria on Jewish day of atonement in effort to take back captured territory.

1979: Egypt and Israel sign peace treaty.

1982: Large Israeli invasion of Lebanon to stop PLO attacks on northern border.

1987–97: First intifada, riots against Israeli rule in occupied territories.

1993: Israel, PLO sign Oslo Declaration of Principles, ending intifada, calling for mutual recognition and the establishment of the Palestinian Authority. Subsequent agreement stipulates withdrawal of Israeli troops, power transfer to Palestinian administration, formation of Palestinian police force. Israel, Jordan sign peace treaty, ending forty-five years of conflict. Violence tapers off, but Israel retains full control over majority of West Bank.

1999–2000: Promising second round of peace talks led by U.S. president Bill Clinton collapses. Hostilities escalate. Second intifada begins after Israeli opposition leader Ariel Sharon visits the Temple Mount in Jerusalem.

2001: Gaza Strip plagued by violent clashes. Curfews imposed, checkpoint security beefed up as Israeli forces launch campaign against Gaza Strip, triggering retaliatory attacks. Unemployment rate soars, economy suffers.

2004: Sharon reveals plan for phased evacuation of Gaza Strip, sparking internal resistance in his party, protests by tens of thousands of right-wing Israelis. Parliament approves withdrawal plan. Arafat dies, replaced by Mahmoud Abbas.

2005–06: Israel carries out unilateral disengagement from Gaza Strip, ending nearly four-decade-long presence. Some Jewish settler families forcibly removed by Israeli military, police. Sharon in coma after stroke. Israeli forces reenter Gaza in June 2006 to free an Israeli soldier captured in a raid by Palestinian militants.

CONFLICT STATUS: ACTIVE

Due to corruption and dissatisfaction with ruling Fatah Party (founded by Yasser Arafat) the more militant Islamic Resistance Movement or Hamas party comes to power in the 2006 Palestinian elections. Because Hamas is considered a terrorist organization by Israel, the United States and the European Union, financial support to the occupied territories is stopped, creating a humanitarian crisis. In March 2007, Fatah and Hamas form a unity government to attempt to end the financial boycott of the occupied territo-

ries, but in June factional fighting between the two groups escalates. Hamas
fighters capture Fatah's security headquarters, a symbol hated by Hamas for
representing the bloody crackdown against the organization in the 1990s.

Eventually Hamas takes military control over the entire Gaza Strip while
Fatah consolidates its power on the West Bank, effectively creating two separate Palestinian enclaves, one dominated by Hamas, the other by Fatah.
Palestinian president Mahmoud Abbas formalizes the split by dissolving the
unity government. The United States, Israel and European nations move to
bolster support for Abbas and the more moderate Fatah by unfreezing financial assets earmarked for the Palestinian Authority. Gaza, however, remains isolated and international organizations fear a humanitarian crisis
for residents there if food, medicine and other critical supplies are not allowed into the strip.

MYANMAR (FORMERLY BURMA)

DEAD: 13,320 (since 1985)
DISPLACED: 540,000
REFUGEES: as many as 121,000

TIMELINE

1937: Burma granted autonomy as colony in British Empire. Opium industry
draws laborers from India, China. British leaders had ignored calls by
minorities—especially Karenni factions—for ethnic independence; di-
verse population (135 ethnic subgroups) splinters further under imperi-
alism.

1942–48: Japanese forces invade Burma (supported by Aung San and Japanese-
trained Burma Independence Army, which later becomes Anti-Fascist
People's Freedom League, or AFPFL). Britain withdraws to India but
later frees Burma from Japanese rule with Aung San–led AFPFL, which
switched sides. Burma's independence again declared, first parliamentary elections held. Aung San and interim government members
assassinated by political opponents, causing instability. Karen War of

Independence begins, causing eight thousand casualties during guerrilla insurgency over several years.

1948-62: U Nu named prime minister. U Nu assassinated, General Bo Ne Win leads Burmese army coup.

1972-74: Ne Win is declared president. Regime represses dissent, leaving Burma isolated from international community.

1975-76: Minority groups (former guerrilla insurgents) found National Democratic Front (NDF) to oppose Ne Win's regime.

1981-82: New law denies nonindigenous people full citizenship, public office opportunities.

1987-89: Fierce rioting waged against government. Military quashes widespread prodemocracy uprisings and demonstrations, killing three thousand to four thousand, injuring twelve thousand. Military government now called State Law and Order Restoration Council (SLORC). Burma renamed Myanmar; capital, Rangoon, renamed Yangon. Aung San Suu Kyi, leader of the opposition National Democracy League (NDL) party, placed under house arrest for first of many times. U.S.-backed sanctions imposed.

1990-95: Aung San Suu Kyi and NDL political bloc overwhelmingly win first free multiparty election in almost thirty years, but ruling military junta ignores results, refusing to surrender power. General Than Shwe becomes SLORC leader in 1992, earning reputation for ruling with iron fist. Shwe troops launch offensive against ethnic Karen enclaves, leading to allegations of numerous human rights abuses.

1996-98: SLORC changes names to State Peace and Development Council (SPDC). SPDC offensives displace twenty thousand Karen people.

2000-04: A handful of high-ranking NDL leaders released from house arrest following U.N. intervention. Government, Karen National Union (KNU) agree to cease-fire.

2005-06: Constitutional convention continues, but NDL boycotts forum because Aung San Suu Kyi still under house arrest. SPDC curiously decides to move the capital from Yangon deep into the Myanmar jungle to Pyinmana.

CONFLICT STATUS: FRAGILE CEASE-FIRE

The Myanmar government remains unresponsive to international sanctions and pressure to release NDL leader Aung San Suu Kyi from house arrest, end human rights abuses and attacks on ethnic regions. Myanmar is prevented from becoming a complete pariah nation through political and economic alliances with China, Russia and India. Despite a cease-fire with the Karen National Union and its military wing, the Karen National Liberation Army, sporadic violence continues. Myanmar's massive drug trade, problems with human trafficking and diseases such as HIV/AIDS also continue to be obstacles to peace and stability.

NEPAL

DEAD: as many as 15,000 (since 1996)
DISPLACED: 100,000–200,000 (est.)

TIMELINE

1990: Civil unrest leads to new constitution and legalization of political parties. King Birendra cedes some power.

1994–95: Communist government emerges after elections but soon dissolves. Series of unstable coalition governments fail, breeding frustration and turning some to radical Maoist philosophies. Aggravation over stifled economic and infrastructural development also radicalizes moderates.

1996: Communist Party of Nepal—Maoist (CPN) and its People's Liberation Army (PLA) declare a "People's War" against royal government. Rebels wage violent decadelong insurgency to overthrow king and his forces.

2001: Crown Prince Dipendra massacres much of royal family, commits suicide while in drunken rage. Prince Gyanendra becomes king.

2003–05: Maoists announce withdrawal from seven-month truce in August 2003, leading to major escalation in violence with Royal Nepalese Army; more than one thousand killed in subsequent four months, marking most lethal period in civil war. King dismisses government and seizes absolute power for monarchy under pretext of defeating insurgency.

Censorship, house arrest, extortion, land seizure, torture are common-
place. Nepal severs relations with other countries as international watchdogs denounce the practices of both the government and Maoist rebels.

SPRING 2006: People's Movement street protests against the monarchy are met
with violence: twenty-one Nepalis killed, hundreds wounded. Protes-
tors demand the king cede power, reinstate parliament. Surprisingly,
King Gyanendra complies. Cease-fire declared.

2006–07: Seven Party Alliance formed (includes Maoists, Nepali Congress,
Communist Party of Nepal—United Marxist Leninist, among others).
New parliament votes for secular state. Maoist rebels, new democratic
government sign peace accord in November 2006, officially ending civil
war. Maoist leaders join transitional government and rebels begin disarming under U.N. monitoring.

CONFLICT STATUS: TENTATIVE PEACE

Operating under an interim constitution, Nepali political parties are negoti-
ating proportional representation and integration of rebels into government
army. However, because of the mixture of poverty, corruption and weapons,
violence continues with as many as sixty killed in the first several months of
2007.

RUSSIA (CHECHNYA/BESLAN)

DEAD: 150,000–500,000 (est.) (since 1994)
DISPLACED: 204,000
REFUGEES: more than 100,000

TIMELINE

1991–92: Chechnya becomes breakaway republic by declaring independence
from Russia, adopting constitution.

1994–96: After several attempts to oust Chechen president General Dzhokhar
Dudayev, Russian troops invade Chechnya to snuff out independence
movement, beginning First Chechen War. Major extended air strikes
launched in Grozny, leveling the capital. Up to one hundred thousand

killed, including substantial number of civilians. Dudayev killed in Russian missile attack. Russian troops suffer a series of humiliating losses and eventually withdraw. Peace accord is signed, ending the fighting.

1997–98: Chechnya, Russia sign formal treaty but issue of independence left unresolved. Warlord, separatist Shamil Basayev named acting Chechen prime minister and then deputy commander of armed forces but clashes with Chechen president Aslan Maskhadov. Basayev resigns, allies himself with jihadists.

1999–2000: With intent of establishing independent Muslim state in Chechnya, Islamic extremists led by Basayev and supported by Muslim mercenaries launch assaults on Dagestan. Hundreds killed. This prompts the start of the Second Chechen War. Russia redeploys armies and uses "cordon-and-bomb" strategy against Chechen villages. Russian troops capture Grozny. Refugees flee in droves. Russian president Vladimir Putin places Chechnya under Russia's presidential jurisdiction.

2001–03: Human rights watchdogs criticize Russian brutality during the conflict with allegations of massacres and torture. Pro-Moscow strongman Akhmad Kadyrov installed as president of Chechnya. Chechen rebels take seven to eight hundred hostages in Moscow theater. About 120 hostages and most of rebels killed when Russian security forces storm the building after pumping it full of a sedative gas that some blame for the high death toll.

2004: President Akhmad Kadyrov, others killed in Grozny explosion during military parade. Russian-backed Alu Alkhanov declared president.

SEPTEMBER 1, 2004: About thirty-two armed Islamic radicals loyal to Shamil Basayev seize a school in Beslan, North Ossetia, and hold 1,200 students, teachers and parents hostages for three days in the school gymnasium, demanding withdrawal of Russian troops from Chechnya. The incident ends in tragedy when the roof catches fire and collapses during a botched rescue effort by Russian security forces. As many as 344 civilians, including 186 children, are killed. Russian forces say all but one of the hostage takers were killed in the assault. Only one was captured alive.

2005–06: Clashes between Russian forces, rebel fighters continue. Kremlin-backed candidates win majority of seats in Chechen parliamentary elections. Basayev and other rebels are killed in a convoy explosion; uncertainty over whether incident was accidental or Russian special operation.

CONFLICT STATUS: ACTIVE

Pro-Moscow Ramzan Kadyrov, son of assassinated president Akhmad Kadyrov, is installed as Chechen president in spring 2007. Critics say he is the Russian government's own warlord thug and that his personal security forces are responsible for many human rights violations in Chechnya. Minor attacks occur daily, but there has been a significant drop in the number of conflict-related casualties during the last year despite the continued separatist violence, armed banditry and extensive, unbridled organized crime networks. Rebuilding is under way in Grozny, but the capital is still filled with the skeletons of bombed-out buildings—and many people still living amid the rubble.

SOMALIA

DEAD: up to 1 million (since 1991)
DISPLACED: 400,000
REFUGEES: 395,000 (est.)

TIMELINE

1949: After World War II, Allied powers allow Italy to continue acting as administrator in Somalia for ten years.

1959: Somalia granted independence. Border disputes with Kenya, Ethiopia follow.

1969–75: Mohammed Siad Barre seizes power in coup after president assassinated. Somalia declared socialist state. Nation battles starvation when drought hits.

1981: Under Barre's tyrannical dictatorship, clans excluded from government. Allegations of bias thrive, opposition organizes. Violence breaks out across country. Civil strife leads to collapse of Somali state, disintegration of infrastructure.

1989–93: Siad Barre overthrown by coalition of the warlords, United Somali

Congress (USC) in 1991, leaving Somalia without official leadership for about a decade. Power struggle ensues among warlords. Somaliland secedes, declares independence. Violence erupts, leaving hundreds dead, thousands wounded. Agricultural production halts, contributing to widespread famine. U.S.-led humanitarian mission, Operation Restore Hope, initiated but fails to curtail violence or famine.

OCTOBER 3, 1993: U.S. military raid to capture deputies of Somali warlord Mohammed Farrah Aidid turns into major battle when Somali fighters shoot down two U.S. Black Hawk helicopters. Eighteen American soldiers are killed and seventy-three wounded while as many as one thousand Somalis are killed and three thousand wounded.

1995: U.N. forces withdraw after intervention mission fails to stabilize area.

1998–99: Puntland secedes, declares temporary independence.

2000–03: Transitional government established, Somali warlords (supported by Ethiopia) form opposition group. Eritrea enters the fray, supporting anti-Ethiopia factions. Proxy wars perpetuate conflicts.

2006: Spring marks deadliest violence in almost a decade during militia clashes in Mogadishu. Union of Islamic Courts (UIC), supported by Eritrea and, some contend, Al Qaeda, wrests power from transitional government and U.S.-backed warlords. Fighting results in more than 1,200 killed. UIC takes control of Mogadishu for a short period before being forced to retreat by Ethiopian troops and forces loyal to the transitional government.

2007: United States launches air strikes in southern Somalia against what it says are Al Qaeda bases. Interim government declares state of emergency.

CONFLICT STATUS: ACTIVE

Turf battles between warlords and attacks in the capital of Mogadishu still occur daily and have increased since the Ethiopian-backed interim government pushed out Islamist militias in late 2006. African Union forces were deployed to the area in early 2007 for another peacekeeping mission that will eventually grow to eight thousand troops. Many in the international community worry that Islamic fundamentalism will grow stronger in Somalia in the face of persistent poverty, violence and the absence of an effective and stable government.

SRI LANKA (FORMERLY CEYLON)

DEAD: 78,600–100,000 (since 1983 with at least 43,333 civilian casualties)
DISPLACED: 500,000–600,000
REFUGEES: 300,000

TIMELINE

1956-58: Solomon Bandaranaike (Buddhist Sinhalese nationalist) elected prime minister. New legislation marginalizes Hindu Tamil minority. Protests spark waves of violence, fatal riots.

1959-70: Bandaranaike assassinated and succeeded by widow, who proceeds with nationalist agenda. Opposition party elected, begins reversing Sinhalese-centric program. But Bandaranaike's widow takes power again, halting dismantling of program.

1972: Ceylon changes name to Sri Lanka.

1976-77: Separatist group Liberation Tigers of Tamil Eelam (LTTE) forms as ethnic tensions escalate. Frustrated minority factions soon launch violent campaign against government aimed at securing autonomy for Tamil-dominated regions in north and east. Anti-Tamil riots kill as many as one hundred Tamils.

1983-85: Tiger rebels kill thirteen soldiers in ambush in 1983, setting off chain reaction of retaliatory attacks, hundreds of LTTE fatalities during attacks on capital of Colombo. Tigers consider it start of First Eelam War. Sinhalese mobs attack Tamils, destroy property. Peace talks break down.

1987-90: Sri Lanka and India sign accord offering Tamils autonomous province in northeast and Indian Peace-Keeping Force (IPKF) to enforce terms. But dispute between government and IPKF over accord implementation sparks more LTTE violence. Indian troops withdraw after fighting in north intensifies. Clashes between government and separatist rebels escalate, Second Eelam War begins in 1990.

1991–96: Indian premier Rajiv Gandhi assassinated, LTTE implicated. LTTE bombing kills Sri Lankan president Ranasinghe Premadasa. Chandrika Kumaratunga takes power. Third Eelam War beings in 1995 when rebels sink naval craft. Government renews assaults, drives separatists out of Jaffna, the provincial capital in the north.

1998–2002: Tigers bomb country's holiest Buddhist site, capture key northern town. Government rejects LTTE cease-fire offer. LTTE suicide attack on Bandaranaike Airport one of most brazen guerrilla assaults against government, destroying military aircrafts, blowing up empty civilian aircrafts and killing more than a dozen people. With Norwegian diplomacy efforts, government, Tiger rebels sign cease-fire agreement.

2004–06: LTTE splits after eastern commander, Colonel Karuna, quits Tigers. Suicide bombings in Colombo. State of emergency declared after foreign minister assassinated by suspected Tiger rebel. After Tiger suicide bombing of Colombo military base, Sri Lankan military launches air strikes on Tamil-held regions. Sixty-four civilians are killed when their bus strikes a mine. The government blames LTTE. Tigers deny involvement. Government resumes air strikes on rebel-held regions in north and east.

2007: Tigers reveal they have airpower with first-ever aerial raid on military base near international airport.

CONFLICT: INEFFECTIVE CEASE-FIRE

A cease-fire agreement technically remains in place, but heavy fighting has continued since mid-2006. Tiger rebels demand that the region in their control, Tiger Eelam, be recognized as an autonomous or independent state. The Sri Lankan government has not been able to dismantle or control the largely self-sustaining and well-developed Tiger territory, but LTTE forces have weakened because of the Karuna split and ongoing violence. LTTE is recognized as the first militant group to employ suicide bombers, called Black Tigers, and many international entities, including the European Union, have designated it a terrorist organization.

SUDAN

DEAD: 2.2 million–2.45 million (est.) (since 1983)
DISPLACED: 5.3 million–6.2 million
REFUGEES: 640,000–700,000

TIMELINE

1956: Sudan granted independence from joint British-Egyptian rule. Religious, racial, ethnic and political diversity breeds tension.

1960s: Unrest in south escalates into civil war with Anya Nya movement (guerrilla force) fighting government. October Revolution creates a national government—toppled by the May Revolution five years later, which installs a military regime headed by Jafar Numayri.

1970s: Peace agreement between government, Anya Nya ends civil war, grants south qualified autonomy. Oil discovered in south.

1983-85: Sudanese People's Liberation Movement (SPLM) and its Sudan People's Liberation Army (SPLA), a southern-based rebel group supported by Uganda, launch campaign for autonomy or independence from northern government. Islamic sharia law imposed after Muslim influence takes root in regime. Numayri deposed during backlash, but successors also unwilling to compromise on southern autonomy.

1986-89: Transitional governments, coups cycle through.

1990-95: SPLA seizes control in south, but splintering leadership allows government to regain power. National Democratic Alliance (NDA, antigovernment alliance of rebel factions) forms, joins forces with weakened SPLA. One hundred thousand refugees flee to Uganda during Sudanese army-led campaign against SPLA.

1996-2000: Government, seven ethnic-based SPLA breakaway groups sign peace agreement. Transition from military to civilian rule, subsequent reforms don't placate rebels. Peace talks stall. SPLA steps up attacks. United States launches missile attack against a Khartoum pharmaceutical plant following bombings of American embassies in Kenya and Tanzania; claims it was making elements for chemical weapons. Sudan begins exporting oil, which helps fund fight against SPLA.

2001–03: Humanitarian crisis emerges with impending famine; U.N.'s food program struggles to feed three million needy. SPLA signs landmark cease-fire agreement followed by Machakos Protocol on ending decades-long civil war. But cease-fire terms violated as hostilities continue. Rebels in western Darfur rise up to fight the government over long-term neglect of the region.

2004: Army deployed to squash rebel resistance in Darfur; hundreds of thousands of refugees flee. According to United Nations, the same government-supported Arab militias (Janjaweed) that terrorized the south are also massacring villagers in Darfur. Tens of thousands killed, millions displaced as struggle for land, power intensifies. African Union mission in Sudan deployed but unable to bring security as government refuses to crack down on Janjaweed.

JANUARY 9, 2005: After compromises on division of wealth and resources, SPLM/A rebels sign peace accord with government for conflict in south. Power-sharing requirements, military integration conditions included. Mandate says national referendum in six years will determine whether Sudan will stay united or split into two distinct regions if south decides to secede.

2005–06: New constitution ratified, new government sworn that includes formerly exiled NDA. Former rebel leader from the south, John Garang, is named vice president but dies in a plane crash one month later. Main rebel faction in Darfur is Sudanese Liberation Movement (SLM) signs peace accord with government, but smaller rebel groups continue fighting.

CONFLICT STATUS: ACTIVE

Sudan's conflict has been the longest civil war in African history. Implementation of the 2005 agreement is progressing, but disagreements and violence continue. Allegations of genocide in Darfur also continue. In April, Sudan said it would accept partial U.N. troop deployment to bolster peacekeeping efforts of the African Union. The perpetual war has decimated the economy, stalled education and health care efforts and reduced Sudan to one of the least developed nations in the world.

SYRIA

1963: Arab Baath Party takes control, remains in power today.

1960s–1970s: Syria, Israel clash in territory dispute before Israel seizes Syrian-held Golan Heights and attacks Syrian air force. Subsequent attempts to retake it fail. Syria capitalizes on instability sparked by Lebanese Civil War by intervening in 1976 and exercising political, military muscle. Peace talks between Syria, Israel stall when Syrian president Hafez al-Assad demands Israeli withdrawal from all Arab nations.

1980–82: Iran-Iraq War begins. Because of hostility between Baath leaders in Syria and Iraq, Syria supports Iran. Israel annexes Golan Heights. Thousands killed during Syrian military crackdown on Muslim Brotherhood after uprisings.

1987: Syrian troops redeployed to Lebanon to enforce cease-fire in Beirut.

1990: Iraq launches invasion of Kuwait. Syria joins U.S.-led effort to oust Iraq from Kuwait.

1999–2000: Syria, Israel resume talks about status of Golan Heights. Short-lived Damascus Spring (intellectual democratic movement) movement starts when Assad dies. Conservative backlash soon squelches movement.

2001–04: In face of mounting anti-Syrian sentiment, Syria moves troops out of Beirut to other areas. U.S. officials call Syria threat through alleged support of Iraqi insurgents following U.S.-led invasion in Iraq.

2005: Facing intense international pressure, Syria withdraws troops from Lebanon after Cedar Revolution. U.S. Marines initiate Operation Matador to kill and capture insurgents they say are entering Iraq through Syria.

2006: Thousands of Lebanese refugees flee into Syria during Israel's month-long war with Hezbollah. U.S. embassy attacked in Damascus by four gunmen; three are killed and one is captured.

CONFLICT STATUS: POLITICAL TENSIONS

Political relations with the United States continue to be tense because of allegations of Syrian involvement in the assassination of former Lebanese prime minister Rafik Hariri, complaints Syria is not doing enough to patrol its common border with Iraq and its support for the Hezbollah militia in Lebanon. However, the European Union has reopened dialogue with Syria, and U.S. House Speaker Nancy Pelosi met with President Bashar al-Assad in Damascus in April 2007, signaling potential for better contact through Democrat-controlled Congress.

UGANDA

DEAD: more than 100,000 (since 1991)
DISPLACED: 1.7 million (25,000–30,000 children abducted)
REFUGEES: more than 34,000

TIMELINE

1962–63: Under Prime Minister Milton Obote, Uganda granted independence as former British protectorate. Obote becomes president and increasingly authoritarian, although country remains multiparty democracy.

1971–73: Obote toppled in coup led by army chief Idi Amin. Amin dissolves parliament, grants himself absolute authority. Up to 400,000 killed, 60,000 noncitizens forced to leave Uganda. Economy plummets. Border clashes with Tanzania.

1978–81: Uganda invades Tanzania. Tanzania invades Uganda. Uganda National Liberation Front (UNLF) formed to unify anti-Amin forces. Amin ousted by UNLF with support of Tanzania. Obote rises to power again through fixed elections.

1985–86: Obote deposed through internal military coup and forced into exile. Tito Okello replaces him. The National Resistance Army (NRA), later to become the Ugandan People's Defense Force (UPDF), formed to oust Obote but now fights against successor government. NRA rebels take the capital of Kampala, and leader Yoweri Museveni becomes president.

1991–98: In northern Uganda an insurgent group called the Lord's Resistance Army forms, led by Joseph Kony, and seeks to create Christian government based on Ten Commandments. Uganda troops help Laurent Kabila overthrow Zaïre dictator Mobutu Sese Seko, then switch sides and aid groups trying to topple Kabila's new government.

1997–2000: More than three hundred civilians killed in several LRA attacks. Government launches unsuccessful sweeps of guerrilla strongholds to dislodge the cultish rebels. LRA assaults begin targeting schools, where hundreds of students are abducted. Estimated twenty-five thousand children kidnapped to fill LRA ranks and work as soldiers, servants and sex slaves. LRA leaders employ brainwashing, mutilation, murder to further brutal campaign.

2000–2001: LRA labeled terrorist organization by United States.

2002–2005: Operation Iron Fist launched by Ugandan government to definitively crush rebels, but LRA counterattacks. Ugandan army relocates four hundred thousand civilians because of fighting. LRA massacres more than two hundred people at one relocation camp. International Criminal Court issues arrests warrant for Kony, other LRA rebels.

2006: Museveni retains power after first multiparty election. Election fraud widely suspected.

CONFLICT STATUS: ACTIVE

The LRA continues to wage attacks even though it is largely depleted of manpower and resources. Kony remains at large. Substantive peace negotiations are stalled. In November 2006, the government rejected a U.N. report that concluded the army used indiscriminate and excessive force in ongoing clashes with rebels. There are also allegations that many of the mostly northern Acholi people, relocated to displaced persons camps by the army, are living in squalid, disease-ridden environments where hundreds die each week.

VIETNAM (AMERICAN WAR)

NORTH VIETNAMESE DEAD: 1 million–1.1 million
NORTH VIETNAMESE WOUNDED: 600,000
SOUTH VIETNAMESE DEAD: 220,000–250,000
SOUTH VIETNAMESE WOUNDED: 500,000–1.2 million

AMERICAN DEAD: 58,100–59,000
AMERICAN WOUNDED: 153,300
COALITION FORCES DEAD: 4,900–6,300
COALITION FORCES WOUNDED: 14,000

TIMELINE

1945-46: Ho Chi Minh declares independence of Vietnam after Viet Minh guerrillas seize power when occupying Japanese troops surrender to Allied forces. French forces attack Viet Minh.

1954: France agrees to peace talks after Viet Minh forces attack French command post at Dien Bien Phu. Three thousand French killed and eight thousand wounded in two-month siege. Vietnam split into North, South at 17th Parallel during Geneva conference. France withdraws.

1957-62: Northern fighters infiltrate into south. Guerrillas assassinate hundreds of South Vietnamese officials. United States increases military advisors in south to twelve thousand.

1963: South Vietnamese president Ngo Dinh Diem overthrown by South Vietnamese military with approval from United States.

1964-66: An alleged attack against a U.S. destroyer in the Gulf of Tonkin provides excuse for United States to begin bombing North Vietnam. U.S. troop levels in Vietnam reach half million.

1968: Viet Cong, North Vietnamese army launch Tet Offensive with simultaneous attacks in the south. Although Tet is tactical defeat for communists, it becomes turning point and contributing factor to eventual U.S. withdrawal.

1969-72: Ho Chi Minh dies. Number of U.S. troops significantly reduced as U.S. opposition to war spreads. U.S. troops begin training South Vietnamese army, transferring authority to locals. U.S. President Richard Nixon orders heavy bombings in north to force peace talks.

1973-75: Peace treaty signed to establish sovereignty for north, south. United States withdraws. North Vietnamese guerrillas invade south and force surrender.

1976-80: North, south unify. Country renamed Socialist Republic of Vietnam. Vietnam invades Cambodia and overthrows Pol Pot's genocidal

Khmer Rouge regime. China invades Vietnam in response but withdraws after fighting with Vietnamese troops.

1986: Nguyen Van Linh (economic liberal) named party leader. Market forces, private enterprise introduced.

1992–2000: New constitution loosens economic restrictions but communist influence still strong. United States lifts trade embargo after three decades, reestablishes diplomatic relations with Vietnam. U.S. president Bill Clinton visits Vietnam in effort to normalize relations, pledges aid for deactivating land mines, which have killed nearly forty thousand.

2003–05: First U.S. warship, commercial flight since end of Vietnam War arrive in Vietnam. Vietnamese prime minister Phan Van Khai is first leader to visit United States since war.

2007: Vietnam joins World Trade Organization after dozen years of negotiations.

CONFLICT STATUS: PAST

As one of the world's fastest-growing economies, the country is developing at a breakneck pace and has seen an influx of foreign investment, tourist dollars and industrial expansion. But a sizable economic disparity between urban and rural areas still exists, and issues of suppression of political dissent, religious intolerance and marginalization of ethnic minorities persist.

SOURCES FOR APPENDIX C

Amnesty International
BBC News Country Profiles
Center for Defense Information
Encyclopaedia Britannica Online
GlobalSecurity.org
Human Rights Watch
Internal Displacement Monitoring Centre
International Crisis Group
International Institute for Strategic Studies
Iraq Body Count
Landmine Monitor
Library of Congress
National Archives
Refugees International
ReliefWeb
UNICEF
UN Refugee Agency—The United Nations High Commissioner for
    Refugees
U.S. Committee for Refugees and Immigrants
U.S. Departments of Defense and State
World Factbook, CIA
World Vision

Appendix C was researched and written by Jessica Young.